A TEXAN
LOOKS AT LYNDON

A Study in Illegitimate Power

by

J. EVETTS HALEY

PALO DURO PRESS

P. O. BOX 390

CANYON   TEXAS

1

" . . . power, well established and entrenched, claiming authority but methodically destroying the values of the common good, is diabolic in character. The satanic aspects of such government combining power (a divine attribute) with wickedness and irrationality are usually underscored by a quality of confusion."

—*Kuehnelt-Leddihn*

Copyright 1964 by J. Evetts Haley

All rights reserved

Published by

The Palo Duro Press
P. O. Box 390   Canyon, Texas

Printed in the United States of America

CONTENTS

Preface 5

Introduction 7

I.   L.B.J.—Congressman 11

II.   "Landslide" Lyndon 21

III.   "Lady Bird's Business" 55

IV.   "The Power to Tax Is . . ." 83

V.   Friends and Favors 103

VI.   Aftermath of Fraud 125

VII.   Counterfeit Conservative 157

VIII. Toward the White House 185

IX.   Power to Incite and Coerce 205

X.   Man and Character 231

*To those who seek the truth
and love liberty
And are willing to struggle
to find the one
And fight to hold the other*

"Authority comes from above . . . legitimacy comes from below. [This] . . . explains why democracy cannot be legitimatized without an internal spiritual unity if all the people are not in agreement both on the principle of legitimacy and on the great moral and religious principles of life. If that unity does not exist, the right of opposition becomes the battleground for a struggle to the death."

—*Ferrero.*

PREFACE

When the great Italian historian, Ferrero, traced *The Principles of Power* in his profound and penetrating book, he pointed out that the basic human trait underlying all illegitimate governments is that of fear. But more than that he proved that this fear is obsessive, playing no favorites, holding ruled and rulers alike in its grim clutches.

The one sure and certain characteristic of illegitimacy in government is this two-pronged terror—the ruler's fear of the people, and the people's fear of the ruler. This fundamental principle, as Ferrero proved, lives in history from Julius Caesar to Lyndon Johnson.

On the other hand government devoid of fear — whatever the form, from an hereditary monarchy to a constitutional republic — is firmly embedded in the principle of legitimacy. When this prevails, confidence and unity, outward calm and inner peace, are reflected in the lives involved, whether subjects or citizens. It naturally follows that any country, lacking respect and consent on the part of the people, and restraint and concern for all on the part of those in power, is sick and in serious trouble.

Then no drummed-up psychosis of continual crisis, or prefabricated image of dynamic leadership, based primarily on power and government spending, even when served up with demagogic platitudes, can substitute for a diet of truth — for honest news. Nothing like this can cure the dangerous internal lesions, nor fill the spiritual void and restore domestic tranquillity.

On the contrary, healthy, moral people, even when denied the facts of national life — the truth essential to their survival—intuitively sense that something is wrong. Since confidence is a two-way street, their confusion leads to suspicion, suspicion to distrust, and distrust to national disunity. At this point the confidence between government and governed is destroyed by mutual fear. At such an advanced stage of national dissolution, disunity is not a cause, but a natural and inevitable result of illegitimate government.

Nor can it be cured, that is, can spiritual unity and national strength be restored, by any false front. The shallow deprecation of "hate" as the cause of national tragedy; the villification of patriots as "extremists"; the preaching of peace while appeasing evil, are dishonest resorts which exacerbate instead of healing the malady. Such fear cannot be banished by propaganda. It can only be restored by principle; principle based on moral character.

For a number of years America has been a victim of fear. She is now ruled by an illegitimate government.

By defalcation of Congress on the one hand and Judicial usurpation on the other—with the connivance and ready support of the Executive branch—the Federal Government has been corrupted into a vehicle of vast and unrestrained power over the lives, the effects and the affairs of the American people.

Just at this fateful period in our national life, as if by diabolical design, there has been thrust into the presidential office a man who knows the meaning and the uses of power; not power based on mutual confidence and consent, but the power of political pressure and of blackmail. Thus we are faced with illegitimate power in the hands of a ruthless ruler.

It would therefore seem proper to review the significant steps in this man's life so as to understand how he rose to preeminent power. Careful consideration of the record could possibly be of import to the future of our country.

INTRODUCTION

Lyndon Baines Johnson, the restless man who is now President of the United States, is not so much a product of Texas as of the strangely deranged times that have set the stage for his ambitious desires, his vanity and monumental egotism, his vindictive nature and his evil genius. In an age of mass action and managed news, slanted to special privileges and pragmatic ends, Johnson emerged, not as a product of the rough but sunlit Southwestern hills, but of political sophistication, cynicism and expediency. His position is not so much a reflection upon himself as upon the electorate of Texas and America.

Federal bureaucratic pressure, state demagogues, intellectually elite, labor, money and criminal tactics combined to elevate him to high office in Texas. His special talents as a wheeler-dealer and political fixer have kept him there. Herein he has always had the financial support of a segment of main-street socialists, who are perennially paraded, for political purposes, as "Texas conservatives." In truth, they are often aligned with the worst of labor leaders, with essentially the same lack of moral and political principle—the same dedication to special privilege and expediency.

Throughout Texas however, among those who have no political axes of their own to grind, and of every political point of view, there is a deep suspicion and distrust of the man who is now President of the United States. It was generally conceded, prior to the assassination of Kennedy, that, despite Lyndon's alleged political magic, Texas would be swept from the Democratic ticket in 1964 if Goldwater were the nominee. The signs were so conclusive that the Johnson forces themselves were privately admitting it.

Whether or not the inane and sometimes vicious pride
of simply having "a native son" as President, which is
being played upon by the so-called Texas "business leaders"
as a great business asset, will, with their financial pressure
and support, be able to overcome the sense of political
betrayal and righteous indignation which augured the defeat of the anticipated Kennedy-Johnson combination, is
now a matter of conjecture. The one thing certain is that
no moderate, "modern" Republican can take his measure.

What tens of thousands of Texans, grown weary of
Democratic duplicity, were thinking and saying the first
few days after Kennedy's death would never do, in view
of Johnson's position of power, to put into print. A special
correspondent of *The Dallas News*, after covering the
presidential party's visit in Austin, November 21, observed
that he "could not find a person—man, woman, or child,
who was for Lyndon Johnson."

There are, however, two widely diverse views in his
native state. On the early afternoon of November 22, 1963,
a mechanic in the West Texas oil town of Odessa, upon
hearing the news, thoughtfully paused and remarked:
"That means Lyndon Johnson is President. He's stolen
out half of Texas; I guess now he'll steal out half of the
United States." Whatever the reason for this attitude, a
casual survey of Texas opinion will disclose its deep and
indubitable hold upon thousands of Texas voters, who feel,
with an abiding passion, that Johnson is devoid of principle.

At the other extreme is the all but idolatrous regard
which the wealthy and "practical" men of Main Street
have for Johnson, best illustrated by Houston Harte, of
San Angelo, whose genius has built the most extensive
and powerful newspaper chain in Texas. In a special article
for the North American Newspaper Alliance shortly after
Lyndon's accession, Harte laid bare his adoration for the

President in many ways, but especially as "a man who knows the value of a dollar," and whose "economic conservatism ... will be reflected, as well, in the conduct of our government." Mr. Harte's article actually reflects, as it was calculated to enhance, the image of the "conservative" Johnson in the mind of the business community.

In simple essence, herein are the opposite poles of the Texas attitude toward Lyndon B. Johnson. The one that of the oil-field roughneck, the "little man" without prestige, fortune, or influence to hazard and lose in the political arena, speaking his honest and open mind; the other a Main Street multi-millionaire of immense power and prestige, writing a laudatory article about another man who has become a multi-millionaire while spending his adult lifetime upon the public payroll, glibly proclaiming the President's "economic conservatism," despite the mountainous proof that Johnson is one of the most irresponsible public spend-thrifts in history.

What influence and historic impact do these two actual incidents have upon the political thinking and future of America? The one is staggering in its implications; the other nil. Houston Harte's views, as an intimate and "long-time close friend of President Johnson," were read by millions of Americans. The frank appraisal of the oil-field mechanic was heard by one voter—the owner of a car.

Yet everyone familiar with the public mind and spirit of Texas knows that these two points of view are deep-seated; that these two basic attitudes divide the Lone Star electorate. The real Texas conservatives are frequently shocked to hear those in other regions refer to Johnson as a "Southern conservative." Yet Lyndon Johnson is no less detested by the hard-core Texas liberals, who are convinced that his vaunted liberalism is that of the head instead of the heart.

The significant and indisputable fact, however, is that these two radically different points of view do exist among the people of Texas who know Lyndon Johnson best. But the man is no longer simply a Texas politician; he is the President of the United States of America at the most critical period in our existence. Not only that, but he is a man with the most complete knowledge of, skill in and ruthless resort to power that has ever been in our highest office in troublous times. Hence the basic attitudes of Texans toward the man, and the reasons therefor, become a matter of national interest and concern.

At such a time it would seem that the duty of the historian is to gather and marshal the facts that explain these militant and completely antagonistic points of view on the part of the Texas electorate. In doing so, he should not be deceived by what is sometimes a slanted and debauched press, nor led astray by the exaggerated or prejudicial judgments of the articulate unknown.

After almost forty years of research into the historic past of Texas, with a growing concern over America's future, I have undertaken this inquiry into Lyndon Johnson's ambitions, methods and career, touching too upon some of his prominent associates. It is not a prideful record. But it seems to me that another "native son" should do no less in atonement for the shameful part Texas has played in foisting this devious and designing man upon the American public.

J. Evetts Haley
Canyon, Texas

I
L.B.J.—CONGRESSMAN

In 1932, Richard Kleberg, of King Ranch fame, was running for Congress from the 16th Texas District against businessman Thurman Barrett of San Antonio, when Lyndon B. Johnson quit teaching and attached himself to the Kleberg campaign. The race was hot and close; the outcome much in doubt. Lyndon was getting his first real taste of politics, in an area and of a brand that was to serve him well in later years.

In San Antonio a group of enterprising young men had organized a political bloc called the Citizens League, which turned out to be a "whale of a good local machine," as one observer put it, and "they did what any bunch of reasonable politicians would do—they tendered their support for $4000 in cash and the promise of the postoffice for one of their group." When Barrett spurned the offer, the same proposition was made to the Kleberg forces, who with a more tolerant background accepted with alacrity. The story is still told that Lyndon Johnson, the new but eager Kleberg confederate, flew in by private plane with the cash the same day and delivered it in person to the leaders of the Citizens League. The League went for Kleberg, Kleberg went to Congress, and the post office went to one of their leaders, who has held the lucrative post ever since.

Johnson went to Washington as Kleberg's secretary where much has been made of his precocious aptitude for politics; an ambitious young man definitely on the make. There is no question that he learned and he learned fast; that he relished the political atmosphere; and that he took to the techniques of influence and pressure like a kitten to a warm brick.

On a visit to Austin in 1934, he met and shortly married Claudia Alta Taylor, the daughter of an East Texas country-store keeper, who had just graduated from the University of Texas. The following year President Franklin D. Roosevelt appointed him as Texas state director for the national Youth Administration—a gigantic boondoggling, political venture for the youthful unemployed. Johnson moved to Austin and proved his talents by converting the NYA to effective use in the political campaign of 1936.

In February 1937, the veteran congressman from the Austin district, James P. Buchanan, died and there was a rush of candidates in an election called for April 10 to fill the place. Lyndon announced and the big guns of the New Deal got behind him. Aubrey Williams, the notorious communist-fronter who was National Administrator of the Youth corps, praised him as "one of the ablest state directors we have ever had." Lyndon, heart and soul a New Dealer, promised to back Roosevelt all the way, even to his court-packing proposal. With eleven candidates in the race, he invoked the help of the extensive federal bureaucracy, especially that built around the Lower Colorado Authority and the NYA, and led the field.

Prominent in the federal machine was Alvin J. Wirtz, late state senator from Seguin and an influential New Dealer who became Undersecretary of Interior as an underling of President Roosevelt. He was closely and profitably associated with the Lower Colorado Authority, and became an ardent supporter and intimate friend of Congressman Johnson, who at once proved his "economic conservatism" by taking this tremendous socialistic project under his wing.

He pushed it untiringly in Congress. Vast millions were spent upon the spectacular development for "recreation and flood control," for "public power" and for popular vote, while its illegitimate economic off-spring, the Pedernales Electric Cooperative, became "the largest rural electrification project in the world."

Even now as President, betimes beguiling gullible corporate executives of America with his "conservative" views, Lyndon speed-boats upon the dark and far-reaching arms of the Colorado from his ever-widening and adjacent ranch holdings, and boasts that the Colorado River Authority and development—still the biggest and most expensive example of national socialism in Texas—is his "proudest accomplishment."

As promised in his campaign, Congressman Johnson went all out for the New Deal. By way of personal encomium he still says that he was "more liberal than Eleanor Roosevelt," and Franklin was his "ideal"—"he was like a daddy to me." Such a thing as modestly waiting in the wings for seniority and its cue was contrary to the Johnson ways. He rushed to capitalize upon his vain and obtrusive talents—especially that of building an image in the reflected but effulgent light of Roosevelt's fame.

The conviction in Texas grew and not without reason, that he was something of a power at the close left hand of the New Deal throne. The devious ways of Washington were duck-soup for him, while back in Texas he revelled in the Roosevelt glory and grew in favor, especially with many wealthy and influential Texans who had axes of special privilege to wield or grind.

With the strong but hardly benign influence of House Democratic Leader, Sam Rayburn, Lyndon's career began to glitter like burnished brass. He readily learned the parliamentary ropes; he slid with ease through the intricate measures of deceptive maneuver; and he became, in his specialized way for special interests, a highly effective congressman.

With Rayburn's ready help he ingratiated himself with Texas oil men by defending the depletion allowance. Yet Johnson's support of depletion was not for free. It gained him the animosity of many party radicals, such as Senator Proxmire, but it paid off in Texas, where he and Rayburn shook down the subservient fat-cats "for the good of the party," or sometimes simply in gratification of personal vanity and pride in life-long tenure on the public payroll. Witness the marble mausoleum called the Rayburn Library, built in part by political shakedown, "in honor of Mr. Sam's service," and in undoubted testimonial to his character and his power.

It is alleged that the relationship between Lyndon and Rayburn was in part ancestral, resting upon friendship for and support of "Mr. Sam" by Lyndon's father while he was pursuing his own liberal but undistinguished career as a Rayburn colleague in the Texas Legislature. However that may have been, it fits in with the Johnson genius of warping time and coincidence to his political purpose—such as having Johnson City "named for his grandfather" when it was not named for his grandfather —to further build his image without regard for the facts.

Lyndon became Rayburn's protege; their relationship a fusion of experience and political sagacity with youthful ardor and enthusiasm, with no appreciable enhancement of the ideals and ethics of either. Skilled in the sense and use of power it became a formidable and effective political combination, with the personal preferment of Johnson and promotion of the sadly defiled Democratic Party cause as the joint, indivisible objective.

In this connection it might be well to analyze the Johnson credo, which has been published repeatedly of late and incredibly with acclaim.

"I am a free man, an American, a U. S. Senator, and a Democrat—in that order," he has written.

"I am also a liberal, a conservative, a Texan, a taxpayer, a rancher, a businessman, a consumer, a parent, a voter . . . and I am all of these things in no fixed order.

"I am unaware of any descriptive word in the second sentence which modifies, amends or is related by hyphenation to the terms listed in the first sentence. In consequence, I am not able to define my political philosophy by the choice of a one or two-word label."

This seems fair enough in objective evaluation. And yet in the light of the record, it is a devastating personal indictment! For the most exacting logician can search the Johnson utterances and public record and find no conclusive evidence of dedication to any eternal verity; no statement of basic spiritual belief; no yardstick based on moral principle by which his personal life is guided, or by which public policy is measured and determined.

It might be thought that this, his claim to being a free American, would indicate regard for and dedication to the spiritual principles of the Declaration of Independence; to the Bill of Rights and their unalienable protection for the individual; to the Constitution and the Republic that he has so repeatedly sworn to uphold. By his record and utterances he would hardly seem to realize that they exist.

At times he contends that the basis of his philosophy is simply what is best for America. But what is best for America seems always equated with what is best for Lyndon Johnson. He is skilled in double-talk. He would seem to agree with Talleyrand that the purpose of language is to "conceal thought." His description of politics as "the art of the possible" and his strictly political invocation of the Scripture—as in "come, let us reason together," sounds well. But at times he gives the stubborn, the recalcitrant, and the "unreasonable" who oppose him the full treatment, from political destruction to personal blackmail.

While warmly in favor with Roosevelt, Congressman Johnson became close friends with the palace guard—with Ben Cohen, Tom Corcoran, Harry Hopkins and Henry Wallace. He was re-elected to Congress in 1938 and 1940 without opposition, and of all the members of the Texas delegation was considered closest to the President and his policies. He became a member of the Naval Affairs Committee; supported the NYA and Civilian Conservation Corps; strongly supported the farm program, as conceived by the Communist cell in Agriculture; and helped get the first slum clearance appropriations for his state.

When Texas Senator Morris Sheppard, the dean of Congress, died April 9, 1941, Governor W. Lee O'Daniel set June 28 for a special election to fill the vacancy. A host of candidates jumped into the race. Congressman Martin Dies, who had gotten under the Roosevelt skin with his investigation of communists in government, announced. Gerald Mann, a former Texas football idol, became a candidate. Johnson, already anticipated as the FDR favorite, called on the President to set the stage from the White House. From the steps of the mansion immediately afterward, he announced his candidacy with the endorsement of the President. At his press conference a few minutes later, Roosevelt parried the implication of involvement in a Texas election, but "to be truthful," which was something, bore down on the fact that "Lyndon Johnson is a very old, old friend of mine."

The Dallas News headline noted that "F.D.R. Picks Johnson to Defeat Dies." With Harold H. Young, Henry Wallace's assistant, as his campaign manager, Johnson opened headquarters in the Brown Building, of Brown and Root fame at Austin, while Governor O'Daniel kept the political talk buzzing as to his possible entry into the race. At last O'Daniel brushed his troublesome legislative problems aside and did announce to help stoke the fires of bitter partisanship and get the campaign under way with a real head of steam.

As a proudly avowed "Roosevelt man," Johnson's theme was undeviating "unity" behind the President in time of crisis. Joseph Alsop and Robert Kintner came to Texas to praise his stature and his candidacy in articles of national circulation, spreading the word that he had conferred with Roosevelt, Rayburn, and Harry Hopkins before announcing; that he had come to Texas with their blessing; that the outcome was of real concern to the President.

Strikes in defense industries were currently serious. In his opening speech, Johnson dwelt on the danger of war and the questionable "right" of labor, capital, the farmer and government "to strike" at such times, in a palpably dishonest implication that all were equally guilty. It was to become a favorite Johnson technique that, somehow, was designed to confuse the public and confute the enemy. He suggested ample federal power to "prevent both capital and labor from taking advantage of the national need."

Unblushingly, in the next breath, he called for full parity for the farmers, the care of mothers and children by the federal government, and pensions for all over sixty, but under federal instead of state control to prevent their exploitation politically. In conservative stance, he opposed federal control of oil as "entirely unnecessary."

As the campaign progressed, Johnson's commitment to federal control became more sweeping; the coordination with Roosevelt's desire to take over Texas politics more obvious. On May 24, 1941, Lyndon called for the declaration of a state of national emergency, with dictatorial war powers in the hands of the President. He advocated immediate delivery of war supplies for Britain, and our overt military occupation of such key Atlantic bases as Iceland, the Azores, Cape Verde and Dakar—suggestions obviously relayed to him directly from the President.

On the domestic front he urged the organization of home defense, the raising and equipping of an army of 2,000,000 men, and, most drastic of all, the drafting of management and brains, of unemployed men and unemployed women and girls for training as nurses and use in defense work. In effect, he advocated a regimented national life on a war-time basis while Roosevelt was assuring the American public there would be no war.

Washington paid off politically by aiding in the Johnson buildup. Roosevelt shortly wired Lyndon that he had signed the bill guaranteeing agricultural parity prices of eighty-five percent. Then, on May 27, the President announced his sweeping declaration of a war-time emergency —as candidate Johnson had suggested three days earlier —and his determination to deliver vital supplies to Britain.

The Texas campaign had a month and a day to run. The timing was good for Lyndon, and utterly cynical in building support for a President determined to plunge America into the conflict, while assuring the country that American boys would never be sent to die on foreign fields.

Lyndon never missed a cue from Washington. He too loved peace and "hated war." Yet he preached subservience to the leader, contending there was no choice for the country except to stand "unified behind the President." As for himself, he repeatedly pledged and always to wild applause: "If the day ever comes when my vote must be cast to send your boy to the trenches, that day Lyndon Johnson will leave his Senate seat to go with him." But his subsequent action, in face of his pledge and his vote, was hardly less cynical than that of his idol and mentor.

There was grave doubt as to the outcome right down to the deadline. Governor O'Daniel, without organization, but with his confounding combination of popular appeal to the masses and support from a considerable segment of solid business, needled Johnson as "that boy who is so friendly with the President . . . he can just walk in the White House and fry his eggs on the White House stove." O'Daniel went easier on his other opponents, "because," he said, "there are twenty-eight of them, and when you get to fighting too many snakes at once, one of them will sneak up and bite you." But he jumped on Roosevelt as a man weakened "by a gang of back-slapping, pie-eating, pussy-footing professional politicians who couldn't run a peanut stand." Meanwhile he kept up his fight with the Legislature, promising, once in Washington, "to put the Texas politicians on probation."

Johnson hit back by invoking the shades of the New Deal great, pointing out Hull, Rayburn, Willkie, Wallace —with Jesse Jones and Tom Connally thrown in for good measure—as the sort of men O'Daniel claimed "couldn't manage a peanut stand." To prove that he was close to the heart of Washington and should know, he kept waving wires and letters from President Roosevelt, Vice President Wallace, Secretary Ickes and other ardent symbols of liberalism before the voting public. By the time the campaign raged to a close, the federal influence and power had become so obvious that the *Fort Worth Star-Telegram* which supported Johnson, admitted that "the spirit of the Hatch Act may have been twisted" in its candidate's favor.

In spite of all pleas for national unity; of complete support for the President in time of peril; the active intervention and admitted appeal of Roosevelt, himself; the pressure, money and pull of the New Deal machine; O'Daniel edged him out. It was a shock to liberalism; a decided jolt to the pragmatic left. Lyndon Johnson, the political wonder boy who, in the popular mind, had all it takes, went down in Democratic Texas before "Pass the Biscuits Pappy" O'Daniel, the flour-salesman Governor who had apparently voted Republican all his life. It still does not make political sense.

Johnson returned to his seat in Congress. O'Daniel went on to fill the unexpired term of Senator Sheppard, while Coke Stevenson moved up from the office of Lieutenant-Governor to fill out O'Daniel's term.

By the time of the 1942 election Roosevelt, as planned, had America at war. Former Governor Dan Moody left his extensive practice of law, and ex-Governor James V. Allred stepped down from the federal bench, to take the field against Senator O'Daniel. The conservative Moody lost out in the primaries as the New Deal support went to Allred. In the runoff O'Daniel was again the victor and went back to Washington to serve the regular six-year term in the Senate.

With the country at war Lyndon B. Johnson took leave of Congress, not as a private with the boys in the trenches in Europe, but for a commission as Lieutenant Commander in the United States Navy. After a very short period of pampered, well-publicized activity in the Pacific, he returned to Congress in the spring of 1942 with a citation for his service and left the dying to others.

II

"LANDSLIDE" LYNDON

When Senator O'Daniel did not announce for reelection in 1948, Johnson was all set to run. His chief adversary for the Senate seat was a product of the hills of Texas, Governor Coke R. Stevenson, who had advanced steadily in public life without fanfare in his buildup. He knew the meaning of hard work and had been a freighter, cowboy and country lawyer. From the office of county attorney he was elected to the Legislature and became Speaker of the Texas House; next Lieutenant-Governor, and then succeeded Governor O'Daniel when he resigned to take Sheppard's unexpired term in the Senate.

Stevenson, an inveterate pipe-smoker and a deliberate man, was a close student of the Constitution. His conservatism was evident from the fact that he had never voted for a tax bill. He was a popular figure and knew Texas and politics, but had gathered the enemies and animosities that follow long tenure in office. He was anathema to the ultra-liberal New Deal elements and the pseudo-intellectuals who had swarmed around the University of Texas President, Homer P. Rainey, in his ambitious political battle against the Board of Regents.

Throughout the war years, however, the influence of Lyndon Johnson "among the people who count"—that is, among the wealthy and influential of Texas—had grown. His ability to "get things done" for prominent people who needed things done had become legendary. His connections with Brown and Root, the Texas contractors who supported his campaigns so generously, and who in turn had prospered so fantastically on wartime government contracts as to become world-wide operators, was more than a legend—it was a scandal.

But Johnson had stood firm in the face of pressure against the oil industry. He had sped the flow of drastically scarce, wartime newsprint to his favorite publishers. He had kept vast federal funds flowing freely into Texas. He had mastered the political techniques of "the Hill" in Washington. He had maintained the support without the trust of the ultra-liberal fringe, and had, untrammelled by any too rigid regard for honesty and ethics, kept his popular image bright with the voters.

In the mind of the Texas public, with Governor Stevenson and Congressman Johnson as adversaries, the issue between conservatism and liberalism was clearly drawn. Johnson, the restless wheeler-dealer, the plausible advocate of progressive change based on federal power, the symbol of youthful glamour and ultra-liberalism, took to the hustings in a helicopter equipped with loud-speaker and furnished, it was reported, by his extremely wealthy Houston oilman friend, Wesley W. West, in one of those ironic quirks of politics. For the late J. M. West, Sr., Wesley's father, with character and genuine dedication to conservatism, had hated and fought Roosevelt's New Deal, its false nostrums and its political prostitutes with deserving passion.

Again the Washington machine, aided and abetted by a bigger sector of the business community, wealth and labor and Mexican and negro blocs marched to the primary polls, July 24, 1948, to register their enthusiastic support of the close friend of "the late great and immortal Democratic President, Franklin D. Roosevelt."[1]

The final count in the primary showed Stevenson with 477,077 to 405,617 votes for Johnson. Since Stevenson's lead of 71,460 votes did not constitute a majority

[1] Dr. S. S. McKay, *Texas and the Fair Deal,* 1945-1952, give a step-by-step account of this campaign.

over the entire field, the runoff was set for August 28.
Stevenson, apparently overconfident and always deliberate, failed to step up his campaign in keeping with the
furious tempo and grandstand tactics of the Johnson elements, diverse and incongruous as to cohesive qualities,
but ardently fused behind their candidate.

Johnson continued to cover the state by air, his force
augmented by a ten-star company of "Hollywood enter-
tainers." New Deal politicians everywhere in Texas were
tireless, and Johnson gave close personal attention to the
controlled Mexican vote section from San Antonio south.

Stevenson, too, had his supporters with political experience, such as fiery, former Congressman Thomas L.
Blanton of Albany, Texas. On August 13, Blanton hit Johnson with a devastating open letter charging that he was a
close friend of Henry Wallace, the man who had not only
"fraternized with Communists," but was still "supported
by Communists," and who insisted on giving "Russia our
Atomic Bomb secret."

More than that, Blanton continued, in 1944 Johnson
had done all in his power "to have Henry Wallace nomi-
nated for Vice President," and, had he succeeded, Wallace
would then have been "the President of the United States."

He reviewed Johnson's part in boosting the pay and
provision of pensions for Congressmen and Senators. He
reminded Johnson of hearings through which "Congress
was furnished evidence ... that the National Youth Administration, whose affairs you later handled in Texas,
was under domination by Russia and was a disloyal, sub-
versive organization." Most scathing of all was his attack
on Johnson's war record in which he charged:

> Being a Congressman enabled you to procure
> a high commission in the U. S. Navy, but when
> President Roosevelt held that Congressmen could

not hold two positions, you thought more of your
$15,000 job in Washington than you did of war-
service to the Nation, and you took off your gold-
braided uniform, and gave up your commission
in the Navy.

Have you any right to brag continually about
being a Veteran of World War II [he continued],
when you fail to tell the GIs that at the time you
got the Navy to issue you a high commission, you
then thought that you could be a Congressman
at the same time, and when early in the war you
learned that you could not hold both positions,
you became convinced that our brave GIs and
Gobs could win the war without your help, and
you quit the Service and hurried back to your
marble-floored, plush-lined Congressional fox-hole
there to sweat out the war while GIs and Gobs
did the fighting?[2]

Congressman Blanton's blast, put in the form of in-
terrogatories, failed of answer. Johnson simply blazed on
with his helicopter, his retinue of movie stars, and his
emphasis on hoopla and sex appeal.

Shortly thereafter *The Dallas News* showered down
on Johnson, charging that his platform was "all things to
all men." *The News* editorially reminded Texans of the
polyglot political backing of this "New Dealingest New
Dealer" who was being supported by Drew Pearson, University of Texas radical professors, and a "variety of busi-

[2] Thomas L. Blanton to Lyndon Johnson, August 13, 1948.
Johnson declined to answer but since explains, in his
authorized biographies, that the President "felt the country
could not give all its men to the front line," and "called
all members of Congress serving in the military to return
to Washington." See Leslie Carpenter, *Profile of a President*, 1964, p. 27.

ness tycoons, left-wing laborites, corporation lawyers, New Dealers, anti-New Dealers, et cetera." *The News,* which admitted it was deeply puzzled as to "what Mr. Johnson stands for," had "offered its editorial conference room, rent free" to this queer combination, "so they might discuss among themselves just why they are riding the same band wagon."

It too reminded its readers that Johnson had "gone right down the line with the Henry Wallace wing of the Party," and that in 1941 Wallace had sent his own "political mentor, Harold Young, to Texas to head Johnson rallies and pay for Johnson advertising." It marvelled at Johnson's ability to reverse himself so quickly from his rabidly pro-labor stance in the past, invariably carrying CIO boxes, to become a supporter of Taft-Hartley, now. Johnson was contending that Stevenson was pro-labor and was soft on subversion while he, Johnson, was promising more in REA, roads, water, wages, pensions and farm income from the Federal Treasury and at the same time "a more economical Federal Government."[3]

In ordinary times it would have been an incredible political phenomenon. But these were not ordinary times. They were times showing the effect of sixteen years of steady erosion of American character through sordid appeal to the most selfish traits in human nature. They were times showing the results of sixteen years of contrived ideological confusion, economic fraud and bribery and dangerous appeal to class warfare and hatred. They were times in which our national unity was being destroyed, and our social structure shattered through the cynical undermining of pride and principle by the man whom Johnson still calls his "spiritual leader," Franklin D. Roosevelt.

---

[3] See *Dallas News,* August 22, and the final week of the month, 1948.

The Johnson support was understandable in the light of history. Like the terrible excesses of the French Revolution, it was a product of the lusts and passions of the times. The response to his synthetic glamour and glib demagoguery was the direct result of lack of moral leadership in high places. It was the seed of corrupt federal policy designed for lifelong tenure of ambitious men in office, instead of the perpetuity of the Republic on the basis of high national policy and moral principle. It only seemed strange. It was natural, and it is still terrible.

Big money was thrown into South Texas by the Johnson forces, reportedly $35,000 into Bexar County (San Antonio) alone. Johnson personally guided the San Antonio setup under his politically-potent leaders, Sheriff Owen Kilday and Street Commissioner Jimmy Knight, where they performed the political miracle of converting a 12,000 Stevenson lead into a 2,000-vote favorable margin for Johnson in the runoff.

Initial returns on the 28th confirmed the "spot checks by trained political writers" that the controlled vote, particularly in the Latin-American sections of Southwest Texas, was firmly in the hands of the New Deal machine and that Governor Stevenson was in trouble.

Johnson had moved in to take the George Parr, Southwest Texas section,[4] which had formerly supported Stevenson, and where, with Kleberg's backing, the Governor, despite the concern of his supporters, had felt he need not worry. Herein was a fatal tactical error. For George Parr had been in trouble, and with the easy duplicity of

---

4 The veteran newspaper man and Texas historian, Clyde Wantland, has traced this phase of the campaign in sweeping and devastating detail. I am much indebted to him for his researches. For his fine account, see *The Texas Argus*, April 1962, San Antonio.

his kind, and the flexible conscience and the undoubted power of the Johnson forces to deliver, Parr had decided that if he did not exactly love Lyndon, his personal interests now lay on Lyndon's side.

The switch that Parr engineered in his area of influence and control was absolutely fantastic. His immediate tri-county returns gave Johnson a thirty to one lead —10,547 to 368, with heavy majorities in many other counties adjacent to them and along the Rio Grande.

For days the outcome was in doubt. With 254 Texas counties, many with independent and leisurely ways, even the honest returns are often deliberate and slow. After five days with returns all in but unofficially tabulated, Stevenson was in the lead with 113 votes out of nearly a million counted. Despite this Johnson hit the air with a broadcast on Thursday, September 2, with a "victory speech," interlaced with the continual refrain that "we have won." As Clyde Wantland has written:

> This broadcast alerted and disturbed the Stevenson forces. Johnson's enthusiastic assurance was unreal in the face of all the known facts.
>
> Their fears were validated the following day, Friday, September 3, when a source friendly to Stevenson reported from Jim Wells County that Precinct 13 had been recanvassed and a 'correction' made favoring Johnson with 202 more votes.
>
> Johnson's radio forecast on Thursday, thus became a reality on Saturday. Princinct No. 13 had been corrected from Johnson 765-60 to Johnson 967-61. This gave him a lead of 87 votes, with returns now complete and semi-official.

Thereupon began the historic struggle to validate the steal which gained for Johnson the frivolous nickname of "Landslide Lyndon," and which established his illegiti-

mate seat in the Senate, where his aptitude for compromise
and chicanery put him into the crucial position from which
a diabolical fate catapulted him into the presidency. The
nature of the men involved and the ways in which his
"election" was sealed and delivered, are of more than
passing significance.

The key figure in this drama, which may finally assume the proportions of a historic Greek tragedy, was an
affable, blue-eyed, multi-millionaire criminal by the name
of George Parr. He was a native product of that unusual
combination of corrupt political patronage and warm paternal concern; of ruthless power at the top and friendly
protection at the bottom; and of confidence of the leader
in the support of those willing to be led, that flourishes
along the Texan-Mexican border as nowhere else. At the
apex of this political phenomenon are the hard, tough and
practical political bosses. At its base is the preponderant
Mexican or Latin-American mass leavened with a few subservient Anglo-Saxons, while in between are the lesser
lackeys, leaders, *jefe politicos*, and ward-heelers of the
hierarchy. The pattern of political control in the border
area goes back almost to the beginnings of Texas.

In 1948 George Parr, Duke of Duval County and
undoubted boss of his domain, was in his late forties and
immensely rich by virtue of his own talents and the inherited political power of his father, the late Texas Senator
Archie Parr. Archie had gone to the Texas Senate in 1914,
and had stayed for twenty years. He so dominated Duval
County that he rarely allowed the name of more than
one candidate on the ticket for local office. During this
time and after his son came to control, the Texas Election
Bureau had grown used to near-unanimous returns on all
offices of importance, sometimes "complete" before the
closing of the polls. Why should Texas be concerned?

After all there were plenty of decent counties, and Duval seemed of little moment.

But on the local level, Senator Parr had his enemies, among them one taxpayer who strangely but persistently believed, especially in view of Parr's prosperity, that the County's financial records should be subject to audit. Parr insisted that since they never had been, this was clearly unnecessary to Duval's progress. The local reactionary hired his own accountants and carried his contentions to the Duval courthouse. Understandably rebuffed, he appealed to the State Supreme Court and was sustained. Before the audit could be made, the courthouse caught fire and burned to the ground. Unfortunately, the records went with it!

When the friendly, light blue-eyed, Spanish speaking George Parr, after service as a senate page and a round in university law, returned home, Archie saw to it that he was elected county judge. It was not hard. He was the only candidate on the ticket. George thus became the head of the local political hierarchy at twenty-five.

While Texas officialdom merely winked at Parr's corruption, it turned out that the Federal Attorney of the San Antonio District, Wm. Robert Smith, with a high regard for his oath of office and his duty, did not. In 1932 he secured indictments against George Parr for criminal evasion of income taxes. But the proof of the ways in which Parr got his money was more significant than his evasion of taxes.

Smith proved that in 1928 George Parr had an income of more than $45,000, only $2,700 of which was "from a legitimate source." Some $17,000 had come in pay-offs for protection of illegal liquor and gambling operations and houses of prostitution. And Parr's protection was ample. He was "the political dictator of Duval County," and "controlled the action of practically every other office-holder in the county."

The remaining $25,000 of his 1928 income—he was quite young and just getting started—came in the form of a kick-back on a county road contract, a Duval operation that had been relatively easy. As County Judge, Parr presided over the meetings of the Commissioners Court, which let substantial road-building contracts to W. L. Pierson and Company of Houston. U. S. Attorney Bob Smith found that on May 14, 1928, the County of Duval, pursuant to one of these contracts, issued a warrant for $85,000 to Pierson Construction Company, signed by the County Treasurer and by Parr as County Judge.

Upon its receipt the Company deposited the warrant in its Houston bank, drew $25,000 in cash, "which was placed in a little black bag and was taken by A. A. Sangster," a Company official, to San Diego, Texas, the county seat of Duval, and "on May 24, 1928 delivered said black bag" to the County Judge, George Parr. Such a picayunish matter would never have caused a public ripple in tolerant Texas except that Parr failed to cut the Federal Government in for its share.

Federal Attorney Smith was a determined prosecutor. For defense Parr employed one-time Attorney General of Texas, Tom Pollard. At the last minute Parr threw in the legal sponge and pleaded guilty, rather than have his methods and means further explored and exposed. But Parr's influence already reached far beyond Duval. Federal Judge Robert J. McMillan was lenient. Pressed with the word of prominent people that Parr would recant and reform, the judge imposed a $5,000 fine and an eighteen-month probated sentence to the Federal Reformatory at El Reno, Oklahoma.

Nothing derelict when it came to chicanery and crime,

however, Parr went right on making the most of his golden opportunity and his less than sterling character. He levied on the county school fund to buy himself the famous Dobie ranch; he assaulted J. C. Canales, a Brownsville attorney, in the Duval Courthouse for political speeches that Canales had made against his father; he financed a local wholesale liquor business before repeal of prohibition; he was a party to a $600 monthly pay-off by a local gambling hall, and then had the operator raided and indicted when he became delinquent; and he really went to town in the oil business that was spreading over Duval.

As an extensive land owner through the generous use of county funds and other progressive educational procedures, Parr was prepared to hit it rich. On June 11, 1934, he leased some lands to J. T. Graham and the Texon Royalty Company for a period of one year, with the usual provision that in case of production the lease should run for "as long thereafter" as oil or gas was produced in commercial quantities. The lessees drilled and were rewarded with production. At the end of the year, however, they were appalled upon being hailed into court by Parr for recovery of the wells due to the expiration of the lease. They rushed to the county courthouse and found that Parr had scratched out "as long thereafter" on "oil and gas"—ironically leaving them only the "sulphur," of which he had none—before the original lease had gone on record.

Thus their expensive wells in the flush of production belonged to Parr. All of which was highly improper in the trade, and even fraudulent under Texas law.

Armed with this fresh evidence of Parr's fraud and open violation of Texas law during his probationary period, Federal Attorney Bob Smith returned to Judge McMillan's court and in the light of the evidence petitioned the Judge to vacate Parr's probation.

In a frank statement sadly delivered, Judge McMillan did so. While harboring his doubts as to the wisdom of a suspended sentence at the time of the trial, the Judge admitted he had made a mistake, primarily because of the "strong representations" by people of prominence that Parr "was a man who might be rehabilitated." And Parr did have his points, now proving his outspoken honesty by blithely admitting he had changed the Texon deed, but "did not call the grantee's attention" to it.

Judge McMillan was unmoved by his frankness. As Parr waited transfer from jail in San Antonio, the Judge was presented with a petition signed by practically every high office-holder at Austin—by Governor James V. Allred, the Attorney-General, every member of the Texas Senate and all Justices of the Court of Criminal Appeals —praying for Parr's release. Parr was sent on for reformation at El Reno, from where he continued to run his district. Shortly he was back on his old stomping grounds at San Diego, still the Duke, still the unquestioned dictator of Duval.

As the years passed, with his ready aptitude for oil, racketeering and even legitimate business—for which he really had no aversion when profitable, the vast wealth, power and influence of George Parr flourished and grew. He moved with confidence, often flanked by a couple of Mexican *pistoleros* for a body-guard. He owned the bank in San Diego and another in Alice, county seat of adjoining Jim Wells. He acquired land holdings of some 70,000 acres and built a mansion, where he lived and entertained, somewhat in feudal splendor, with a swimming pool, his own race track and a string of horses. But politics—which his friend Lyndon Johnson has so neatly termed "the art of the possible," was the basis of his money and power.

Through the bloc Mexican vote he took and held control of the 79th Judicial District made up of Jim Wells, Brooks, Starr, and Duval Counties. His influence weighed heavily in Nueces (Corpus Christi), as well as in many other counties that lapped leisurely west and south to include the tier abutting on the Rio Grande.[5] He is reported to have fallen out with his powerful friend, Congressman Kleberg and retaliated by defeating him. Thus, when Johnson called on Parr for support in 1948 and got it, Kleberg was in Stevenson's corner.

At the time of the Johnson-Stevenson campaign, Parr was reported to have had a brother in trouble and in need of added influence. Johnson and his political ally from nearby Floresville, John Connally, had that highly negotiable commodity. When the count from the run-off election was in, Parr had delivered for Lyndon. But though he had dallied in sending his returns while Lyndon kept in close touch by telephone, it finally turned out that they had closed their own count prematurely. Stevenson was ahead by 113 votes.

Johnson made another frantic telephone call to Parr, who indicated that he might pick up what they needed in Precinct 13 at Alice. Thereupon his henchmen "recanvassed the returns," reporting on September 3 the "corrected" total of 202 additional votes for Johnson and one for Stevenson. Thus Lyndon went into the lead by 87 votes out of nearly a million actually cast.

By Texas procedure the next step was the meeting of the State Democratic Executive Committee, which was to convene at Fort Worth on September 13, in advance of the Party Convention, officially to canvas the returns

---

[5] Dr. McKay, *Texas and the Fair Deal*, as cited, 240, speaks of Parr as "the ruling power of the 18-county Twenty-Seventh Senatorial District.

and certify the nominees. In the meantime, however, its
sub-committee met in Austin to tabulate the vote and
immediately announced its acceptance of the "corrected"
returns from Box 13.

When he had challenged in vain acceptance of the
report by the sub-committee, Governor Stevenson sent two
of his best campaign workers, Kellis Dibrell and Jim
Gardner, ex-FBI agents and young Texas lawyers, post-
haste to Parr's country to investigate. They went by Laredo
to pick up a guide who knew the land and its ropes, and
were joined at San Diego on Monday by Governor Stevenson. But when they called on Parr at his office, they found
that Johnson's campaign manager, John Connally, who is
now Governor of Texas, had beat them to it. As Wantland
wrote, "He had arrived the preceding day and was busily
cementing the theft," though Parr publicly stated that
the run-off in his district "was as clean an election as had
ever been held." Possibly so, *in his district*.

Stevenson demanded that Parr show them the Duval
poll lists and the returns of the election judges, which
reported a vote of 4622 to 38 in favor of Johnson. Parr
feigned astonishment. Why should they ask him? He was
not an election judge; he knew nothing about the returns.

From Parr's office the Governor and his party hurried
into adjacent Jim Wells County, and at Alice found that
"Harry Adams and H. L. Poole, newly elected chairman
and secretary, respectively, of the Jim Wells County
Democratic Executive Committee, were already trying to
upset the 'correction' from Precinct 13, that had been
made and reported by the old committee officials."

These two, who had seen the "corrected" list on the
previous Friday, and had sat in on the meeting of the
committee for the "recount," told Stevenson that the 202
new names had been added alphabetically in blue ink,

whereas the original list was in black. The old secretary, Tom Donald, an employee in Parr's Texas State Bank, carefully kept the list despite the protests of the new officials.

Donald locked the list in the vault of the bank and continued to refuse to turn it over for public scrutiny. Thereupon Governor Stevenson and his party made plans to get possession of this "public record" when the bank opened next morning.

South Texas, in keeping with its history, traditions and the mercurial temper of its people, was still an explosive and dangerous country. When Dibrell and Gardner sent out "an urgent call for help to check the entire voting lists, and recruits began arriving hourly," wild rumor spread that the Governor's party were all well-armed FBI men. The newspapers reported that an emergency call for Texas Rangers had been relayed to Austin. Stevenson did call the noted Ranger, Captain Frank Hamer, to come down and keep the peace.

Next morning before the bank opened, Parr's forces commandeered the entrance with Winchesters. The historian Clyde Wantland has told the story of what happened and told it well:

> Governor Stevenson wisely ordered his forces to appear in public in only their shirt sleeves [to prove they were unarmed].

> As the hour approached for the bank doors to open, armed men sauntered onto the scene and took positions with an ominous silence.

> Governor Stevenson and his coatless investigators arrived, escorted by Ranger Captain Frank Hamer. Not a word was spoken as the Ranger Captain took position directly before the bank door. The veteran Captain was well known to

every man there. He was known as a stern, inflex-
ible officer who exacted, one way or another,
prompt and stern obedience to his orders.

He waved the armed men to fall back from
the bank door, and they did. Very promptly! The
doors opened and Governor Stevenson and his
men entered. Captain Hamer forbid any other
to follow. None tried. Witnesses said later the
Captain never lifted his pistol, nor even touched
it, but Johnson charged him with force, threats,
and intimidation.[6]

Inside the bank Tom Donald produced the list for
the Stevenson party to see. Dibrell and Gardner concen-
trated upon the added names, having determined in advance to memorize as many as possible. Donald conferred
with the County Attorney who, after a few moments, gave
the opinion that Stevenson should be allowed only to look
at the record, not to copy or make notes therefrom. Donald
repossessed the record and again locked it in the bank
vault.[7]

Stevenson left to confer in private with Adams and
Poole. Gardner and Dibrell, hurriedly scribbling down
their remembered names, left on investigations of their
own—the identity and whereabouts of the added "voters."
They found grave difficulty in locating the addresses they
had jotted down except three, "whose last known address
was the cemetery," one of whom, according to the church
records, had been there for four years. At least two of
those they did locate swore they had not voted, while
others shrugged off their questions with the frank ad-

---

[6] Wantland, as cited.

[7] James Gardner, Affidavit to the Sub-Committee on Privileges and Elections of the United States Senate, November
12, 1948.

mission that people in Parr's province who did not talk prospered better and lived longer than those who did.

On the local level the battle now revolved around the efforts of newly-elected Democratic Chairman Adams and Secretary Poole to take over the Jim Wells poll lists and re-certify the returns. In the light of the irregularities, they hoped to get the County Committee to eliminate returns from Box 13 completely, which would have thrown the election to Governor Stevenson. At a private meeting on the night of September 9, they decided they had the commitments necessary to do so. They issued a call for the full committee to meet at eleven on the following morning, Friday, the 10th, to sanction the proposal and to report their official action to the State Committee, which was to convene three days later.

But John Connally had virtually assumed command of the Parr and Johnson forces, for which the prevailing county chairman and secretary, Clarence Martens and Tom Donald were the local front. They relayed the news of the proposed meeting to Johnson and his lawyers, who sped into a friendly jurisdiction to stop it.

Shortly after ten o'clock on Friday all members of the Jim Wells Executive Committee, Governor Stevenson, Frank Hamer, and Kellis Dibrell were served with notices of an injunction issued by Judge Roy Archer in Austin. It forbade the County Committee to meet. It brought the Stevenson counter-attack to a standstill.

Johnson's petition and Judge Archer's restraining order are exceptional documents even in Texas jurisprudence. Obviously Johnson was desperate. He contended that he had received a majority of the votes "in the recent election." He charged that Stevenson, Hamer and the Committee had "entered into a conspiracy" to have Box 13 "thrown out on the grounds of fraud and irregularity . . .," which would take from him enough votes to change the election.

He charged that Adams and Poole were "acting under threats and intimidation" of Captain Hamer. His petition argued that the county Committee lacked authority to take any action in the premises. He admitted that it had met once for the purpose of correcting the returns, but that it had no legal right to meet again and reconsider, "to hear and pass judgment on charges of illegality or irregularity of any nature . . ."

He pleaded that the "resident Judge of Jim Wells County . . . cannot be reached in sufficient time," and that therefore "a restraining order without notice" to the defendants—that is, to Governor Stevenson and the County Committee, should be granted. All this he contended, in effect, was urgent and necessary to keep his rightful "seat in the United States Senate" from being stolen from him. Judge Archer forthwith signed the order.

This obvious perversion of the law, distortion of the truth, brazen action and political perfidy, were characteristic of Johnson. But even for Texas it was a high point in low and dirty dealing. It set something of a record.

"For the first and only time in Texas history a Texas Ranger was forbidden to preserve the peace and maintain order and discharge his lawful duty," on the specious and wholly dishonest claim that Hamer had used "threats, force and intimidation" to further the alleged conspiracy. The historical record shows that "Captain Hamer had conducted himself with impartial restraint, and that he was on hand to prevent violence and bloodshed. This he had done. Nothing more!"

The record further reveals that Judge L. Broeter, of Alice, was in his resident district on Friday morning and readily available had Johnson desired him. In view of the obvious chicanery, Mr. Wantland raises the pertinent question that has burned in the minds of Texans ever since.

Just why Johnson and Connally presented the petition to Judge Roy Archer in Austin, two hundred miles distant from Jim Wells County, raised a serious question, not alone of honesty and fair play, but also the more serious fact of swearing to a falsehood when Johnson knew it was a lie.

Just why Judge Archer was beguiled into signing this order in chambers, without notice, thus perverting the vast powers of a District Court to handcuff a victim while ruthless political hijackers mauled and stripped him clean, is a question still unanswered. Maybe it was the legendary Johnson charm and personality. Maybe the decision stemmed from the law of heteronomy rather than the law of Texas. Judge Archer alone has the answer.[8]

Time was of the essence. Had the action in Judge Archer's chambers been delayed more than an hour, it is highly likely that the Jim Wells Democratic Committee would have met, thrown out Box 13, and restored the electoral decision in Stevenson's favor. But with the State Democratic Executive Committee meeting in Fort Worth within three days to canvass the returns and certify the candidates to the Secretary of State for printing of the ballots for the November election, the blow to the hopes of the Stevenson forces seemed fatal.

They girded for a forceful and factual presentation

[8] Clyde Wantland, "The Story of George Parr's Ballot Box No. 13," as cited; Josh Groce, ms., 7 pp.; Kellis Dibrell and Jas. Gardner to J. E. H., Jan. 6, 9, 1964; Gordon Schendel, "Something is Rotten in the State of Texas," pp. 13-14, *Colliers*, June 9, 1951.

of the Governor's case, and left for the momentous meeting of the State Committee, set to open at noon at the Blackstone Hotel in Fort Worth, on Monday, September 13. The decisive issue in the battle before the Committee was to be the acceptance or rejection of the sub-committee's report. If rejected it would open the way for the submission of evidence of fraud by Governor Stevenson. If accepted it would automatically mean that Johnson was the party's nominee, certain of election in November since the Republican chances were nil.

Delegates, gathering for the Convention, crowded the Committee meeting, where tempers were high; the battle long and hot. The sophisticated lawyer, Charles I. Frances, of the most powerful political firm in Texas, eloquently and emotionally argued the Congressman's case as the New Deal idol sat smoking his cigarette with an affected air of ennui, while Stevenson puffed on his pipe in obvious concern. The battle raged throughout the afternoon; the Stevenson forces encouraged when the first test showed the committee split down the middle, twenty-eight on either side. But this was broken by the dramatic appearance of C. C. Gibson, the Amarillo Committeeman who flew in to break the tie in favor of the sub-committee report, and hence of Lyndon Johnson.

The Chairman gavelled the session to a close and before night the jubilant Johnson attorneys had the official results on the way to the Secretary of State at Austin for certification of Johnson's name as the nominee. The stunned Stevenson leaders were decimated by the action. A few faithful gathered in their Blackstone rooms that

---

9 The author was a delegate to the Democratic Party Convention and a witness of the Committee's proceedings. For further details see *Fort Worth Star-Telegram,* September 14, 1948.

night in utter dejection. Among them were veteran conservative political leaders who would not quit as long as Stevenson refused to surrender. They pondered their course.[9]

"This race is not a matter of life or death for me." Stevenson said. "If I lost by one vote in an honest count the heavens wouldn't fall in. But some half million good solid Texans voted for me as their Senator and they have been defrauded and robbed. We can do no less than appeal to the Federal Courts."

Thus again a precedent was set in Texas. During the next two days his attorneys worked on an appeal to the Federal Court "raising for the first time in a major case the issue of Civil Rights." Their petition alleged that through fraud and corruption the Governor and those who had voted for him, had been denied the right of an honest count. They drafted a petition for a temporary order restraining the Secretary of State from printing the name of Johnson on the ballot until their evidence could be heard and headed for Judge T. Whitfield Davidson's court to present their petition.

It turned out that Judge Davidson was not in Dallas but at his ancestral farm home in deep East Texas. Despite the late hour C. C. Renfro and Kellis Dibrell decided to drive to the Judge's retreat and present the petition upon arrival. About four o'clock on the morning of September 15, Connie Renfro cajoled his way past the Judge's truculent dog and roused the sharp and genial Southern Constitutionalist from his bed. The Judge brewed a pot of coffee, read the petition and listened to their brief presentation. He then signed the sweeping order and set Federal Court for a full hearing Tuesday, September 21.

His court convened in Fort Worth as scheduled, and in calling it to order Judge Davidson clearly stated that it was for the purpose of hearing an election contest. Lawyer-Governor Coke Stevenson rose to say that he had not subpoenaed witnesses, but that he had plenty of testimony and evidence at hand to support his contentions of irregularity and fraud. His leading counsel, the outstanding lawyer Ex-Governor Dan Moody, was flanked by State Senator Clint Small, C. C. Renfro and five others, all of whom had "volunteered their services," while "at least 100 lawyers" from over Texas had likewise volunteered theirs. Not a member of his array of counsel, Stevenson quietly observed, "had been hired," but had joined the case "because they were interested from the standpoint of the people of Texas."[10]

Standing by were Gardner and Dibrell with the evidence that they had been digging up, ready to testify as to their examination of the poll list for Box 13, with its final 202 names of alleged voters mysteriously added alphabetically, in blue ink, in the same hand, whereas the rest of the list was in black, and in a number of hands.

Besides these, a number of Mexicans on the list were present and ready to take the stand to say they had not voted. One was a girl named Enriqueta Acero, from the State of Yucatan, who was in Mexico at the time of voting, but who had been found and who willingly agreed to come out and testify. Stevenson was ready with affidavits from a number of others, together with the factual proof that only 600 ballots had been officially issued for Precinct 13, while the "corrected returns" claimed 1025 votes had been cast. In addition the Stevenson forces had the dead-wood on a number of other "voters" on the list who, at the time of the election, were resting easy in local cemeteries. All this had been adduced from only the relatively few names that Dibrell, Gardner and Adams had been able to mem-

---

[10] *Fort Worth Star-Telegram*, Sept. 21, 28, 1948.

orize hurriedly from fleeting examination of the list—a "public record" still secure from public scrutiny—still safely locked in Parr's bank in Alice.[11]

Their evidence was devastating; their contentions went unchallenged. Yet an air of superlative self-confidence if not of boredom permeated the Johnson camp as lawyer John D. Cofer and Charles Frances, a prominent figure in Johnson's career, asked that the petition be denied, while they sneered at Governor Stevenson as a bad sport, "a poor loser."

They contended that he had lost in a party contest in which the party managers were the sole authority. These leaders, they argued, had declared him the loser and Judge Davidson's Court was without jurisdiction. "As for his alleged Civil Rights—they couldn't have been violated because he had none. This is strictly a party matter." Which, except for the charges of fraud, Judge Davidson had recognized at the outset. They offered no evidence in rebuttal. The reason was obvious. They had none.

Judge Davidson, in his inimitable courtroom way, observed off-the-record that the citizens of Texas "were entitled to a Senator without any cloud of suspicion hanging over him," and suggested a compromise, adding however that its reception would have no bearing upon his decision. Why not, as a party matter, he asked, let the names of both go on the general ballot in November, leaving the choice to the court of public opinion?

Governor Moody responded that "Stevenson is ready to dispose of the entire controversy in the manner your

11 *Star-Telegram*, as cited; Coke R. Stevenson vs. Tom L. Tyson, case 1640, Federal Court Records, Northern District of Texas; Wantland, as cited; Dibrell and Gardner to J. E. H., Jan. 9, 1964; C. C. Renfro to J. E. H., Jan. 18, 1964; Coke R. Stevenson to J. E. H., Jan. 5, 1964; McKay, as cited, pp. 238-242.

Honor suggested."

John D. Cofer, for Johnson, rose to refuse, with what seems a strangely illogical statement: "Voluntarily to waive that right [did he mean Johnson's 'right' to the 'corrected' returns?] would stultify the right of the people."

Moody retorted that the plaintiff was ready to prove that Box 13 "was stuffed," and prove as well the fraudulent shift of votes in four precincts in Zavalla County, from down on the Rio Grande. But the strategy of the Johnson attorneys simply seemed to be to make the best of the Court as a forum and to continue to berate the Governor.[12] Thereupon Judge Davidson.

> ...arose and angrily cut short the tirade in a manner seldom witnessed in a sedate Federal Court.

> 'There has not been one word of evidence submitted,' he blazed 'to disprove this plaintiff's claim that he has been robbed of a seat in the United States Senate.

> 'If there was not a single law on the books, this man would be entitled to and would get a hearing in this Court.

> 'This hearing shall be held over until September 27; and this Court will appoint a Commissioner to go into Jim Wells County, procure evidence and report back to this Court when the hearing opens again.'

The Court's blistering denunciation and decision to adduce the evidence itself "all but blew the Johnson ship out of the water." Judge Davidson[13] thereupon named Wm.

---

12 *Star-Telegram*, Sept. 21, 1948.

13 The sturdy and venerable Judge Davidson is still on the Federal Bench at Dallas. This incident is taken from Wantland, as cited, and confirmed by others.

Robert Smith, late Federal Attorney and a man familiar with Parr's record and power, to go into the Parr district as Master in Chancery for the Federal Court, to summon and swear witnesses, to adduce evidence, and to determine the truth about the doings in Duval. He likewise sent James McCollum Burnett as Commissioner, since evidence was to be taken in Duval and Jim Wells simultaneously.

At once the Texas newspapers carried stories that apparently the fight would be resolved by a write-in campaign between Stevenson and Johnson, who was then triumphantly crossing the state as an honor guest on President Harry Truman's campaign train.

This sudden turn threw his camp into panic and completely dispelled the assumed air of ennui—all appearances of boredom. Johnson rushed back into the fray while Truman, well aware of the possibly disastrous effects on his own cause, especially with the Southern rebellion of Fielding Wright and Strom Thurmond drawing off scores of Democratic Texas leaders and thousands of voters, repeatedly dropped word to the party faithful as he crossed Texas that it must be Johnson "at any price."

With the resolute Bob Smith, armed with the authority of the Federal Court, moving to dig out the voting records and take the sworn testimony of those involved, Johnson was in serious trouble. He frantically called George Parr, who was at his office with Duval County Democratic Chairman, T. C. King, pleading: "George, don't burn those ballots. It'll be a reflection on me."

But Parr, who like Harry Truman, knew the psychology of his henchmen and the code of loyalty in their protection, shouted back:

"To hell with you. I'm going to protect my friends."

Commissioner Burnett opened his investigation in the

Duval Courthouse, with the prominent and veteran Texas courtroom attorneys Joe Montague, Oliver Fannin, Jr. and C. C. Renfro, with plenty of local help from Jacob Floyd and others, examining the unwilling witnesses summoned into court. Most were election judges or otherwise officially connected with Duval County, carefully coached in advance by Judge George Parr. Hours of penetrating examination revealed little more than the appalling ignorance of the witnesses; proving the eternal aptness of the Spanish phrase in answer to embarrassing questions—*"quien sabe?"* —"who knows?"

But as a matter of official record the Commissioners did establish certain historic facts about Duval County elections that everybody in South Texas, from Mexican sheepherders to State Senators, already knew. They brought out the fact that despite the Texas election laws there had never been an official return by a precinct chairman to the county chairman, and that the keeping of actual poll lists was unknown. Attorney Montague eased County Tax Collector Clemente Garcia into admitting, in his broken English, that poll taxes had been bought in bales in Duval County, "yes, many several thousands." But when George Parr, who sat directly behind Montague, vigorously shook his head, Clemente forgot completely "who had paid for them." Commissioner Smith sent him to his office for his legal authorizations. Clemente returned sadly to report that he could not find them.[14]

What of the all-important lists kept at the polls at the time of the recent election? They too "showed up missing." It developed later that County Chairman, T. C. King, a Parr enterprise employee, had grown nervous over the vast disparity between the election returns and the

14 Wm. Robert Smith to J. E. H., Jan. 10, 1964; Joseph Montague to J. E. H., Jan. 18, 1964.

poll taxes issued—about two to one—and had taken the
lists home for safe-keeping. There his wife, in her commendable zeal of housecleaning, had apparently consigned
them to the fire. Thus the attempt to get at the actual
voting in Duval ended in futility, in complete frustration.

Over in Princinct 13 at Alice, in Jim Wells County,
the investigations went little better. Commissioner Bob
Smith issued a subpoena for Tom Donald, the Parr bank
employee who was Democratic County Secretary at the
time of the election, but he was in Mexico "on business."
He issued another for Luis Salas, presiding judge in the
election. He had been called to Mexico "on business."

The poll list, too, failed of subpoena. Commissioner
Smith impounded the County's ballot boxes and found
them empty. "Why?" Obviously, it was suggested, the
industrious Mexican janitor, ignorant in the premises, must
have emptied the boxes and burned the ballots. Thus the
same pattern of evasion and frustration prevailed as in
Duval. "Nobody knew nothing."[15]

The interest over the state had grown to a fever pitch.
Sam Rayburn had called a caucus of New and Fair Deal
leaders at his Bonham home, determined to meet Truman's
demand that it be Johnson "at any price." Johnson and
his attorney had flown to New Orleans to petition the dismissal of Judge Davidson's order by the Fifth Court of
Appeals, where Judge J. C. Hutcheson, Jr., held that their
case must be heard by the entire Court and set an early
date.

With time so urgent, and aware, as no one else, that
the ultimate power lay with friendly forces in Washington,
Johnson by-passed the Court of Civil Appeals, while his
attorneys made only a perfunctory defense at Judge Davidson's hearing, which re-opened on September 28th. John-

15 W. R. Smith to J. E. H., Jan. 9, 1964; Wantland, as cited.

son flew his case directly to that ex-Ku Klux Klansman
and noted police judge on the Supreme Bench, Mr. Justice
Hugo Black.[16]

Justice Black belonged to the club. At once, on September 29, 1948, he issued a sweeping order on behalf of
Johnson, staying Judge Davidson's temporary injunction
and ending the Fort Worth hearing, where the iron curtain
tactics of South Texas were about to be proved in Federal
Court.

In adjourning Court, Judge Davidson observed that
the Supreme Court was without jurisdiction; that this was
not a dispute in a general election, but in a State primary
over a party nominee, where even the Senate was without
power to act; and that Stevenson's only "recourse was in
my court." As a part of the nation's responsible judiciary,
he had no choice except to suspend the hearings and
adjourn court in view of Black's ruling. But with charac-
teristically outspoken courage he added:

"The United States Supreme Court has altered my
opinion, but it hasn't changed my mind."[17] He was also
heard to remark that Black's order was unduly hasty "and
probably unlawful."

The Black order, hurriedly issued in chambers, evidently without clerical or stenographic help, since it was
dated in his own hand, has been likened to that of a judi-

16 The high-placed New Deal attorneys, Abe Fortas and
Thurman Arnold, along with Charles I. Frances, represented
Johnson in Washington. Alvin J. Wirtz was designated his
leading attorney in Texas, though John Cofer, who was to
represent Johnson in all sorts of business from defending
a friend charged with murder to the defense of another
named Billy Sol Estes, took the lead in the hearings before
Judge Davidson. See *Fort Worth Star-Telegram*, Sept. 16,
18, and 21, 1948.

17 *Fort Worth Star-Telegram*, Sept. 28 and 30, 1948.

cial bulldozer. It over-rode one of America's foremost Constitutionalists and Judges, who had, in the light of fraud, simply stayed the election contest long enough to give each side time to present its case in evidence. It over-rode a distinguished Circuit Federal Judge who had held that the full Court of Appeals should hear Johnson's petition, and had set an immediate date to do so. It peremptorily denied justice to Governor Stevenson and nearly half a million Texans who had voted for him. It brazenly abridged the Constitution and the Bill of Rights, especially in their guarantees of States Rights and the limitations on jurisdiction. But perhaps most terrible of all, it sanctioned corruption as public policy. There is nothing in American history like it.

Lyndon Johnson went on to the Senate and his truly meteoric rise to power. But the trouble in South Texas continued as local leaders rose to challenge the domination of the powerful and much-indicted George Parr, still the Duke of Duval. His oil holdings grew with scores of new wells and he entertained his prominent friends, such as Tom Clark, now a Justice of the Supreme Court, on the Dobie Ranch.

The many charges against him never seemed to hinder his influence or operations, and somehow his rare convictions in court seemed certain of reversals, especially by the Federal bench, where Johnson's friends had become Judges as often as vacancies occurred. Only recently the last of many true bills against him was dismissed on motion of the present Federal Attorney Ernest Morgan, who had publicly admitted that he got his appointment through the close friendship of Vice-President Lyndon Johnson.

For years the veteran Jim Wells attorney, Jacob Floyd, fought to break the Parr control. He had some effective help. When a young courageous, crusading newcomer, W. H. Mason, joined the Alice station KBKI as a news commentator, he immediately discovered and began to expose the local corruption, especially as it pertained to Parr's Jim Wells County Sheriff, H. T. Sain and his deputies. Anonymous threats stirred Mason's ardor instead of deterring him.

Among his exposures was the ownership of what was deliciously known as *"Rancho Alegre,"*—"The Ranch of Joy," a hall for drinking, dancing and prostitution stocked with quite young and pretty Mexican girls, located on the edge of the town of Alice and owned by the Sheriff's Deputy, a giant half-breed Mexican by the name of Sam Smithwick.

Bill Mason repeatedly exposed the operation and when threats did not stop him, two of Sain's deputies waylaid and beat him up, stripped him of his trousers and left him half naked in the street. Mason retrieved his pants and flew them from the radio station flagstaff as an indication that he had not surrendered. Shortly thereafter, July 29, 1949, Smithwick met him on the street, removed his great hat as in token of Latin grace, whipped out his .45 behind it and shot Mason to the ground.

After some delay the Smithwick trial was thrown on change of venue into Central Texas, where a young and fearless prosecutor by the name of Jim Evetts had never failed, in a case originating in his native county of Bell, to get an indictment. Smithwick came to trial in January, 1950, confident that the pervasive Parr influence would still prevail. But Jim Evetts rounded up an array of witnesses, among them a number of seductive figures from the late *Rancho Alegre*. He exposed the official corruption and connections of the Jim Wells-Duval machine, and in a sweeping and devastating attack had Smithwick apprehensively looking down the corridor to the electric chair.

Something had to be done to cause a mistrial, and that something was the ultimate, age-old resort of illegitimacy in desperation—assassination!

When District Attorney Evetts drove home the night of January 23, 1950, and stepped out of his car, a man rose from hiding in a hedge beside the garage and opened up on him in the darkness with an automatic Colt's .45. But illegitimacy lives in fear and the gunman, obviously nervous, missed two shots and fled when his gun jammed. Evading apprehension, like his confederates in time of trouble, he too crossed the river, on business in Mexico.[18]

Jim Evetts failed of the death penalty but did send Smithwick to the penitentiary for life. His appeal was denied and at Huntsville he languished in solitude, with a growing resentment against the South Texas powers, that he had faithfully served, for not getting him out. He wrote a letter to former Governor Stevenson, urging Stevenson to come and see him, saying he was ready to tell the true story of what had happened in Jim Wells and Duval. Within a few days, before Stevenson could make the trip, the prison guard, while making his morning round on April 16, 1952, found Smithwick dead in his cell, an apparent suicide, though many in Texas still refuse to believe it.[19]

Shortly thereafter the long battle to recover that fair and fascinating land from Parr's control took an even more tragic turn for the embattled Alice attorney, "Jake"

18 Juan Barrera Canate is suspected as the would-be assassin. Captain Alfred Y. Allee to J. E. H., Feb. 2, 1964.

19 Judge James K. Evetts to J. E. H., Jan. 14, 1964; Captain Alfred Y. Allee to J. E. H., Jan. 8, 1964; *District Court Records*, Bell County, Sam Smithwick case; *Dallas News*, Jan. 24, 1950; Gordon Schendel, in *Colliers*, June 9, 1951, as cited; Coke R. Stevenson to J. E. H., Jan. 5, 1964, Kellis Dibrell, as cited.

Floyd, who had proven so persistent and effective that
the machine decided upon his assassination. But at the
last minute, on the night of September 9, 1952, a Mexican
by the name of Nego Alaniz, one of the co-conspirators,
weakened and frantically phoned Floyd to call a taxi and
come to the edge of town, as he had vitally important
news for him. Floyd agreed to come. Again Alaniz warned:
"Take a taxi! Don't go for your car! They are waiting
there to kill you."

Floyd called for and left in a cab. Almost immediately
his youthful son, Jacob, Jr., reached home, and upon
hearing of his father's hurried departure, and apprehensive
of his safety, rushed for the family car to follow him. In
the darkness the assassin mistook him for the father and
shot him down.

Sometime later "El Turco" Mario Sapet, the Mexican
murderer, was quietly hustled from deep in Mexico by a
Texas Ranger—without benefit of extradition, in the sometimes mysterious but effective ways of the Texas Border,
and delivered for trial in Brown County. He was sent to
the penitentiary for life. Nego Alaniz, who had warned
the father, was tried on change of venue in Waco, Texas,
as accessory to the murder of the Floyd boy. His defense
attorney was the noted Houston criminal lawyer, Percy
Foreman, at a "$25,000 fee" reportedly paid by Parr.

In the years since, violence and corruption have so
spread to the national stage as to relegate Parr and
Duval to a relatively minor role. In a last futile effort
Stevenson did appeal the fraud to the United States
Senate Sub-Committee on Privileges and Elections. But
the battle was over, the deal was done. Judge Davidson's
views were confirmed. Stevenson's "contest complaint was
not considered since it was not presented to the Senate"
at the time. And for two very good reasons; "the Senate

was not in session," and in a state primary, Washington had no jurisdiction.[20]

More than once in public addresses thereafter Governor Moody boldly charged, in the proper jurisdiction, that "if the District Attorney here had done his duty, Lyndon Johnson would now be in the penitentiary instead of the United States Senate." And there was no action for libel.[21]

The profound significance of this remark was, first, that the lawless underworld was in league with the highest echelons of the Federal Government, and second, that fraud and corruption had come to be tolerated if not admired by authority on the State level. In such a climate and environment, the adept Lyndon B. Johnson systematically and securely enhanced his power.

Unresolved however were the bitter and ineradicable effects of the steal—albeit validated by Black's nefarious order—upon the minds of Texans. Unsettled yet is the sense of betrayal, the smouldering resentment and righteous indignation of moral people, which sixteen years later still burns with passion in the hearts of thousands of Texans who think that the duty and province of the judiciary is to mete out justice, after "full and impartial" hearings, rather than, in Star Chamber proceedings, to serve as a mantle for criminality.

Given a healthy society, the perversion of character in individuals can be contained. But the perversion of justice, with its reaction upon all a country's institutions, has historically placed nations and even civilizations beyond recall.

20 Recently, however, the Supreme Court, in its Georgia, Tennessee, Texas and related cases on Congressional redistricting, has swept these Constitutional guarantees completely away.

21 *Star-Telegram*, Sept. 28, 1948, for the Stevenson remark. The author himself heard Moody repeat this statement.

Times change, but not the motivations of human nature; not the moral and spiritual principles upon which civilized society depends. The celestial spheres sail on in their sure and certain orbits, suggesting something Eternal, while America sports and plays on, engrossed with "social progress," and the dirty Duval deal is "past history."

Coke Stevenson, a forgotten man, lives sadly in seclusion on his remote ranch in the hills of Texas. George Parr, citizenship restored by President Truman, flourishes and prospers—still a tremendous political power in South Texas, while the prominent figures who fought him hardest are gone, some having paid with fortune, blood and life. Justice Black still sits on the Supreme Bench, a leading figure in its steady and unspeakable usurpation of power, while John Connally, Lyndon's right hand man in the Duval steal, is Governor of "the great state of Texas."

And Lyndon Baines Johnson, the master devotee of power and politics as "the art of the possible," is President of the United States at the most critical period in history.

In its incipiency, public sanction of immorality, assassination and illegitimacy may seem a local if not a minor matter. But the malignancy spreads! What a strange coincidence that Lee Harvey Oswald, on his return from Mexico shortly before the Kennedy assassination, detoured from Laredo to stop and spend the night in "search of a job" at Alice, in Jim Wells County, Texas, before proceeding to Dallas and his world-shocking deed!

All thoughtful men who have read the record of mankind can but stop, ponder and probably shudder. The judgments now will not be rendered by an impartial judiciary, which is apparently gone. They will be found in the distant verdicts of history, most likely written in red.

III

"LADY BIRD'S BUSINESS"

As an example of the whirlwind tactics of Lyndon
Baines Johnson, James Reston, of *The New York Times*,
while being given the works at the 400-odd acre "LBJ
spread"—with the 6000-foot paved jet runway—at Christmas in 1963, wrote admiringly of the sudden presidential
decision to buy a ranch. As a play for the press it was a
typical Johnson stunt. But as a reflection of the way
ranches are appraised and bought, the story must have
brought a sardonic smile to every farmer and ranchman
who read it—if any did.

As they were driving along a highway the President
glanced off at a piece of land and suddenly decided that
he wanted to buy it. Shifting his hand from the steering
wheel, apparently without slowing down to the legal limit,
or even spilling his beer, he picked up his mobile phone,
called his ranch manager to get the details at once and
brief him before he left for Washington, within a few
hours. After attending to a host of other matters, Lyndon
flew out on schedule, but not before his manager breezed
in to report on the deal, though Reston neglected to say if
he delivered the deed.

This is hardly the way ranches are appraised and
bought, at least in Texas. It probably made a good story
for those who knew no better, as *The Times,* with all the
news that's "fit to print," ran it. But beneath its shallow
sensationalism lay a basic fact. Lyndon Johnson is now
an extremely wealthy man; by some thought to be among
the wealthiest in Texas. Therefore the Reston suggestion
that he may buy a ranch on impulse is financially sound.
His known ranch holdings are extensive and his other
interests, tending at times to the legendary, are fantastic.

All of which would be nobody else's business except for his public position. Here is a man who by reliable report and public record, puts in every full day of his life at nothing but the pursuit of politics. He has been on the public payroll his entire adult life, at a comfortable salary to be sure, but not one to make a man rich, much less to make him a multi-millionaire.

It is true he has had ample "opportunity"; his close connections with Brown and Root, Wesley W. West and moneyed men in all fields—as with those who tried to retake the California tidelands—is bound to have brought "good deals" in his direction. In addition he has been tied-in with such fabulous promoters as Billie Sol Estes, Morris Jaffe and Bobby Baker. Yet he was rich before these past-masters in the art of getting ahead built empires of their own; and always close at hand as his political friends ladled out the government gravy.

Where and how did Lyndon Johnson get rich? Inherently the public has a right to know, for the facts have an impact on the public interest which no sudden cynical shift of the "LBJ Company" to trusteeship can divert or dissolve.

While the designedly distorted and obscure record poses its research problems, much could be written on this phase of Johnson's career alone. The first of his early wealthy ventures, which likewise illustrates his business ethics, methods and policies, is the LBJ Company, the name of which has just been changed for obvious political purposes, back to its original title of The Texas Broadcasting Company.

Its lucrative base is the Johnson politically and perhaps financially dominated capital city of Texas, where his monopoly of television has long rankled the citizens of Austin. Here the truth is in interesting contrast to the picture so carefully contrived in the public mind. For years this enterprise has been represented as the product of the inherited wealth and the rare business ability of Mrs. Johnson. Granted her sharp and practical business mind and "the iron beneath the velvet glove," this too hardly squares with the major recorded facts. Johnson acquired his original holdings in Austin through one of the foulest political deals, upon one of the greatest Texans, on record.

First, to the well-worn fabrication that the President's wealth is founded on his wife's inheritance. When Johnson married Claudia Alta Taylor, November 17, 1934, her father was the keeper of a general country store at the village of Karnack, in East Texas. He lived in an old and substantial brick house that made no pretensions of being a mansion, but was ample and comfortable. His first wife, a veiled and retiring, if not a shy woman, who struck the neighbors as "being strange" had long since died. Taylor educated his children and tended to business, advertising himself as a "dealer in everything," adding to his real estate holdings as the depression accelerated the East Texas rural decline and lands came on the market at a bargain.

When Mrs. Johnson's mother died September 6, 1918, the inventory of the estate, as reflected in the probate records at Marshall, Texas, showed that the interest of the three minor heirs, Claudia Alta and her two brothers, was principally in the Karnack store and 11,966.4 acres of Harrison County lands. Their half of the estate under the Texas community property laws, had a "probable value" of $40,762.50 in land and $8,627.50 in the store.[1]

During the children's minority T. J. Taylor married again; a union of short duration. He then married a young

[1] *Probate Records*, Harrison County, Marshall, Texas, **Vol. 139, p. 541.**

woman named Ruth Scoggins, who renovated the house, adding the columns in front and giving it some pretentions of "the mansion where Lady Bird was born"—as glowingly reported in many articles since she became "the first lady of the land."

Mrs. Johnson was the youngest of the three children by seven years. Antonio Taylor, her oldest brother, with disabilities of minority legally removed, first had his third of the estate settled upon him in amount of $26,000. In 1924 T. J. Taylor, Jr., was next paid $40,500 as his enhanced third of his mother's estate.[2] The years passed without settlement of the interest of Claudia Alta, who had been raised by an aunt, had graduated in journalism from the University of Texas and married Lyndon, who shortly afterwards was elected Congressman.

On the 6th of November, 1936, Claudia Alta was joined by her husband, Lyndon B. Johnson, state director of the communist-ridden National Youth Administration in Texas, in acknowledging receipt of $21,000 in notes from her father, T. J. Taylor, to be paid off at $7,000 annually, beginning November 6, 1937, as settlement in full of her interest in her mother's estate. Thus her "inherited wealth" from her mother's estate, as repeatedly mentioned in the press, consisted of a total of $21,000 in notes. In 1937 Lyndon B. Johnson, made his successful race for Congress, according to one of his intimate biographers, on $10,000 loaned by his wife out of her inheritance, though by the official records she had not yet been paid a penny from her mother's estate.[2a]

[2] *District Court Records*, Volume X, p. 95, and *County Court Records*, Vol. 130, p. 106, Harrison County.

[2a] *Deed Records*, Harrison County, vol. 221, p. 183. Of late this story has been revised to the effect that the campaign money was "borrowed from her father against the inheritance." *U.S. News and World Report*, May 4, 1964.

With the outbreak of the War Congressman Johnson's influence not only paid off for Brown and Root—the financial angels of his campaign—but for many others in Texas as well. It just happened that the extensive Taylor lands around Karnack, adjacent to Caddo Lake, and the most valuable Texas assests in his wife's paternal inheritance, proved to be the best site for the vast war-time Longhorn Ordnance Plant—though there were scores of others available. Washington decided to locate it there.

Johnson knew that this "might not look good"; that politically it would hardly do. Thus the impartial testimonials of the Harrison County *Deed Records* show that on July 27, 1942, Lyndon Johnson and his wife "quit claimed" all right and title to a certain portion of the Taylor land and that exactly nine days later, August 5, 1942, Mrs. Johnson's father and stepmother conveyed 2,887.6 acres of this land to the Federal Government for $70,000.[3] The plant was located within a few hundred yards of the Taylor store. Thus the Longhorn development, combined with inflation, enhanced the value of her father's estate.

The records show that upon her father's death, October, 1960, he left some land and the Taylor home to his wife, with a life-long trust to provide for her, and that he remembered his daughter, Claudia Taylor Johnson with only "the brick building ... in Mauldin, Missouri, in fee simple."[4]

Thus, with the evidence that Mrs. Johnson received only $21,000 from her mother's estate, the doubting public has been left to wonder how Lyndon B. Johnson has managed to become a multi-millionaire while devoting all his

---

[3] *Deed Records*, Harrison County, Vol. 249, pg. 415.

[4] *Probate Records*, Harrison County, will of T. J. Taylor, Nov. 17, 1959.

time to politics, simply "with his wife's money."[5]

What then are the facts behind this story that in 1943 she invested, as variously reported, between $15,500 and $75,000 "in a small radio station" at Austin "that was losing money;" and that she "assumed its debts" and "worked day and night" upon it "until it began to show a tiny profit?" Could this story have been started and kept alive by her husband for diversionary political purposes? Perhaps something of its actual history will explain.

The author of this book happens to know, at first hand, its history and the sequence of events by which it fell as a luscious financial plum into Lady Bird Johnson's lap. That history is as follows:

On January 9, 1939, after three years of effort, an East Texas graduate of Yale, Dr. James G. Ulmer, associated with others as the Texas Broadcasting Company, was granted a permit by the Federal Communications Commission to build and operate station KTBC at Austin, Texas. After long experience in communications, Dr. Ulmer had gone into the radio business in 1930 with a station at Tyler, Texas. Through the years he obtained additional permits and with local associates spread his operations to include stations in at least half a dozen other Texas towns and cities before acquiring the Austin permit.

Then J. M. West, Sr., the rugged son of an East Texas tenant farmer, who had fought his way to the top from a hand in a lumber mill to become one of the richest men in Texas, heard of the Austin permit. He called in his general ranch manager, the author of this study, whom he used in various capacities, and sent him to Austin to see Dr. Ulmer, to investigate the station's potentialities,

---

[5] For one of the latest elaborations on the shopworn story, see the authorized biography by Leslie Carpenter, *Profile of a President*, pp. 24 and 39.

to learn whether Dr. Ulmer would sell and if so to ascertain his price.[6] This West employee learned that Dr. Ulmer would sell, subject of course to the approval of the Federal Communications Commission. His asking price was $150,000.

Dr. Ulmer met with West at Houston late in August and settled upon a price of $125,000. West thereupon turned the matter over to his lawyers, Platt and Stevenson, who drew the option contract for signature on September 1, 1939. But on that day war broke in Europe, and West, a far-seeing, conservative man, anticipating America's involvement and resultant war-time controls on honest media, told Ulmer that he wanted to call the trade off.

Ulmer countered with a drastic cut in his price. He offered to take $87,500; with $2500 in cash to bind the bargain and the balance upon approval of the transfer by the F.C.C. West agreed and the contract was signed on that fateful day. Incidentally, but significantly for this history, Roosevelt appointed James Lawrence Fly, of Dallas to chairmanship of the F.C.C. on the same day.

Jim West, a ruggedly individualistic giant of impeccable business character, had never wanted anything before from Washington except to be let alone. More than that, in his quiet but effective way he had never been timorous in letting the world, especially Roosevelt's world, know exactly where he stood. Though the deal with Dr. Ulmer was perfectly legitimate and above-board, the matter dragged. Somehow the approval of the Commission was not forthcoming.

But J. M. West was a determined man who had decided that he wanted a voice for American freedom. He sent his general range manager, the author of this book,

6 The author went to Austin on the initial investigation in August, 1939.

back to Austin to negotiate the purchase of a struggling little newspaper, its circulation and its archaic plant. He then contracted for and built a handsome six-story structure adjacent to the Texas Capitol grounds, equipped it with a modern press and launched what he called *The Austin Tribune*, because of his admiration for the great Chicago paper. The Tribune Building was also designed to house the office and facilities of Station KTBC when the F.C.C. approved the Ulmer sale.

He hired the able Dan Moody, who could handle almost any intricate legal matter, to push the approval of the permit by the Commission and, in keeping with his imaginative genius, told Dr. Ulmer that he would give him three-quarters of a million dollars for all the radio stations he owned or controlled, and retain him to run the business—after the Austin sale was approved. His idea was a network, with headquarters in the Tribune Building. But his problem with the government was one of politics, not technicalities of the law, and Governor Moody, who likewise had spoken his mind about Lyndon and the New Deal, could not turn a bureaucratic wheel.

Thus the matter dragged until February 7, 1940, when Dr. Ulmer, while driving from Austin to Houston, was astounded and appalled to hear the news on his car radio that the Commission had just revoked the license of every station in which he was interested. Hurriedly, from Huntsville, Ulmer called West at his offices on the 20th floor of the Sterling Building, in Houston, to discuss this sudden and startling turn in his affairs. West had already heard the news. The F.C.C. was alleging violations of various administrative rulings, the chief complaint being that of "hidden ownership."

There was outside ownership with Dr. Ulmer in the Austin station, which was well-known and is worthy of recall. A. W. Walker, then of the University of Texas Law Faculty and now, as a practicing attorney in Dallas, perhaps the greatest authority on oil and gas law in the world, was one of the KTBC owners; the late State Senator of Fort Worth, Bob Stuart, was another, while Robert B. Anderson, then State Tax Commissioner, later director of the vast Waggoner Estate and still later a prominent Cabinet member under Eisenhower, was President of the Company. They had not put up any money, but had agreed to take a twenty per cent interest. Ulmer had built and operated the station and with options on their stock had their authority to sell.

After the revocation order the F.C.C. allowed Ulmer to continue operating his stations, while Commission Chairman Fly ordered extensive investigations and hearings on the Texas scene. These continued for weeks, accompanied by much unfavorable and unjustifiable publicity. With America's entry into the War, government controls became general, and KTBC's application for transfer was still unapproved. After many months of effort and expense—an estimated $50,000 expenditure on West's part, with Dr. Ulmer kept from the active supervision of his stations while being choused around in public hearings, KTBC and the balance of his properties were in drastic financial condition.

In desperation he turned to a source of influence, to Lyndon Johnson's old campaign manager and close friend, Austin attorney, Senator Alvin J. Wirtz. They went to the Driskill Hotel for dinner where they ate leisurely, talking long and late. Dr. Ulmer laid his legal and business problems before Wirtz in professional detail, especially in regard to KTBC and the contract for its sale to J. M. West, and told Senator Wirtz he wanted to retain him in his efforts to get F.C.C. approval of the sale.

He told Wirtz that when the revocation order came and his associates thought the Commission was after him, he had, in March, 1940, given a quit-claim deed to them in hopes that this adverse action of the Commission might not affect the West trade.

But undoubtedly the news of J. M. West's interest in buying all of Ulmer's stations had reached Washington, and in view of West's ready cash and rugged character, about the last thing the powers in Washington wanted was for him to own a daily in the Texas capitol, tied in with an extensive radio chain. Dr. Ulmer just happened to be the unlucky pawn the politicians were ruthlessly playing to block the West plans.

Wirtz showed interest, inquiring as to what KTBC was really worth. "A million dollars," Ulmer replied, which must have seemed ridiculous. But Ulmer was an imaginative operator who knew the business, and time has abundantly proven him right. He offered to pay Wirtz $10,000 if he could get the F.C.C. to approve the sale; $2,500 down ,$1,000 a month through five months and the balance upon approval. Wirtz agreed to the retainer and asked Ulmer to meet him at his office at nine in the morning.

Ulmer went to his office at the appointed time, took a seat in the waiting room, and waited and waited. Prominent on the wall of Wirtz's office was a large and handsome picture of Congressman Lyndon B. Johnson, warmly autographed with a sentiment which Ulmer probably never forgot: "To my friend, Alvin J. Wirtz," it read, "who can do anything better than anybody else."

Finally a secretary came to report that Senator Wirtz was out and suggested Ulmer return in the afternoon. He did. The secretary said she was sorry; the Senator had suddenly left for Washington on urgent business. "His address there? The Mayflower Hotel." For several days

Ulmer tried to get him by phone. But he never returned the call and Ulmer never heard from him again.

J. M. West, Sr. died in 1942 and Dr. Ulmer was at the end of his rope, his station in dire debt, the man himself broke. His Austin associates, unable to put up cash for their agreed purchase of stock, had given him $15,500 in notes, which he had endorsed to his Tyler financial backer as collateral, who in turn assigned them to the Austin bank which was carrying KTBC's operating expenses.

Meanwhile Lyndon Baines Johnson had "discovered" the station's plight; Lady Bird had made application for its purchase with an accompanying statement of her net worth December 21, 1942; an agent was sent to Wesley W. West to see that the West estate was out of the picture; the F.C.C. approved the sale in January, 1943 and Lyndon and Lady Bird Johnson picked up the station for the $15,500 in notes against it and were at once on their way to immense wealth.[7]

When the first TV permit was issued for Austin, it came to KTBC on a silver platter as a result of being on the ground floor with its radio operations. Many cities much smaller than Austin have several TV stations, but this has been a privileged and monopolistic range for Lyndon Johnson's family ever since. No other station has

[7] Johnson called in Ted Taylor for advice on operations, and to negotiate the withdrawal of the West option—if still in force. For some of the more obvious detail, see *U.S. News and World Report*, May 4, 1964, and the *Wall Street Journal* series.

In further emphasis of the totally political nature of this business, it should be noted that the F.C.C. subsequently granted and renewed a total of 14 permits for Dr. Ulmer, among them that for the 50,000 watt station KCUL at Fort Worth, which he sold to Gov. Ed. Rivers, reportedly for $450,000.

been able to get a permit and authorities say that now
the coverage has been so scientifically rigged that without
a revolutionary revision of the patterns of the surrounding
stations, none ever will.[8]

The conversion of KTBC to television was expensive,
but the Company was in a position to make it really pay,
primarily because of its complete control of the Austin
market, and because of Lyndon's undoubted influence and
aptitude for pressure. As for the political risk, he always
had an out; someone was always in between.

Except for a few small blocks of stock, closely held
by employees, the station is owned by his wife and daughters. Ever since it became a public issue, he has claimed
he owned no interest in it. Yet on October 3, 1956, when
it turned up that he had joined Mrs. Johnson in transfer
of stocks to their daughters, J. D. Kellam, the station's
manager, in an amendment to its ownership reports, explained to the F.C.C. that this was done by Johnson and
his wife "to avail themselves of the split gift provisions
of the Internal Revenue Code." But if he was not one of
the owners, how could he legally take advantage of the
gift tax exemptions? Again in a restriction-of-stock agreement placed on file with the Commission, January 10,
1956, Claudia Taylor Johnson was joined by her husband
as "stockholder."

Irrespective of the implications and the suggested
juggling for political and preferential tax purposes, the

_____
[8] Johnson's contention is that one VHF television channel
was allocated for Austin in 1948, that there was no other
applicant and that it was granted to KTBC in 1952. Neil
McNeil, of Scripps-Howard, explored the Johnson TV operations in some detail in February, 1958 issues of their papers.
See also *Texas Observer*, Feb. 28, 1958. In 1951 Lyndon
seriously considered selling out instead of converting to TV,
but seasoned advice convinced him against doing so.

LBJ Company is definitely in the family. As of F.C.C. record in 1962, KTBC-TV with 593 shares of stock outstanding, Mrs. Johnson was shown as chairman of the Board with 338, and their daughters with 160 shares, or just over 84 per cent of the stock. The balance was held by Johnson associates and employees; primarily by Jesse Kellam, the president, Walter Jenkins, treasurer and Paul Bolton, ultra liberal newsman, vice-president.[9]

KTBC's expansion under Jesse Kellam, an old Johnson associate from his NYA days, followed the same ruthless Johnson tactics that had become known to politicians in Washington. Stories of pressure bordering on blackmail have been current in Austin for years, but it took a Congressional investigation of Johnson's boy, Bobby Baker, to vest them with the privilege of publication and kick them into the press.

This however is not to discount Mrs. Johnson's ability and influence. Company officials and other employees, even after the family operations spread extensively, were amazed at her intimate knowledge of local personnel, costs and income. While Lyndon was out beating the political bushes, after the receptions she might be found at the station discussing business, and concentrating on the balance sheets, leaving the impression of a sharp, cold and calculating business mind—perhaps "the real mind behind the President."

Unlike most women, her primary interests are not her children and home, but business and politics. Her youth was a sheltered and cultivated existence; her favorite books and expressed preferences in literature not deep in nature, but far above her husband's, who seems to have none. She is obviously more popular with men, as women often find her " 'corney,' 'calculating' and 'cold-eyed,' " damning

9 *Texas Observer*, Feb. 21, 1964.

"all those y'alls and 'all those LBJ's' right down to Little
Beagle Johnson."

After an hour with her in the 1960 campaign, one
public relations man "felt that she cared more about her
husband's career than her husband. She's got very darting
eyes . . . I had a feeling of somebody who was making all
kinds of long mental notes, almost a human tape recorder
going.[10]

Women of her home section smile at the stories only recently heard but now widely disseminated, that her Southern mother was a social liberal, believing in and practicing
racial integration. Search of old-time memories in the
Marshall section turns up nothing to support this obvious
pitch for negro votes.

Many cultivated women intuitively resent her. In
reference to her obsessions with money and politics, one
Southern lady, versed in Shakespearean wisdom and allu-
sion, sharply wondered: "Is Claudia Taylor Johnson a
gentle Portia who outwitted Shylock, or is she more interested in power such as Macbeth's wife wielded?" Thus to
some she does suggest Lady Macbeth's consuming ambition for the growth of her husband's power. Yet women
journalists eulogize her as another Eleanor Roosevelt, perhaps more calculating and colder than that ubiquitous
lady, but decidedly more attractive.

In her own right she too is now a multi-millionaire.
From the initial KTBC radio station in Austin, converted
to TV, Mrs. Johnson's interests prospered and spread, and

[10] Nan Robertson, "Our New First Lady," *The Saturday
Evening Post*, Feb. 8, 1964. There have been a rash of
articles about her. See others by Maggie Savoy, *Arizona
Republic*, Dec. 11, 1959; Frances Lewine, *The Nashville
Tennessean*, Jan. 5, 1964; Mary Jane Maddox, *Marshall
News-Messenger*, Dec. 22, 1963; Flora Rheta Schreiber, *Cos-
mopolitan*, Feb. 1964.

with them spread the suspicion of Lyndon's ethics and tactics as a politician-businessman. Whether or not his position had any influence on the fact that she got the first, which has remained the only TV station in Austin, may be left to popular imagination—and precious little imagination at that. Three facts are pertinent. It was one of the first channels the government released after the war-time freeze; it went to Lyndon-Lady Bird Johnson; and it is still the only one in a city of more than 200,000 people—whereas many smaller cities have three to four competing stations. Perhaps it was providential circumstance; not politics. Anyway, it's so![11]

Next the Johnson interests spread into Waco. The F.C.C. records reflect that from there Wm. J. Boswell had written Senator Johnson, February 4, 1952, inquiring as to procedure in applying for a permit from the F.C.C., and outlining plans of the proposed owners of a local station, KWTX-TV. Johnson relayed the request to the F.C.C., all in the apparently proper routine duty of any Senator for any constituent. Over a year later Johnson wrote the Commission again, enclosing a Waco testimonial in support and urged consideration of "the problem, based on its merits." What passed by telephone is not of record.

KWTX-TV of Waco won the permit over a competitor, but when asked about it Walter Jenkins, Johnson's "man Friday," bore down in answer that Johnson's part was merely "routine."

Nevertheless Johnson was forearmed with knowledge of the Waco situation, and his Company shortly acquired Waco's ultra-high frequency radio station, KANG. There-

---

11 The notorious Drew Pearson, who now serves the President so submissively, once wrote that the application was filed one night, granted the next. McNeil of Scripps-Howard said it was on file for four months and uncontested.

upon KWTX-TV began to feel the competition and on
April 29, 1955, filed a protest against the F.C.C.'s granting
an increase in power and range to Johnson's Austin station
without so much as a hearing. It charged that this station,
armed with the major networks and just ninety-six miles
away, "has violated and is continuing to violate the Sherman Act and the Clayton Act . . . against undue concentration of control . . . and [was thus] depriving the public
of a free choice of television programming . . . to the great
financial detriment of KWTX-TV. . ."

The LBJ Company denied any effort at monopoly
as well as the allegations of a broadcast overlap. The politically-minded F.C.C. ignored the complaint, which was
then withdrawn. Within less than a year the Johnsons had
disposed of radio station KANG and showed up with
twenty-nine per cent of KWTX-TV's stock.[12]

In view of the well-known and vindictive nature of the
Senate Majority Leader, and the life and death power of
the politically-minded F.C.C. over every station—power
to wipe out fortunes at its whim and caprice—it is not
surprising that the Waco station did not seek relief in the
courts, even had it been of a mind to do so. The basic
facts are simple. Senator Johnson was in a position of real
power, the squeeze was on, and the LBJ Company wound
up as partial owner of the Waco station. But what the
records do not reflect and what many people wonder, is
just how much of the transfer of stock was a legitimate
deal and what proportion may have been a payoff.

The next station to fall to the Johnson technique
was KRGV-TV in the little city of Weslaco. It was owned
by O. L. "Ted" Taylor, a young enterpriser who, after
seasoning with a pioneer Amarillo station, had organized

---

12 See the McNeil articles, as well as a summary in *Texas
Observer*, Feb. 28, 1958 and Feb. 21, 1964.

the Taylor Broadcasting Company of Wichita, Kansas and had later extended his interests into the southern tip of Texas to include the station at Weslaco.

After litigation over and loss of his channel at Wichita, Taylor found himself in need of additional capital. He called on the Murchisons of Dallas, who investigated but decided against the loan. Taylor then turned to Johnson interests, who for a loan, variously reported at $243,000 and $400,000 exacted in return an assignment of fifty percent of Taylor's stock. The first figure is reflected in a letter of March 12, 1956, wherein the Johnsons "asked the F.C.C. for permission to take over" half the Weslaco stock. Forthwith permission was granted.

Taylor brought in new management and reorganized his operations in an attempt to pull the station out. But with the burden of the Johnson debt added to an unlucky start, it was too little and too late. By report Ted Taylor was boxed in, and forced out. With the tough Jesse Kellam, who was known among the Weslaco employees as Johnson's "hatchet man", wielding the axe, the station was taken over lock, stock and barrel by LBJ's assumption of "the debt," plus Taylor's retention as "consultant" for a reported fee of $25,000 annually for five years—a sometimes convenient contrivance by which purchasers in a high tax bracket advantageously set up a portion of the purchase price as expense, instead of declaring it as capital investment. By this time the LBJ Company was probably looking for tax advantages, as it was really in the big money.

Thereupon in March, 1959, the Johnsons applied to the F.C.C. for permission to assume complete control of the Weslaco station. Their statement on file then showed that the Weslaco assets "had increased $400,000 since December 31, 1956," when they made their Shylock loan. The permit was granted and Johnson had again proven that he "knew the value of a dollar."[13]

The years had proven profitable for KTBC-TV. By the end of 1956, the Company's reports to the F.C.C. showed that it was really "hitting the black," with total assets of $1,516,516 and a surplus and profit for the year of $1,029,531. Thereafter each year was bigger and better.[15]

Eight years later Alvin J. Wirtz, whom Johnson had praised as a man who could "do anything better than anybody else," was dead, but the business he had helped discover in Austin for his close personal friend had exceeded, in fantastic degree, the optimistic predictions of its forgotten and unfortunate founder. But Lyndon B. Johnson, whose family owned it, as President of the United States, was faced with the embarrassing fact that he was the man who had discovered, cultivated and really made the redoubtable Senate Democratic Majority Secretary, his friend Bobby Baker.

Bobby Baker was the New Frontier model of Horatio Alger's successful American boy, imaginative and enterprising and an eager student of his boss's methods and operations. He dealt in everything: brokerage on American beef to Haiti with Texas millionaires; big and questionable building promotions in Washington; business with notorious Las Vegas gamblers; and especially, lucrative friendships with the choicest call girls, sometimes thereby laying the groundwork for tolerance, if not for outright blackmail, of some of the Congressional stud-horses on Capitol Hill. Bobby Baker was in position, with influence to peddle, and he believed in peddling it at a profit. On a $19,600 job, he had in a relatively few years parlayed his influence into a two million dollar estate.

Meanwhile the calculating Kennedy brothers, the cold

---

13 For comment see *Texas Observer*, Dec. 18, 1959.
15 *Texas Observer,* Dec. 18, 1959.

and ruthless Attorney General and the President, adept themselves at midnight maneuver, knew what was going on. They, their ivy leaguers and their Irish mafia, had never trusted Lyndon and had never been happy with the political shotgun wedding that had dictated his choice as running mate. Consequently they had so relegated the Vice-President to the wings that he had become a national television joke—the worst kind: "Lyndon Johnson? Who's that?"—"Where's he?"

He was on one of many senseless foreign junkets as "the President's special emissary," mainly for the political purpose of getting him out of the country and out of public mind, which was difficult enough, what with his corny, egotistical exhibitionism in the Taj Mahal and such exotic props as camel drivers from Pakistan. While anything like this rarely gets of record, the evidence seems conclusive that the Kennedys had decided to ditch him as their running mate in the coming election—despite all the usual disclaimers to the contrary.[15a]

The sharpest political observers in Washington were dead convinced of their design, to be effected probably in January. The Kennedys calculated the way in which to make him a thorough political liability, even beyond Democratic redemption, was to expose his close friend whom he had made Secretary to the Democratic Majority—this free-wheeling peddler of everything from favors for organized gamblers to the ardor of the fairest and youngest in public prostitution.

While any suggestion of intimacy between the two is anathema to the White House now, in the past Senate Majority Leader Johnson had left no doubt of his admiration for Bobby Baker. Before the Senate on August 30, 1957, which was after Baker's involvement in the John-

---

15a Walter Trohan, *Chicago Tribune*, March 7, 1964.

son insurance deal, the Majority Leader lavishly praised
his protege as "the most tireless and indefatigable man on
this floor..." Speaking from personal knowledge and with
prophetic insight, he continued with his praise of Bobby
as "a young man who has gone farther in life than many
others ... and is just getting started..." Warming to his
subject Johnson went on: "He gives himself unsparingly
and without regard to what he will get in return ... his
first thought is always those of us he serves ... and I consider him one of my most trusted, most loyal and most
competent friends." In the light of the record, who would
gainsay Lyndon Johnson; who could have known better?[16]

Thus in the fall of 1963, with the apparent blessing
of the Kennedys, the Senate investigation got under way,
the juicy news hit the front pages with a vengeance,
Vice-President Johnson rushed back from his junket to
Scandinavia and Bobby Baker, with Abe Fortas, Lyndon's
own lawyer and friend as counsel, resigned his post. Everything seemed set for a regular Roman holiday as the deep
and far-reaching corruption became obvious.

Shortly thereafter Kennedy and Johnson made their
political trip to Texas, to try to re-stretch the fatally
sagging Democratic fences, from which Johnson flew back
to Washington as President. Thereupon Abe Fortas hurriedly resigned as Baker's lawyer to return to Lyndon.
With the well-known influence of Johnson "on the Hill"
the searching inquiry hit high-center and threatened to
grind to an immediate standstill. Which might well have
been except for the determination of Senator John Williams
of Delaware and an obscure insurance broker who was one
day called to the witness stand.

Then the half-hearted Senate investigation, from its in-

---

[16] Requoted from Ted Lewis, "Capitol Stuff," March 19,
1964.

nocent launching pad, inadvertently set off an explosive missile in the President's direction, sending a lot of White House folks into orbit. Yet it simply confirmed, in the minds of thousands of Texans, long and outspoken convictions about Johnson's business methods and principles.

In 1955, Senator Johnson had suffered a heart attack while on his way for a convivial week-end with his old Texas political crony, George Brown, of Brown and Root, at his estate near Middleburg, Virginia. As the ever handy Walter Jenkins explained, after the Senator's recovery the LBJ Company decided to buy heavy insurance on his life to protect Mrs. Johnson's "control over the company, in event of Johnson's death."

Thereupon Bobby Baker, with powerful influence inside, as well as opportunistic friends on the outside, suggested the need to an insurance broker named Don B. Reynolds. As a true pal Reynolds' intimate dealings with Baker had ranged from actual business deals to getting specific advice on abortion for a girl friend who needed to find "some way to get rid of the baby." And Bobby Baker—whose lurid business activities had included a plush motel, which was opened with a bevy of lush and scantily dressed beauties as hostesses and Vice-President Johnson as guest of honor—knowing the problems as well as the powers of call girls, was able to help.

With Bobby's tip Reynolds set out to sell the LBJ Company insurance on the life of Senator Johnson. As a "sweetener" in the deal, Reynolds testified under oath, Bobby suggested the gift of a fine stereo-recorder set, one that cost $524.25 wholesale, to the Senate Majority Leader, Lyndon B. Johnson. The commissions on $200,000 of insurance on a man of Johnson's age and condition were considerable, and Reynolds, an agreeable if not a prudent man, reasoned that the idea was sound. He swore he bought

the set after Mrs. Johnson's personal selection and paid for
its installation in Johnson's palatial Washington home.

Still there was the ubiquitous Walter Jenkins, in Senator Johnson's Washington offices, who was likewise Treasurer of the LBJ Company back in Texas. In order to meet
a competitive bid on the policies, Reynolds swore that he
had to agree, at the insistence of Jenkins, to kick-back
$1208 of his commission for advertising on the Johnson
family station.

Reynolds, a Silver Spring, Maryland insurance man
with no possible use for advertising in Texas, peddled the
credit at a discount to Albert G. Young, of Mid-Atlantic
Stainless Steel, who had pots and pans to sell everywhere.
Thereupon Young, summoned before the Senate Investigating Committee and placed under oath, confirmed the
advertising deal. From under the near-immunity of the
presidential wing at the White House, Walter Jenkins
denied, finally with a sworn statement, the whole business.

At first the White House had answered that it was
obvious from the Committee's record that the President
"never had any conversation with Mr. Reynolds..." Of
course not! Such crude stupidity is not the Johnson way;
such business now is always handled by a subordinate
or confederate by word of mouth or telephone.

As the issue of certain perjury on the part of either
Jenkins or Reynolds was aired on the waves and in print,
the President himself had to take notice. He suddenly
called the press into the White House "Fish Room" and
in an equivocal, typically Johnsonian statement, that would
have been taken to pieces by any jack-leg attorney in a
JP Court, blithely observed that Bobby Baker's family,
with whom they had exchanged gifts before, "gave us a
stereo set." After all, Johnson drawled, Baker "was an
employee of the public, had no business pending before

me and was asking for nothing, and so far as I knew expected nothing in return..." Except for confirmation of the purchase of the insurance policies, the President had answered nothing.

He refused to entertain questions and peremptorily closed the matter with the press. Over on Capitol Hill the issue of perjury seemed forgotten while Bobby Baker repeatedly "took the fifth," and some Senators cooled off on the inquiry, apparently anxious to pull the cover over the whole mess, especially over the call girls. By now it was a major political issue.

Meantime in the House, Congressman H. R. Gross, of Iowa had been raising persistent and pointed questions about the propriety, the ethics and the legality of Johnson's Radio-TV operations, which by now had grown to include other stations.[17] A number of applicants for entry into the Texas Capital by cable and closed-circuit TV, for individual contract to customers, had been blocked by Johnson's dominant business, financial and legal tentacles, operating through the Johnson-controlled City Council of

---

[17] Besides the Waco interests, these include heavy interests in Brazos Broadcasting Co., Bryan; Victoria Broadcasters, Victoria, Texas; Texoma Broadcaster, Ardmore, Oklahoma; and an option for 50% of Capital Cable, a subsidiary of Midwest Video, of Little Rock, Arkansas, of which Hamilton Moses, the senior member of Senator John McClellan's law firm, is President. Thus with Senator McClellan, a close friend of President Johnson, the Chairman of the Senate Operations Committee and Chairman of its permanent Sub-Committee on Investigations, the likelihood of any real investigation is extremely slim. Only recently Capital Cable, with a contract to use KTBC's Austin tower, was given the green light by the Austin City Commission, dominated by Johnson men. Thus in every phase is the Johnson monopoly at Austin maintained. See *Dallas News*, Jan. 29, 1963, and for an extended review, *Texas Observer*, Feb. 1964. The Weslaco station had been sold.

Austin. The Council gave the permit to a Johnson affiliate, in action so flagrant as to cause an old Johnson lawyer-friend, retained by a contesting company, to wise-crack right in the Council meeting, that "Variety Magazine called it 'Lady Bird's gravy train.' The gravy train now has a cable connection..."

With Johnson's accession to the presidency, the family-owned LBJ Company was hurriedly placed in trusteeship, "removing it from Mrs. Johnson's control," in an effort to reassure the critical public that there would be no ground for suspicion of conflict of interest. Unanswered however was the persistent question: "If this is proper and valid while he is President, then what of the twenty-two years in which he and his family had owned it while he continually held other high and powerful public office?" Something is illogical here; something haywire somewhere.

On December 9, 1963, Gross put his finger upon the vital spot: "I submit" he said, "that every member of the Federal Communications Commission is going to be aware of the interests of the Johnson family in the field of radio and television. And I further submit that in the case of the F.C.C. the chairman holds office at the pleasure of the President."[18]

But it remained for the boss, who knows the full use of power from the ingratiating "come let us reason together" approach, right down to the Machiavellian art of pressure, to prove what was in store for those who oppose him. It so happened that insurance man Don Reynolds had had some troubles of his own, record of which had gone on file in the Pentagon and the FBI. But in no way were they pertinent to his sworn, and in part corroborated testimony of his shakedown by the Johnson interests.

[18] *Congressional Record*, Dec. 9, 1963; *Dallas News*, Dec. 13, 1963.

The White House "leaked" these secret files, this privileged material on Reynolds, through Drew Pearson, who like a lot of other liberals, from detesting Johnson as "a Brown and Root Senator," had turned into one of the President's self-abased idolators.

The enormity of this dirty business is staggering in its implications, though done with but one immediate purpose in mind; to compromise the character of Reynolds, discredit his testimony and divert the public attention from his revelation of the Johnsonian ethics and business tactics. Here was his personal air force record, classified, privileged information meant only for the military forces, which was pulled out, not for the Senate Committee, but for the press. Only after repeated but futile White House efforts to get reputable writers to take it, did Johnson's tacticians turn the smear over to Pearson, who broke the story.

Senator Hugh Scott demanded an investigation of the "leak" of "the raw FBI files, (which) could only have occurred at the instance of some person . . . higher than the FBI in government." FBI Director J. Edgar Hoover denied a leak to any unauthorized source. Veteran newsmen pin-pointed it directly on the White House—which in a matter of this importance, meant the President himself. This drastic if not diabolical use of power provoked Columnist Ted Lewis, of the *New York Daily News*, to put the question that was probably uppermost in every critic's mind:

"Does the White House have the authority—ethically, anyway—to order J. Edgar Hoover to turn over its secret files any time the Administration wants to crack down on an embarrassing witness or a political opponent?"[20]

20 The story can be traced through the daily papers, and is summed up by Edward Hunter, in the monthly newsletter, *Tactics*, Feb. 1964, Arlington, Virginia.

Americans everywhere were shocked and surprised except
for those who knew Lyndon Johnson in Texas.

For nowhere in the millions of Johnson's words that
embody the Johnson record can recognition of any positive legal, moral or Constitutional limitation upon his concepts of and lust for power be found. With Johnson, authority needed, if politically prudent and possible, is authority assumed. This is explicit in his record. This is
basic in illegitimate government.

In an ironic way Don Reynolds may be said to have
done a public service. He had touched the Johnson nature
at its two vitally sensitive spots; disclosure of its ruthless
use of power on the one hand, and its infinite greed on the
other—as well as its lack of ethics and principle in both.
He had given another example—though more should hardly
be needed—of the terrible power of blackmail, and what
may be used on any man who dares stand in Johnson's
way, even with the truth. Finally, he had added further
proof of the historic principle that a nation ruled by illegitimacy is a nation ruled by fear.

Strangely, it all started with the entirely proper and
businesslike idea of hedging against forced liquidation of
Mrs. Johnson's empire for tax or other reason, by heavy
insurance on her husband's life. Which may leave some
public wonderment as to just how badly the LBJ Company's treasurer, Walter Jenkins, really needed that embarrassing $1208 kick-back on the commission. His Com-
pany's annual statement to the F.C.C. in 1959 should be
fairly conclusive for those who abide the judgments of
the balance sheets.

As of the year ending in March, its "fixed assets"
were reported to be $1,229,341.52; more than double what
they were in 1956. It owned $226,256.52 worth of "other
property," $276,349.51 of stocks, over $69,000 worth of

automobiles, and showed "deferred charges" of $10,131
on 'prepaid life insurance.'" On hand were $520,563.60
in cash, $812,747.98 in "receivables," and a surplus of
$1,063,713.94. Its total assets were listed at $2,569,503.39
its long-term indebtedness at only $155,000, and its ac-
counts payable $505,369.60—which seemed only a book-
keeping entry as to what its fully-owned Weslaco station
owed the home office. Its declared profit was $430,-
432.24. [21] So it would hardly seem that the help of Don
Reynolds was needed, though apparently he was but one
among many of the Company's prudent and reasonable
customers.

Thus with practically no indebtedness, with an increase in fixed capital assets of over 100% in three years,
with more than $1,333,000 in cash and receivables, with
over another million in surplus, and with a declared profit of over $430,000—up some 350% in three years, ap-
parently the LBJ Company was not doing so badly. Its
current value is estimated to be at least $7,000,000. Aft-
er such a showing who would dispute the claims of his
wealthy main-street socialist friends that Lyndon B. Johnson—on the personal level—"knows the value of a dollar?"

Back of all this however, is another element, the tough
and tremendous drive of determined men, most of whom
have been with him for years. Those at the top are close
to the boss and once enmeshed within his personality and
power, become a part of his machine and seemingly never
quit. The tempo is ever one of pressure from above; of
relentless drive upon those below. His organization is
really a striking human phenomenon. [22]

A former employee of rank has observed that "their
business philosophy," simply boils down to this: "We have

a few key people who are well paid. We expect their un-
divided devotion and loyalty. All others are 'peons' who
are expendable. When they reach the end of their use-
fulness, throw them away and get some new ones."

Since Lyndon "has it made," his main-street friends
like to point to his "business success" as proof of his
"essential conservativism." But his political philosophy
never squares with the exacting standards of his balance
sheets. These prove nothing but the avarice of his family
and the wealth of the man. Others will even contend that
the placing of his properties under trusteeship, in removing them "completely from Johnson family influence and
control," is proof of high-minded purpose, which alleged
divestment of personal interest has been favorably reported
in the press. But somehow certain shadows still hang over
the scene, uneasy skeletons rattle in the closets and the
stench from Bobby Baker's and many other odorous doings
persistently blows down the winds from Washington.

---

[22] See *The Wall Street Journal*, March 23-24, 1964. It is
interesting to note that the LBJ Company, despite Johnson's
open alliance with Reuther, Meany and other top figures in
labor, is still not unionized. Also that in view of his vast
concern for the "under privileged," as this is being written
his company is being sued for an accounting, and for an
amount estimated between $50,000 and $75,000 by 38 former
employees, under the company's profit sharing and incentive
plan. *Austin-American-Statesman*, Feb. 29, 1964.

IV
EXCEPT WITH FRIENDS,
"THE POWER TO TAX IS..."

"Politics is the most important pursuit of man."
                                    —Spengler.

Beyond his understandable interest in helping an ambitious and enterprising friend along, Lyndon B. Johnson really had no business need for the imaginative Bobby Baker. Lyndon had been cozy with real wheeler-dealers for years, and for himself he already "had it made." First and closest among his big business friends were his original financial angels, Brown and Root, of Houston, Texas, of whom George and Herman Brown were the dominant figures.

When Lyndon ran for the Senate in 1941, and again to steal the election in 1948, Brown and Root, having spread their operations extensively, primarily on government contracts, really laid the cash on their candidate's line. Their marvelous expansion and success were understandable. With ready access to the best Washington sources, with advance information on proposed public works from which to estimate and figure, and with ready and telling influence when the contracts were let, they were in superb position to skim off the gravy, and did—especially at "cost plus." Progressing from local operations around Austin, the world became their oyster. In a liberal sort of Texas way, there was really little that was criminal or illegitimate about it. It was open federal policy, approved by the great white father and sanctioned by a representative Congress elected by a people who obviously did not give an infinitesimal part of a damn. Racketeering was hardly suspect; preferential treatment had become public policy. Brown and Root prospered.

Still there was an element of public conscience, strangely but not completely lost, which prompted some idealistic agents with the Bureau of Internal Revenue to launch an investigation into their tax returns. A lot of deep and productive digging was done by the investigators, and they hit pay dirt at Houston in thick and successive layers. They shot their reports to Washington where they seemed to get lost in more important business. In time the fact that Brown and Root was being investigated became a matter of news of Brown and Root dimensions.

On May 13, 1944, James M. Cooner, Internal Revenue special agent in charge for Texas and Louisiana, was busy relaying additional details to Washington bearing on the investigation—especially as to how Brown and Root's tremendous contributions to Johnson's 1941 Senatorial campaign were being taken as tax deductions. The same day Congressman Johnson and former Undersecretary of Interior, Alvin J. Wirtz, representing Brown and Root, called on President Roosevelt.

Johnson later denied that they had talked about the Brown and Root investigation. Nevertheless Roosevelt called in Assistant Secretary of the Treasury Elmery Irey the next morning, and at once a treasury agent was on his way from Atlanta to Texas, quietly to pull the cover over the Brown and Root investigation, as usual leaving the little men at the bottom, the more or less unknown investigators, holding the sack.

How many were fired or quit in disgust is not of record, but as perverse fortune willed it, a store of their documents wound up in the hands of the columnist, Drew Pearson, who then detested Johnson and his big business backing, and who, when it served his purpose, was not altogether averse to printing the truth. The tumultous

years hurried by and the time seemed ripe when in the
spring of 1956 Senator Johnson "had adroitly maneuvered"
a threatened Senate probe of "the natural gas lobby"
out of the hands of Senator Hennings, of Missouri, to
arouse the ire of the liberals and with reason.

Following the War the government had, quite properly, put its war-time, government-built Big and Little Inch
Pipelines, reaching from the Texas Gulf fields to the
Atlantic seaboard, up for sale. Of current tremendous
worth, they were, in view of the impending industrial
development, potentially of fantastic value. Houston attorney Charles I. Frances, Lyndon's close friend who had
rendered distinguished service in the Duval deal, handled
the vast and intricate sale, to assure his own independent
fortune and to further the vast enrichment of Lyndon's
angels, Brown and Root and associates. They wanted no
investigation. Lyndon reciprocated by cutting the ground
from under the Henning's probe of the gas lobby, to the
disgust of Lyndon's present bosom pal Drew Pearson, who
thereupon hit the pages with his revelations from the
squelched tax investigations of Brown and Root.

To make the timing even more effective, an election
reform bill was pending before Congress designed to regu-
late and publicize campaign contributions. Senate Majority Leader Johnson opposed it, especially its application
to primary elections; first not for its flagrant unconstitu-
tionality—as he has so often proven, but because, if applied
only to general elections, Texas would be virtually exempt
from embarrassment in the primaries, which were always
tantamount to election. Second, he opposed it because
disclosure of his own might be politically suicidal. Since
Lyndon Johnson would not let it happen to himself, Drew
Pearson, with understandable relish, did it for him.

Not in the usual Pearson way, but in straight reportorial style, as if sobered by unusual confrontation with the truth, he dipped into the devastating records of the Revenue investigators which he had somehow acquired and broke his present disclosures.[1]

After pointing out Johnson's well-known intimacies with George and Herman Brown; their political support of the Senator; his frequent use of their private plane; his visits to the Middleburg estate—as at the time of his heart attack the previous summer; their unbroken participation in government ventures, such as in the recent billion-dollar contracts on naval and air bases in Spain; he got down to the meat of the matter—how they had so handily financed Lyndon Johnson's campaigns. The disclosures left no doubt as to why Senator Henning's proposed probe might have blown the Big and Little Inch deals clear out of the ground, and why Senator Johnson opposed the disclosure of contributions in the primaries.

The records of the Internal Revenue showed that the handiest device Brown and Root "used to finance the Johnson campaign was to make out checks to employees of Victoria Gravel Company," one of their subsidiaries, who in turn cashed them and contributed the money for campaign purposes.

As an instance, on May 26, 1941, a check for $5,000 was made out to J. O. Corwin, Jr., of Victoria Gravel, "and charged off as a business expense." Corwin apparently cashed the check in Lyndon's home town of Austin, and later, under oath, admitted that he had mailed half of it to Johnson's campaign headquarters.

In similar fashion, a check for $2,500, issued to another Victoria employee, Randolph Mills was deposited in his own bank. The same day he withdrew the same amount,

[1] These were printed in Pearson's columns of March 26-27, 1956.

which was given to J. Frank Jungman, Johnson's Houston
campaign manager. In turn, as the Internal Revenue records showed, Jungman deposited it in The Second National Bank in Houston for the Lyndon Johnson Club.

As the contributions grew larger, the procedure sometimes became circuitous. As an example, the Revenue
agents found that Brown and Root, through Victoria
Gravel, had issued checks in the amounts of $5,000 on
May 26, and two more, for $3,000 and $4,500 on June 7,
1941 to Edgar Monteith, a Houston attorney. He seems
to have "distributed" $10,000 of this "as a profit" between
himself and his law partner, A. W. Baring, who then re-
paid the full amount to Monteith, who in turn put it into
the Johnson effort by writing checks to pay for radio time,
printing and other campaign expense—all of which the
Internal Revenue had from the Second National's photostat files.

When asked specifically about the matter, Senator
Johnson said he "had never heard of Monteith," much
less his financial support, though Monteith was the brother
of a former Houston mayor.

Monteith refused to testify, which provoked the observation by the special agent in charge of the investigation that:

> It is quite obvious that Monteith aided and
> abetted Brown and Root, Inc., and Victoria
> Gravel Company in showing that political con-
> tributions for which he was the conduit were at-
> torney's fees. This would make his income tax
> fraudulent...
>
> I seriously doubt that he was afraid of in-
> criminating himself in connection with his own
> tax liability, but believe that he was afraid he
> might be involved in a conspiracy in connection

with the evasion of taxes by Brown and Root, Inc., and Victoria Gravel Company.

The most interesting disclosures were the oddly-timed bonuses that Brown and Root's books showed had been paid to its officials, and then how these tax deductible windfalls had been used. They found that L. H. Durst, their purchasing agent, was paid two bonuses of $3,500 and $2,000; W. M. Powell, vice-president, $4,000; Carl Burkhart, office manager, $5,000; D. B. Young, secretary, $9,500 in three checks; and L. T. Bolin, vice-president a whopping $30,000. But these "bonuses" were not given toward the end of the year—in keeping with usual business practice, but between March 28 and May 20, 1941, which just happened to fall in the very middle of the hot Johnson-O'Daniel Senatorial campaign.

Significantly there was no explanation for these sudden bonuses. Under investigation the employees themselves could give none. More than that, with the possible exception of Bolin, they seemed to have cashed their checks the same day they got them and could give no explanation of what they did with the cash. For successful businessmen, their memories were woefully short.

In the case of Vice-President Bolin and his $30,000 bonus, he did admit that he had made a cash contribution to Johnson, but could not recall the amount. The agents found a check for $1,150 for printing, and another for $1,870 as contributions to the 1941 campaign. As for the rest, there is nothing more elusive than campaign cash.

This was the nature of the material on Brown and Root's tax deductible contributions to Johnson's campaign that was rolling into Washington when, on January 14, 1941, the investigation was shut down by no less than President Roosevelt himself.

Still the evidence suggesting criminal fraud was on

file, potentially dangerous should it eventually fall into honest or unfriendly political hands. Almost unnoticed in this connection was the sordid nature of what happened to the Collector in that district, and the fate of the files of income tax returns for the years in question.

In a situation like this, the importance of having "agreeable" men in the "right offices" is of paramount importance. For years Johnson had been dominating the appointment of key figures to the most important places in Texas—U. S. Judges, commissioners, attorneys, marshalls, postmasters, and so on,[2] as well as a multitude of administrative boards. But there was one vital place still unfilled by a Johnson man.

In 1933 President Roosevelt had appointed a Texas Democrat of the old school, Frank L. Scofield, to the job of Collector of Internal Revenue for the First District of Texas, with headquarters in Austin, and with jurisdiction over Houston. With not only the Brown and Root but a number of other important investigations pending, or subject to recall, Frank Scofield was far from the sort of man the Establishment needed. Impartial administration refuses to be a party to blackmail and is inconsistent with illegitimate government. The decision was reached that Frank Scofield had to go, and the device seems to have been that simple resort of ruthless power, a plan to "frame him."

In the middle of the 1950, off-year Democratic campaign the party loyal in Texas, led by that bumptious bag

[2] Texas patronage, which Lyndon dominated as Senator and continued to dominate as Vice-President, was one of the biggest bones of contention between him and Senator Ralph Yarborough, a bitter issue with Yarborough, right up to the hour of the assassination. Immediately thereafter he and the new President came to "a meetings of minds"—a modern euphemism for "a deal."

of wind, Mayor Tom Miller, of Austin, planned a Jefferson Jackson Day Dinner for fund-raising purposes at $50 a head, to be held on May 27 at the City Coliseum. The anticipated and successful goal was a $100,000 pot for that same old crusade of progress, Roosevelt's New Deal. The featured speaker brought in from the Potomac to shell the reactionary timbers of Texas from the City Coliseum beside the Colorado was Vice-President Alben W. Barkley, that paragon of Democratic virtue who died wealthy by simply overlooking, for years, the payment of his income tax—an ironic choice in view of what was planned.

The procedure of filling the bull-barn was the usual call to the brass-collared faithful, the "notice" to the recipients of special privilege, and the pressure on the defenseless little people—those hired elements in the bureaucratic machine. One day well in advance of the dinner, Frank L. Scofield, in his office at Austin, picked up his phone, and when he learned that Sam Rayburn and Lyndon Johnson were calling, waved his first assistant to get on the line. The subject was the Jefferson-Jackson Day dinner, the need of money and the necessity of a full house for Barkley, as further positive and irrefutable proof of "making Democracy work." The word was to put the pressure on; to get out and sell the tickets.

Though Scofield had been a party wheel-horse at raising funds before his appointment, this went decidedly against his Texas-cowman grain.[3] Tickets were bought, or small contributions made, by only two members of his staff. But others were hardly derelict, and the crowded coliseum heard Barkley invoke the shades of a virtuous

[3] In his late seventies, Frank Scofield is still a working ranchman, one of the most noted breeders of registered shorthorns in the world, on his ranch near Austin.

and valorous past. Mayor Tom Miller proudly delivered
his $100,000 to the Democratic National Committee and
all seemed successful and serene.

   In the months that followed, however, Charles F.
Herring, the U. S. Attorney, scenting corruption in the
Austin area, got to work and on January 29, 1953, a Federal Grand Jury brought in criminal indictments against
Frank L. Scofield, mainly under the Hatch Act, which
forbids the participation of Civil Service officials in politics. Since over two and a half years had elapsed, a lot of
time had evidently been put in on the case. Scofield was
charged on fourteen different counts, typical of which
was the allegation of "wilfully" soliciting and receiving
"directly and indirectly," "a subscription and contribution
for a political purpose from another officer and employee
of the United States, namely Helen Jester," a cashier in
his office.

   Scofield resigned while his old friend, Ex-Governor
Moody, as counsel, moved the dismissal of the charges.
Federal Judge Ben H. Rice agreed on eight, and ordered
trial on the remaining six. Helen Jester and ten other
employees of the Revenue Office were subpoenaed, the
capias ordering them to bring their cancelled checks showing their contributions, "by virtue of which you received
a ticket or tickets of admission to the Texas Jefferson-
Jackson Dinner." Only two employees had contributed;
one $25, the other $50.

   Nor was this all in the way of high crime Herring
turned up in Scofield's office. The government charged
that employees had given the Collector a refrigerator, and
pointed to a little old office ice-box as proof. This was
readily admitted by the staff, which contended that Collector Scofield kept country hours, arriving early and
sometimes staying at his work until late at night—often

without a bite to eat. Concerned with his health, they had chipped in and surprised him with the gift of an ice box where he might keep milk, fruit and other food for a noon-day lunch.

In defense Governor Moody went to bat on the Constitutional issues. He argued that four of the charges were in violation of the First of the Bill of Rights, "unduly and unreasonably" limiting the defendant's "freedom of speech, [and] the right of people to peacefully assemble and petition the Government for a redress of grievances ..." Likewise, Moody pointed out, they violated the Ninth Amendment, as the Government's action "denies and disparages rights retained by the people from those enumerated in the Constitution of the United States, including the right to engage in political activity." He continued that in like manner, they violated the Tenth Amendment. On June 8, 1954 the Federal Jury brought in its verdict, and Frank Scofield, acquitted on every count returned to his cattle on the bluebonneted slopes above Austin. Thereupon his place in the Collector's office was filled with Robert W. Phinney, Democratic Party Leader Johnson's personal choice.

Sometime later misfortune befell the old and extensive Internal Revenue files in the Austin office, which, in keeping with the Bureau's practice at that time were the only copies in existence. With space a problem for such voluminous records, Collector Scofield had kept them stored in a fire-proof structure. But his successor, with, commendable zeal for economy, shifted them into a quonset building across the river in south Austin, which, as fate would have it "accidentally" caught fire and burned to the ground, June 5, 1953.

Even so the Government was frightfully embarrassed, as everybody's past returns, including Brown and Root's,

"THE POWER went up in act of ... as ... ks

...mes. But who can contest even an ill-timed
Instead of being brought to trial for crimi-
f the tax laws, Brown and Root saw their
dropped; instead of collecting $1,062,184.87
axes, with a fraud penalty of $53,092.45, as
mated against Brown and Root, the papers
t Uncle Sam settled for $372,000. Politics,
ie possible," had paid off. Small wonder that
...ness loves Lyndon.[4]

A strange and incredible, and in its far-reaching implications a terrifying aftermath of character assassination and persecution, levelled at a relatively obscure person, followed the Austin fire. This incident seems to have had its beginnings in Washington, where, under President Eisenhower, his "modern Republicans" and such quondam Democrats as Mrs. Oveta Culp Hobby, the welfare state was free-wheeling along at accelerated speed.

There, in early February, 1954, a House Committee was conducting hearings on H.R. 7341, the Public Health Service Act, which among other features would have placed private nursing homes under the supervision of the Federal Government. Cabinet Member Hobby's Department of Health, Education and Welfare was sponsor. Government doctors and the "director of social insurance activities" for the American Federation of Labor testified in its favor.

Opposing were representatives of nursing groups from some forty-odd states, among them the President of the Texas Nursing Home Operators Association, Mrs. Oscar Yellott, owner of The Palms, a nursing home for the aged

---

[4] For the bare outline of the Frank Scofield incident, see the newspapers of the period and the documents in Case 3744, U.S. District Clerk's Office, Austin, Texas. For an account of the fire, see *Austin American*, June 6, 1953.

and infirm in Beaumont, Texas. Mrs. Yellot
a fight for state licensing and inspection of nu
knew the problems and issues and wanted no pa
eral control. A forceful and articulate woman, s
lenged the government doctors on the stand and ap
before the Committee, February 5, 1954, with a d
tating attack against the bill and some pointed rema
about her fellow Texan, Madam Secretary Hobby, fo
good measure.

The following April 12, John L. Keating, a special
agent for the Bureau of Internal Revenue, called and asked
to look into her safety deposit box, demanded her records,
and began an investigation of her income tax returns, with
the implications of an impending charge of criminal fraud.
Never before had a question as to her tax returns been
raised. She was surprised, but completely cooperative.

After his initial investigation, Keating returned and
frankly admitted he had found nothing adverse, but that
he had been sent by orders from "higher-up," and expressed his regret that she had ever gotten mixed up "in
politics." Despite his findings he said, her case had not
been closed.

Sometime after midnight on April 30, 1954, Mrs.
Yellott had a strange, friendly, but anonymous telephone
call to the effect that "the powers that be" were really
after her. The caller suggested that she "ask those dirty
crooks about the warehouse fire in Austin," adding that
"the FBI can make the man in Atlanta talk. He has plenty
of records. He gets blackmail money . . . They want you
to quit talking." Then the caller hung up.

Mrs. Yellott drove to Austin to investigate the "warehouse fire" and with exceptional pertinacity ran down the
report. Upon her return she told her attorney what she
had done, but his conservative counsel was to drop the

matter completely. Between times she was hounded for additional information on her income for years past, which she managed to produce with much bother and expense.

In July, 1954, the Texas Nursing Home Operators met in Austin, where, as President, Mrs. Yellott was scheduled to talk. And she did. She talked about the investigation launched against her by the Internal Revenue Bureau, with its overtones of criminal fraud, following her forthright attack on the welfare legislation in Washington. She reviewed her past efforts at reform and levelled a broadside at the system, saying:

> The thing that is so diabolic is that an honest person can be put through so much humiliation and expense . . . just because someone sought revenge. I soon realized that I had committed a crime—the crime of loving my country enough to be interested in current events and of exercising my constitutional right of freedom of speech, my right to petition, my right to openly oppose that which I believed with all my heart to be wrong . . . I had castigated high officials for their neglect of our old people. I had dared to expose health inspectors with sticky fingers, and had demanded their resignation and stuck to my guns until they were replaced. I had sponsored a bill for the licensing and inspecting of nursing homes and fought . . . until it was signed by my Governor in my presence.
>
> And alas, but not least, I had committed the crime of going to Washington and opposing legislation which I believed to be the initial step to the complete socialization of the American people . . .
>
> I do not believe that Congress is aware of this kind of persecution of people who appear before

Committees . . . I do not believe America can re-
main a free country without people feeling free
to redress government. I intend to start the ball
rolling by going before Congress and laying my
cards on the table and asking them to determine
just why a special agent was sent to disrupt my
domestic tranquility—to hinder me in my pursuit
of happiness—to front for the accuser who should
have come himself to seize, search and make me
feel insecure, and to make me lose complete confidence in my government.[5]

Following Mrs. Yellott's fiery speech, the group discussed what constituted full and appropriate income tax
records. In disagreement, they decided to have Mrs. Yellott
call the new Collector of the District, Robert W. Phinney
requesting a Revenue speaker to come and advise. An
official was sent.

The problems of the nursing operators, often with
inadequate help, posed the dilemma between properly attending their patients and keeping onerous and extensive
records, which was discussed with animation and then with
heat. At last the agent told them that, "Whether you like
it or not, you are Uncle Sam's junior partners in business," and are expected to keep the "same sort of books
as an oil business or any other big company."

In the over-all irritation a delegate from Houston rose
to demand: "Is it true that our duplicate tax records have
been burned? Was there really a fire?" The surprised
official blanched and admitted, "Well, yes" and grabbing
up his papers hastily left the meeting. After adjournment,
Mrs. Yellott, somewhat abashed, called at Phinney's office
to thank him for the speaker and to apologize for the
unexpected question.

5 Copy of Mrs. Yellott's' speech in files of the author.

Phinney's reception was cordial, and after her apology
she paused to comment on the investigation of her own
returns, and with naive candor and simple honesty related
the anonymous call about the fire—probably, she suspected, by some worried subordinate with the Revenue office—
the truth of which she had confirmed by personal investigation. Thereupon she left the office of the Collector, returned to Beaumont, to The Palms, and to her care of
the infirm aged.

In between there had been many conferences with
Special Agent Keating, who still admitted he could find
nothing tangible, but feared his boss would reject his report, saying "that he had been told he had to get results
or get out.[6]

On August 12, Mrs. Yellott had another anonymous
phone call, to the effect that Brown and Root were in
control of Texas politics; that Lyndon B. Johnson was in
control of the Internal Revenue Service of the State; that
the records had been deliberately moved and burned to
"get Brown and Root off the hook"; that a man in Atlanta
knew the facts, but no FBI investigation had been made;
and that she was slated for more harassment.

On September 5, 1954, a similar call from Dallas
warned that her case was being reinstated because of the
talk she had made in Austin, and that she was really in
for trouble. The following Tuesday the same Special Agent
but "a changed man," John L. Keating—a man who
"acted like he was scared to death," appeared to reopen
the inquiry. Through fall and early winter the case was
bounced back and forth between Mrs. Yellott's accountant,
Marion F. Munro, her attorney, Peter B. Wells, Agent

6 Mrs. Yellott to J. E. H., October 7, 1956; Affidavits, Kathleen Yellott files, Ezra Jarnigan, W. P. Pryor, and Peter
B. Wells, Oct. 1, Sept. 29 and Sept. 15, 1956.

Keating, and the regional office in Dallas where it was finally turned over to Messrs. Patterson and Gray, whom the anonymous caller of August 12 had warned were "Lyndon Johnson's hatchet men."

After some delay they advised Attorney Wells that the case had been referred to the Justice Department for consideration. Upon inquiry there, Wells was told it had already been sent to the United States Attorney at Austin for prosecution. Thereupon Munro, Wells and Bell drove to Austin to see U. S. Assistant Attorney Lonny F. Zwiener, as U.S. Attorney Charles Herring had resigned; his place being taken by Russell Wine. The result: Keating was again sent back for further investigation. Anxious if possible to avoid unfavorable publicity, before leaving Austin Mrs. Yellott's attorneys had got Zwiener to agree that, prior to the filing of any complaint, they would be given opportunity for further conference.

Without notice shortly thereafter, February 16, 1955, a complaint for criminal fraud signed by Keating was filed in San Antonio. Zwiener then called Wells, but claimed it had been done without his knowledge. Thereupon Kathleen Yellott was arrested, posted bond, and, when the next Federal Grand Jury convened in Waco, was on hand with her records ready to go before the jury herself. When it met on March 2, 1955, and her charge came up, it did not even call her to testify. Upon conclusion of the pre-

---

7 This story, in shocking detail, is found in the files of Kathleen Yellott, notably; letters of Marion F. Munro to Mr. and Mrs. Oscar Yellott, Aug. 28 and Sept. 28, 1956; Lonny F. Zwiener to Peter B. Wells, March 2, 1955; Photostat of Complaint by John L. Keating, Feb. 16, 1955; newspaper accounts, March 3, 1955; Affidavits, as cited, including others by Mrs. Pansy Mills, Mrs. Theresia Foote Roller, of Sept., 1956; and extensive review, Mrs. Oscar Yellott to J. E. H., Oct. 7, 1956.

sentation of the case by Zwiener and the Federal agents, the Grand Jury forthwith slapped the Government down. It found "no bill" against the defendant, Kathleen Yellott.[7]

To repeat, these strange and incredible stories of perverted and hence terrifying use of power—the power of blackmail, the ruthless power to destroy the name, the reputation, the economic independence, and hence human personality itself, invoked alike against the big and little, the prominent and obscure, leave a number of questions not completely answered. Why was Kathleen Yellott chosen as an example? What was in her record even to suggest evasion, much less a criminal charge? What explains the strange, anonymous and friendly telephone calls? What did it cost her? What does it prove for other Americans who would face the issues with like candor—unintimidated, unafraid? These merit a measure of summation.

An element of speculation may be admitted in answer to the first, but certain facts are significant. Though a relatively obscure person, Kathleen Yellott, a completely courageous American, forearmed with righteous indignation over disturbing dangers to her liberties, became an articulate adversary of federal corruption and control. Before delegations from forty-odd states and a Congressional Committee, she had shaken her workworn fingers at the paid professional advocates of Federal force; attacked and pierced the pride of a vain Cabinet Member from Texas —the head of the new, subversive-ridden Department sponsoring the legislation; and had made a shambles of the government's case.

More than that, she had told the story of the repressive measures against her in public meeting at Austin, revealed her personal investigations regarding burning of the records to the Collector of the District himself, and let him know that she had sympathetic informers, almost certainly from among his own men within the Bureau. Such a woman was enough to worry any politician.

History indicates that illegitimate power cannot afford to let rebellion grow and spread. Usually it is easily contained among the big people at the top; it can easily get out of hand among the little below. Therefore the assumption that Kathleen Yellott was chosen as an "example."

From the first she had cooperated completely with the investigators. From the first she and her husband had insisted, with her accountants, lawyers and the tax agents, that if any liability could be found, they were ready and anxious to pay it. From the first she had turned her books and files to complete Federal use, even though, under investigation for fraud, she could have stood on her Constitutional rights and told and surrendered nothing. And all concerned, even to the investigators, believed in her. Agent Keating admitted repeatedly that nothing could be found, saying "several times," that he was "under instructions to secure newspaper notoriety in a fraud case in the Beaumont area" as a deterrent, "because Beaumont was a fertile field"; while his assistant Aubrey Logan remarked that "regardless of what we report the decision will be made by men higher up." Despite all these admissions by the government's agents, the prosecution continued. Thus the conclusion that an example was being made of Kathleen Yellott is inescapable.

To the next question; what was in her record to suggest evasion of taxes, much less criminal fraud? Her tax advisor Marion F. Munro, CPA—with twenty-seven years experience with a major oil company and in independent service—had been making her returns for years. In a remarkable letter reviewing the case, Munro declared that during his entire "experience as a tax practitioner I have

never had a client who was more willing to cooperate with
a revenue agent than Mrs. Yellott," and that he had never
found any "evidence of wilful intent to evade taxes . . ."

Finally the charge of criminal fraud, even when
pleaded by the Federal attorney and backed up with two
years of special investigation, proved such an obviously
put-up job that the Federal Grand Jury at Waco did not
even call the waiting defendant, but peremptorily pitched
the real fraud—the Federal charge—into the waste-basket,
and forthwith found "no-bill" against Kathleen Yellott, a
vindicated, but sadly disillusioned American.

The explanation of the anonymous telephone calls
must rest on assumption but on reasoning entirely logical.
The calls were certainly made by individuals with definite,
positive knowledge about men, policy and impending
events within the Revenue Bureau itself. The informants
must have been "on the inside." What could have mo-
tivated them? The answer seems conclusive.

The Districts in Texas were being taken over by
Johnson's political machine. Those subordinates who would
not go along were, likely, either being forced out or dominated into submissive silence. Thus to the element of fear
was added the passion of resentment, while their manhood
rebelled and conscience cried for an outlet. Resentful of
the new buccaneers, the honest could find relief in warnings to hapless victims, somehow hopeful that the truth
would prevail.

What of the question of costs? There is no way to
estimate how much had been spent by the Federal Government. After all who cares? With the failure of its contentions of criminal fraud, this Machiavellian inquisition
rolled on as a civil case, because government is devoid of
conscience and in politics nothing is so bad as failure. At
last, in 1956, Kathleen Yellott paid $1,200 of alleged tax

liability and the case was closed. The conspiracy to prove
that the political power in Texas cannot be defied, and
to make "an example in the Beaumont area," had cost
her heavily; $6,700 in accounting fees alone; overall, more
than $20,000; and finally, as she tragically admitted, it
had cost her "complete confidence in her government"—
the most terrible, because irreplaceable, exaction of illegitimate power.

Nothing could be more obvious than the hard cruel
fact that "the power to tax is the power to destroy"—
not just wealth *per se,* but worse still the durable fiber of
men, ancestral pride and inheritance, confidence, courage,
character—everything! The destruction is far more sweeping than simply that of wealth and material values; the
most terrible tributes are levied on spiritual and moral
character.

Thus by one of the most ironical and horrible usurpations of power in history—that of the honest and sublime
purpose of property to enhance the horizons of men and
set them free—has America suffered a diabolical perversion through the unlimited and immoral powers to tax,
and thus to reduce those who should be highest in a
civilized society to craven servants of an illegitimate state.

But for striking exceptions, no longer are the rich
"independent"; only the poor "can afford" to be courageous and free. In essence, these stood on trial with Kathleen Yellott. And the somber verdict of history is inescapable. When they are gone, the nation follows.

Meanwhile Lyndon Baines Johnson, whose influence
was once largely limited to Texas, now holds the most
powerful office in the world. And more than any man who
ever held it, he knows the meaning and the uses of power
—the ready use of power to intimidate and destroy.

V

L.B.J. — FRIENDS AND FAVORS

When deceit and duplicity become accepted government policy, no sage is wise enough to anticipate the ultimate and possibly violent end. Inherently this means the abrogation of the God-given right of free speech, the perversion and hence destruction of the freedom of the press, and the denial of that indispensable ingredient of all legitimate governments, *the consent of the governed*.

After steady if not studied attrition of these rights and principles through many years, through preferential treatment of some, and coercion and blackmail of others, vast portions of the news media in America have been reduced to sycophantic if not criminal confederates of the Establishment or the man in power. This was no less obvious in the successful buildup of a politically inexperienced army man by politicians and press to the stature of a hero worthy to be President, than in the instant, repulsive reversal of position toward Lyndon B. Johnson when adverse fate elevated him to the presidency.

On the morning of November 22, 1963, except among his favored friends, he was simply a professional politician of indifferent news value at the best, or an object of public jest at worst, distrusted by conservatives and radicals alike. Instantly the treatment and the image changed.

Overnight this inordinately vain, egotistical, ambitious extrovert became at once the most openly human yet complex, the most down-to-earth man of action and yet the most sophisticated in statescraft, the most "realistic" in diplomacy, the smartest in strategy, the most adept in political tactics, and, in idolatrous panegyric, the "man of mankind" from the honest grass-roots of Texas. To read the paeans of praise, one would have thought that nothing like this had happened to the American presidency since the angular Abe stalked in from the prairies.[1]

One wonders if these prostitutes of the media are simply so deluded by their own inflated sense of important position and power as really to believe what they say, or whether they are so devoid of character as to slant and distort the truth for personal expediency, or whether they, like the late utterly cynical Harry Hopkins, simply believe the people are just "too damned dumb to understand." The explanation of this gross perversion of truth and news is possibly a combination of all these human foibles and weaknesses.

The existence of such a phenomenon in such an area of vital interest and concern, with its eventual effects upon the morals of the people and the national character and unity, is staggering in its potential effect. Its surface influence is reflected in the idiom of the street, in the repeated and pervasive comment that "you can't believe a thing you read in the papers!" Nor can this sweeping indictment of a once vaunted "free and independent" press be swept aside as popular caprice or a momentary passion.

It is something of far deeper and more somber significance. It is a combination of the long frustrations of little but honest people who want and seek the truth, of resentment of propaganda and designed deception by those in power, of a sense of betrayal in past deed and action by those of influence and authority! More than that it is cumulative in force and effect. It is impervious to pious plati-

---

[1] Nor was this treatment alone from such known kept men of the news media as Leslie Carpenter — who came up with the "man of mankind," Pearson, Huntley, Brinkley and their ilk, but such others as Holmes Alexander and even Henry Taylor fell under the spell. Walter Trohan has maintained his rugged independence and objectivity, and David Lawrence his sense of perspective. See *U. S. News and World Report*, Henry Gemmill, "Dual Image," p. 95, Feb. 10, 1964.

tudes in political forum, press or pulpit. It is a sign of
national disunity, the dangerous undertones of largely forgotten and inarticulate masses stirring with potential violence—one of the most historic, most natural and yet most
terrifying reactions of people who have been denied the
truth by illegitimate power.

When men are once convinced that they are consistently being denied the truth essential to their survival,
imagination alone is left with which to anticipate tomorrow,
upon which to predicate their future. Even at its most
adverse, an honest and healthy people with national unity
solidly based on spiritual faith and morality can face and
live with reality. With venality on the prowl, and corruption widely condoned if not an actual part of government
policy, public apprehension feeds on imaginative fears, and
the spectre of the gods of wrath and violence hang over
such unfortunate and uneasy lands.[2]

Only in such a frame of emotion and events, of sustained judicial and executive usurpations—combined with
the abdication and default of Congress, can the real significance of the forced shutdown of the Bobby Baker investigation through the pressure of the President be correctly
assayed and understood. The peccadillos of this urbane but professional pimp, the admittedly effective operations to this connoisseur of plush living and lush flesh as
the ready accessories of money, influence and power, even
when wrapped in the magic mantle of being one of "the
most trusted, most loyal and most competent" of Lyndon
Johnson's friends, were not enough to make

---

2 When "managed news" becomes government policy, the
perversion is confirmed and complete. For people no longer
get "news" but propaganda, progressively moving from distortion to outright lying. America passed into this "progressive" phase as admitted and defended policy under
Kennedy.

a ripple on what was once the honest and open stream of American life and affairs.

Once all this would have been diligently smoked out of the devious passages of Washington life into the full and critical view of the American public. Then justice would have been demanded. The President's right hand man, Walter Jenkins, would have been called, either to "take the fifth" or be forced to throw light on the issue of perjury as between himself and Reynolds and Young, whereupon a grand jury could have come up with criminal findings. The President's action in bull-dozing, by sheer executive power and hidden pressure, the investigation to a close, will heighten the suspicions of people generally, confirming the lurking conviction that he could not afford to let the truth come out.

In such a situation in public life, nothing will substitute for candor. Nothing will dispel suspicion, restore tranquillity and confidence, and hence reunify society like exposure of the truth. The denial of this psychological fact does much to explain the influence of other strange if not sordid incidents in shaping the public attitude toward President Lyndon B. Johnson. They are tied, not positively and firmly, but tenuously and mysteriously, to the man throughout his career. Public apathy has combined with fear to keep them out of print.

Thus denied the truth even on matters hardly vital, instead of popular reassurance, suspicion is enhanced and wild imagination inevitably takes possession of the public mind. This was the real significance of President Johnson's action in suppressing the Bobby Baker inquiry. Yet it was not without plenty of precedent in the Johnson record.

One of the strangest of these is the story of an Austin murder. In 1951 a man named John Douglas Kinser owned the Butler Park, a scenic spot across the Colorado River from the center of Austin, where he operated the Pitch and Putt Golf Course. The other man involved was Malcolm E. Wallace, who, as a prominent student at the University of Texas, had helped lead the demonstration that marched on the capitol following the firing of the University President, Homer P. Rainey.

"Mac" Wallace had gone to Washington and by report had worked for Lyndon before moving into the Department of Agriculture as an "economist." Back in Austin thirty-three year old "Doug" Kinser, locally prominent in the Austin Civic Theater, and a "popular golf professional," was going with Lyndon's oldest sister, Josefa, who died suddenly at the President's ranch following a Christmas party some years later. From here on the record is stark, tragic and bare.

At mid-afternoon on October 22, 1951, thirty-year old "Mac" Wallace drove up to the Pitch and Putt course, walked in on "Doug" Kinser at the keeper's house and shot him dead. Wallace fled, but was caught, indicted for murder with "malice aforethought," and released on $30,000 bond. Strangely, no counsel appeared for him at first; only William E. Carroll, "a university friend," who somehow arranged the bond—later reduced to $10,000; while Carroll refused to say who the counsel would be.

Strangely too, District Attorney Bob Long called in a psychiatrist. Wallace, arrogant throughout the hearing, refused to see him. Still with no attorney, but with his "university friend" contending he was being held "without cause," and with bond posted, District Judge Charles A. Betts issued a writ of habeas corpus and released him.

He was brought to trial in the 98th District Court of Travis County before Judge Betts, with John Cofer, Johnson's every ready and able lawyer in times of trouble, and Polk Shelton, as attorneys for the defense. Cofer was not unduly searching in his examination of jurors, but qualified each on his attitude toward the *"suspended sentence law."*

The case went to trial. District Attorney Bob Long—notwithstanding the identity of the car, a bloody shirt and a cartridge of the same caliber as used in the shooting, found in Wallace's possession, and witnesses who heard the shots and saw the departure of a man who fit Wallace's description — described it as "a near perfect murder."

Wallace did not take the stand. No evidence was presented to suggest cause or extenuating circumstances. Cofer simply filed a brief, one-page motion for an instructed verdict, pleading that there was no evidence upon which the State could "legally base a judgment of guilt." Long said nothing whatever in rebuttal. After less than two hours of testimony which was shut off so "abruptly" that it "left the packed courtroom with jaws ajar." Long urged the jury to "punish Wallace in whatever degree you can agree upon."

Thus after one of the briefest and most perfunctory trials of a prominent murder case on record, even in Texas, the jury nonetheless found, March 27, 1952, that Wallace was, as charged, guilty "of murder with malice aforethought." Its penalty, a *five-year suspended sentence*—for murder in the first degree.

Long was on his way out of the courtroom while the verdict was being read. His staff seemed "dumbfounded," but his own comment to the press was no less strange than his action: "You win cases and you lose them . . . usually everything happens for the best." Somewhat understandable, therefore, was the comment of *The Austin Statesman* that this case, "marked from the start to finish by the unusual," had left the people of Austin shocked and "quizzical."[3]

3 *Austin Statesman*, Oct. 23-24, 1951; Feb. 23-25, 1952; and the slim file of Case 27417, State of Texas vs. Malcolm E. Wallace, *District Court Records*, Travis County, Texas.

Wallace returned to his work in Washington and five years to a day later appeared back in the 98th District Court to have his record wiped clean, citizenship restored.

From Austin the stories of the suspect nature of Lyndon Johnson's connections and deals reach far and wide. There is a persistent but completely unconfirmed story that Mrs. Johnson owned one-fourth interest in the giant wartime Sid Richardson Carbon Black plant west of Odessa, Texas; a plant picked up from the government at a small fraction of its cost through the political management of Johnson and John Connally.

There were the far distant Morrocan Air Base scandals, stemming from an $800,000,000 boondoggle where "there was not much doubt in anybody's mind" that the responsibility could largely be laid on Lyndon B. Johnson. Half-way round the world in the other direction, his younger brother, Sam Johnson, graduating—after newspaper exposure—from a $16,000 a year job as "clerk" in the Senator's Washington office, got profitable employment with the Senator's friend and supporter, Edgar M. Linkenhoger of Corpus Christi, on the contract for a government installation on Kwajalein Island.

Linkenhoger started out as a hard-boiled produce trucker in Robstown, Texas. He got into war-time contracting and as a close friend of George Parr, of Duval, and the New Deal Congressman, John E. Lyle, Jr., of Corpus Christi, all of whom were close to Lyndon, was remarkably successful in getting allocations of scarce materials when his competitors could not. From trucking spinach and onions he moved to world-wide contracting as president and principal owner of Transport Company of Texas. He had been convicted and fined of violation of Interstate Commerce Commission regulations, and he had slid out from under a Federal tax charge by pleading negligence and settling for $200,000 instead of going to trial for fraud.

Then came the need of the Kwajalein Island installations. Despite Linkenhoger's background, without competitive procedure the Navy passed over such well-established bidders as Pan American World Airways of New York, Lockheed Aircraft of California and Chance Vought of Texas, giving as one reason the Linkenhoger "company reputation." Though Transport Company of Texas had never put in such an over-seas installation, it got the contract at "cost plus." There were strong protests and lengthy reconsiderations involving various Admirals. Sam Houston Johnson left his clerkship with Lyndon and went to work for Linkenhoger. So did a high ranking civilian employee, Clayton Jones, in the Shore Establishment Division of the Navy, which had been active in the award to Transport of Texas. Linkenhoger's pay was better, and besides Sam Houston was causing stories in the papers.

A racket was raised and the award was reconsidered. Despite the recommendations of a Procurement Review Board that the work be let to Pan American, Rear Admiral Joseph E. Dodson, noting the "urgent" need of speed, re-awarded it to Transport of Texas on an estimate of $5,200,000 for the Kwajalein installation and the contract was signed April 1, 1959. Thirty months later the cost had climbed to $18,500,000 and the Robstown vegetable trucker was a multi-millionaire Texas businessman, flying his own twin-engine plane.

His hard and determined clique set a new and expensive precedent in letting of naval contracts, ruthlessly over-rode the judgment of various high admirals and a Review board and grabbed an $18,500,000 federal windfall for a long-drawn job that might have been done expeditiously for $5,200,000 or less, had the competing companies had an equal chance. Ironically, to cap the climax,

Secretary of the Navy John Connally gave the "award his blessing in a letter to Lyndon Johnson."

At last account Samuel H. Johnson, late of Washington, was "confidential consultant," with such "duties" as "appearing at conferences" with his boss, the tough tycoon, Edgar M. Linkenhoger—the former spinach trucker now living in style on Ocean Drive at Corpus Christi, his family of social prominence. The gossip frequently connecting Lyndon B. Johnson with Linkenhoger's career was happily dismissed by *Fortune* magazine, since "his role seems to have been that of an innocent bystander."[4]

When Linkenhoger was pressed for an explanation, he made his attitude clear. "It's a hell of a long story," he growled. "It's none of the public's business. There's no telling what it would have cost the taxpayers if we hadn't got the contract . . . It looks like that West Coast crowd [i.e., Lockheed and other bidders] thought nobody else should get this business. It apparently was a shock to them and their hirelings began fabricating rumors. But there's no scandal involved."—Naturally not! Only Lyndon's close friends.

When the jerry-built, fantastic financial empire of another "fabulous Texan," Billie Sol Estes, was trembling toward collapse through the long-deferred but honest exactions of the balance sheets, there was much scurrying for political cover, all the way from the dreary alkali Pecos flats to the marble mausoleums of free enterprise along the Potomac.

The full implications of this far-flung and intricate affair have in some respects, stumped the best investigators and legal and business minds that have been brought to

[4] See Herbert Solow's "How Not to Award a Navy Contract," *Fortune*, December, 1960, pp. 167 ff.; *Fort Worth Star-Telegram*, April 2, 1959, and confidential sources in Corpus Christi.

bear upon it. Mention of certain puzzling angles here is simply in illustration of the inevitable effects of political corruption and power, where again, lacking full and impartial exposure, the public suspicion of Johnson's involvement has grown stronger.

For months the remarkable, independent investigations of Billie Sol Estes by the Pecos doctor, John Dunn, had been under way before the first newspaper articles summarizing his findings were published in exposure. He had not only kept in touch with honest and interested local officials, but had counseled with the Texas Department of Public Safety, as well as local FBI agents.

Files of his findings were stashed away with two friends at widely separated points for safe-keeping. Another had been forwarded to FBI Director, J. Edgar Hoover, by his friend and former agent, Dan Smoot of Dallas. Another was in the hands of a prominent U. S. Senator. The involvement of big business institutions, as well as State and Federal officials of high place was definitely known.

When once the fraudulent nature of Billie Sol's operations was brought to light—in other words, when the barest outline of *the truth* became known through the press —the entire structure crumbled like a worn and dirty house of cards, thus again proving the infinitely healthy, cathartic power of the press. But only the surface had been scratched. So many and in such high positions were involved that quite probably only the surface ever will be.

Like many other courageous and honest Americans, John Dunn firmly believed that the truth alone would suffice and prevail and launched his lonely and personally tragic crusade for honesty upon that frail and faulty craft. His miscalculations reckoned not the far-reaching nature of the evil power he had exposed, endangered, and then defied.

The fraudulent business end of Billie Sol's operations

naturally went into the Courts, with bankruptcy and criminal indictments for himself and some close associates and a raft of civil suits over the conflicting interests of many others. But the exposure, the most important need, while nurtured by a few rugged souls, withered and died on the vine.

What was needed most was the exposure of the political policies, philosophy, morals and men behind this whole mess—in a word, the climate in Washington that had produced Billie Sol Estes. For the most gigantic swindle and scandal in the history of Texas was not bred and born on the Pecos. Billie Sol Estes was but the natural product of a system of corruption intent alone upon the growth and retention of power; a system whereby special privilege and legalized theft had become established federal policy.

While there may be no way, as Burke observed, of drawing "an indictment against an entire people," the fact remains that Americans generally, through public apathy and moral delinquency, were responsible for the conditions that produced the evil situation reaching from the Potomac to the Pecos, capitalized upon by the imaginative genius of Billie Sol Estes. That he should be prosecuted and made to pay was entirely proper, but to leave untouched the immoral policies that produced him was like stepping on the eggs and letting the cockroaches go. A bigger swarm was bound to be messing up the place tomorrow.

Dr. John Dunn was certain that the enormity of the national crime he had exposed would force a full and searching Congressional investigation. But Dunn was a product of forthright Texas raising, not of political sophistication. The very enormity of what he had turned up was the sure and certain reason that it would never be investigated and exposed. The Senator who had his files simply sat upon them. Even the sometimes sturdy John McClellan of Arkansas, to whose Senate Committee the inquiry fell, barely went through the motions. For this scandal involved at least one Cabinet member of the Kennedy administration, along with his staff—a raft of high Agriculture officials, two Senators, Representatives, ex-Governors and scores of lesser-fry.

Not high policy predicated on moral principle, but politics alone dictated the decision. In essence this decision was the sacrifice of a few lesser officials, dilatory tactics in the prosecution of Estes, the destruction of Dr. Dunn as diversionary news and a public example, and the profitable takeover of Billie Sol's bankrupt empire for the enrichment of the Establishment. In time the peak of interest passed and the public grew weary of the subject, largely because of its widespread and valid conviction that it had been denied much of the essential truth. It suspected the proven master of political maneuver, the Vice-President of the United States, Lyndon B. Johnson, of not only being involved but of having killed the Senatorial investigation.

The Billie Sol Estes debacle, and Washington's hurried burial of the remains without effective fumigation of the premises, revived a host of suspicions and convictions that Johnson was again the designing master of duplicity. It is doubtful if full exposure, no matter his connection, would have done half the political damage as did this exhibition of power in denying the public the truth. For curiosity and suspicion sometimes grow with insatiable hunger on meager morsels of news, when they would have been completely dispelled by a belly-full of the truth.

Thus in response to the President's defenders that "nothing significant has ever been proven tying Lyndon to Billie Sol," certain strange if not significant stories and incidents keep popping up in the unregenerate Texas mind.

First, to the aforesaid treatment of the chief defend-

ant: Two years after his empire crashed, with two convictions of eight and fifteen years levied, and with a Federal tax bill of $18¼ million against him, Billie Sol Estes
—"jobless, penniless and bankrupt," to quote the Federal
Court—is driving a 1964 Cadillac and is still living "in
style" in a new $50,000 home in Abilene, Texas. Under-
standably the public wonders, "How?" One of his lawyers
Jack Bryant, answers that he bought the place for Billie
Sol. Then who is financing him?[5]

Billie Sol is still free on $100,000 bond pending appeal
of his convictions—which is proper procedure. At times
the Courts do take time. But many Texans, grown cynical
with the political "run-around," will lay "heavy odds that
he will never serve a day." And they will tell you why;
"the influence of Lyndon Johnson." Wherein is the basis
for this belief that borders on obsession? The record is
fragmentary but in the Texas mind significant.

Prominent on the wall of Estes' luxurious Pecos home
hung the pictures of two Texas notables—the first in-
scribed "To Billie Sol Estes with warm regards and best
wishes" from Lyndon Johnson. They were close friends.
The inscription on the other read "To a great friend, true
Texan, grand American, Billie Sol Estes of Pecos with
warmest appreciation," signed by Senator Ralph Yarborough. They were even closer friends.

Undoubtedly those two Texans lent ready political
aid to Billie Sol in his multi-million dollar operations, and
Billie Sol reciprocated, with political support and campaign cash. At the peak of his operations his correspond-
ence with Lyndon and aides, especially Walter Jenkins
and Cliff Carter, dealt not only with the serious business
of cotton allotments, but with the intimate details of personal friends. The Vice-President's letters reflected warm

5 *Dallas News*, Oct. 9, 1963 and Jan. 18, 1964.

pleasure over Billie's visit "with Lady Bird and me" in
their Washington mansion; his enjoyment of Billie's favorite gift, the famed Pecos cantaloupes; holiday roses at
the Christmas season; and his interest in helping promote
Billie Sol's religious and denominational zeal through the
Department of State, "in behalf of the churches" in Tan-
ganyika; and so on.

Among the most important of the many-sided Billie
Sol enterprises was his anhydrous ammonia fertilizer business, which, with ruthlessly competitive procedures, he was
building into a virtual West Texas monopoly. It was
through the handling of the mobile tanks for the distribution of this fertilizer, from their actual construction to
their sale to farmers, and the mortgages upon thousands
of non-existent others, as will be recalled, that Billie Sol
Estes in large degree financed his vast holdings. Closely
tied in with his operations, therefore, was the supplier of
the anhydrous ammonia, Commercial Solvents Corporation of New York City, which was carrying him for fantastic credits in his cut-throat deals that were wiping out
competition in Texas.

Ward Jackson, a high official with Commercial Solvents, attended a business conference with the President,
Vice-President and Cabinet Members in Washington in
February, 1961, and enjoyed the special services of Clifford Carter and a visit with Vice-President Johnson himself. The fact that he wrote Estes that he had discussed,
"in general the situation in Texas and in the overall business area," with Vice-President Johnson served to heighten
the Texas suspicion of them all—Johnson, Commercial Solvents and Billie Sol.

There is a persistent belief that Mrs. Lyndon B. Johnson was a heavy investor in Commercial Solvents, and
thus indirectly interested in the Estes operation, though

the list of stockholders has never been produced in proof. Yet the Johnson influence in Billie Sol's behalf was generally known, though skirted by the press.

For example, Billie Sol acquired cotton allotments from submerged lands and other government expropriated acreages. His practice of illegally applying these allotments to his own land in the marvellously productive Pecos area had become so blatant and notorious that even the tolerant federal officials could not blink them down. From mild dissent they had moved to open investigation of his means and methods. Billie Sol appealed to Lyndon.

On January 31, 1961, Vice-President Johnson wrote to Secretary of Agriculture, Orville Freeman, enclosing a letter from A. B. Foster, Jr., Billie's man in Pecos. On February 20, 1961, Freeman wrote back about "changes in regulations governing the transfer of cotton allotments from farms whose owners have been displaced by agencies having the right of eminent domain."

Freeman, likewise a "reasonable and prudent" man, especially with Vice-President Johnson, gently pointed out that "there have been some abuses of the law in this regard." These "had the effect of an outright sale of the pooled allotment by the displaced owner under subterfuge practices . . . ," which was not the simple transfer of the allotment "to another farm actually owned by the displaced producer in accordance with the purpose of the law."

In view of such evasion and fraud, honest Orville continued, the Department's "regulations had recently been changed." These now provided that before the county committee could act upon "application for such transfer the applicant"—in this case Billie Sol with a basket-full of such—"shall personally appear before the county committee," armed with "all pertinent documents"—which

meant certificates of allotments, field notes and the actual
deeds, "and answer all pertinent questions" bearing on
the transfer. This sounded pretty severe for a man as
deeply immersed in the racket as Billie Sol, unless he had
complete control of the County Committee.

In such contingencies, as Secretary Freeman's letter
to Vice-President Johnson made clear, the State Committee could waive appearance if it "unduly inconvenienced"
the applicant, or because of "illness or other good cause."
In further reassurance and conclusion, the Secretary felt
"sure that the State Committee" would "be reasonable in
passing judgment," should the applicant fail to appear
under the "conditions enumerated . . ."6

With a note typed on a "United States Senate Memorandum" slip, saying "I hope the information contained
in the attached [Freeman letter] will be of interest and
helpful to you," which ended simply, "If I can again assist
you, let me know. LBJ," it was mailed to Billie Sol.

What an understatement, guarded or not; what an
open-ended "out" for Billie Sol! This . . . "of interest and
helpful!" What worried man, with a million dollars worth
of allotments at stake and currently under investigation
with distinct over-tones of fraud, wouldn't already be ill,
as well as handy with "other good" causes. And here it
was signed and sealed by the Secretary, and relayed with
a personal memo by no less than Vice-President Lyndon
B. Johnson, into the eager hand of Billie Sol Estes. How
could he keep from "having it made?"

That fly in the New Deal farm ointment might pos-

---

6 Secretary, Department of Agriculture Orville Freeman to
the Vice-President, February 20, 1961, photostat copy in
files of the author. The writer assumes that everyone knows
that cotton cannot be grown without government permission
— "an allotment," and the richest cotton land is of little
value without it.

sibly be the report made by a subordinate Agriculture official, Henry Marshall. He had been an employee of the
State Agricultural Stabilization and Conservation office,
assigned to investigate the vast jungle of Billie Sol's suspect
cotton allotments. His connection with the case was not
openly known, and his report was buried in Washington.

On June 3, 1961, Henry Marshall was found dead
on a remote section of his farm near Franklin, Texas. Five
days later Justice of the Peace Lee Farmer pronounced
a verdict of suicide *without ordering an autopsy,* despite
the protestations of Marshall's widow, according to the
newspapers, that "he was not the type to commit suicide."
Marshall was buried and his work as an investigator was
unknown to most, and all but forgotten by a few, while
the wheeler-dealer from the Pecos flew on, his twin-motored
plane virtually at the beck and call of important public
figures, from Senator Yarborough and Lyndon's staff in
Washington down to John White, Commissioner of Agriculture, in Austin.[7] After all, "nothing succeeds like
success."

Meanwhile the doggedly-determined Pecos doctor,
John Dunn, in addition to the pursuit of his successful
practice, drove ahead with his own investigations. At last
with the sweeping documentary evidence of Billie Sol's
fraudulent borrowings on non-existent fertilizer tanks firmly in hand, he decided he was ready to nail the sanctimonious Pecos civic leader to the cross of justice. When
Dunn's repeated calls to all political sources had gone
unanswered, he and an associate bought the *Pecos Inde-*

[7] Yarborough readily admitted that Estes' plane was on loan
to him in his 1954 Texas gubernatorial campaign, and that
Estes had been helping finance his weekly Senatorial broadcasts. Estes was doing the same for Lyndon, as indicated
in letters from Johnson's aides, though LBJ made no public
confession. For Yarborough's see *San Angelo Standard-
Times,* May 20, 1962.

pendent and Enterprise, determined at least to give the salt flat folks the acid truth.

He briefed his editor Oscar Griffin, turned over to him his files, and in the February 12, 1962 issue of their modest bi-weekly paper, began the devastating exposure that blew the Billie Sol Estes business sky-high.[8] Farmers, bankers, corporations, finance and fertilizer companies involved, all saw the handwriting on the wall when Dunn's investigations revealed the wild transactions—15,000 alleged tanks for his county alone, and total chattel mortgages of more than $34,000,000 in several Texas counties involved, most of which was fictitious financing. As the full import of the news began to be felt, a closed and frantic meeting of Billie Sol and his creditors was called in Dallas. But the false house built on frenzied and crooked finance, superimposed on a highly productive farming area, and from the first inherent in the immoral Federal farm policy, was already in ruins.

Immediately Estes became a sobering lesson in the utterly ephemeral nature of human vanity, pride and power. From the ostentatious host at two prominently placed $1,000 tables at President John F. Kennedy's "glittering" birthday dinner in Washington, May 27, 1961, and the no less distinguished host at two more at $100 a seat, directly beneath Vice-President Johnson's dais at the first inaugural anniversary dinner, January 29, 1962, Billie Sol was being held like a common criminal in a Texas jail two months later. An avalanche of action had followed Dr. Dunn's disclosures.[9]

Within a month Billie Sol was in jail in lieu of a

---

[8] The exposure continued in the issues of February 19 and March 1, 1962.

[9] In both cases the most prominent guests were Senator Ralph Yarborough and his wife. *Dallas News,* April 1, 1962.

alf million dollar bond;[10] grand jury charges were being
repared; suits and counter-suits were being filed; Yar-
orough and other politicans were anxiously scanning every
ews release; the Vice-President was discreetly silent; fed-
ral Agriculture authorities were making a show of con-
ern as to whether the millions of bushels of government
rain in Estes' storage were intact; while John White,
ikewise long-involved, made an unctuous pretense of pro-
ecting the public by cancelling the licenses of a number
f Estes-owned grain warehouses.

Texas Attorney-General Will Wilson, a candidate for
Governor, moved vigorously into the investigation for the
State; local grand juries met and returned a mounting
ist of indictments; associated West Texas corporations
and enterprises began to tumble with criminal indictments
on the side; the collusion of giant finance and fertilizer
interests became obvious; and after a long closed session
the Senate Investigations Sub-Committee unanimously
voted to probe the far-reaching manipulations in what its
Chairman, John L. McClellan, promised would be "a full,
thorough and complete investigation."

A host of creditors and mortgagors descended on the
Federal Court in Bankruptcy at El Paso to file their claims.
A Committee of Creditors was set up to represent their
interests. The millions of dollars of assets—lands, fertilizer
distribution systems, grain storage facilities and a variety
of other Estes businesses—were taken over. Billie Sol
was brought to trial and sentenced on two counts. The
sacrifice of a few minor Washington officials was made
as a sop to the public and Senator McClellan, after a
desultory inquiry, charitably let the curtain fall on his
"full, thorough and complete investigation."

10 Shortly reduced to $100,000. See the Texas dailies of late
March and early April, 1962.

So the natural and yet sometimes defensive question "Why not forget the matter? Why not let it rest?" Even if men resolutely willed it, subconsciously certain aspects like Banquo's ghost will not sleep, but restlessly wander on to disturb men's minds.

Yet anyone who inquires further is certain to be charged with incitement to disrespect for established institutions and people of prominence, of futile raking of old coals, of scandal-mongering and attempted character assassination. But here again, as in the case of Bobby Baker, what the all but endless newspaper stories, private inquires, jury investigations, indictments and trials disclosed was not, for the public mind, any more significant in inciting the people than what they suspected had been covered up.

The general story is known. But the sometimes vast significance of the apparently insignificant is lost in the mad stampede and never tallied up when the herd is quieted down and the losses counted. Historians of the future can assay the balance sheets and their significance. Our interest here is to expose certain hidden and overlooked incidents and weigh the import of the subtle and the tenuous factors.

First consider a matter of what now seems of minor moment. Just what precipitated this crash when, given a little time, Billie Sol's annually assured income of from $5,000,000 to $7,000,000 from government-guaranteed[11] grain storage alone might have bailed him out and put him on the high road to security and eventual reform? What blew up this business, bringing disgrace to some, financial ruin to many, prison for a few, death to others

[11] The government paid him $5,100,000 for storage of surplus grain for 1962. It was estimated to be at least $7,000,000 in the future. See Vernon Louviere's report, *Amarillo Daily News*, April 3, 1962.

and disquietude to millions of Americans?

Just three little articles in a country newspaper that dared to tell the truth. This is perhaps the most profound significance of the Billie Sol Estes case, his career and his story.

But those articles represented many months of the most intelligent, skillful persistent and courageous investigation in the history of that exacting and adventurous science. Nor were they done for a fee by a seasoned investigator. Instead the first evidence was stumbled upon by a young, skilled and busy surgeon, with intuitive curiosity and sufficient dedication to truth to follow through— as if in search of some fatal human malignancy, which in a measure it was—with the courage to probe to the source of the trouble.

With his files and diagnosis in the hands of his editor, Oscar Griffin, that truth, in quite ordinary literary style, brought the writer distinction and the Pulitzer prize, precipitated an avalanche of fenzied inquiry and shook America from end to end. What was the reward for the man who was really responsible? What measure of public gratitude, esteem and renown was bestowed upon him? That in itself is an equally significant story.

There is nothing more vicious than mass depravity with a cultivated veneer when its own image is exposed to public contempt, scorn and justice. In the smug and "successful" circles of his home town, it was John Dunn who had committed the unpardonable crime. He had exposed the leading churchman, the financial genius and the "most promising" citizen of the city of Pecos.[12] Therefore

12 E.g., former Pecos City Manager L. A. Patterson said: "You have to remember that Billie Sol was like a god in this town. It was freely reported that anyone opposed to him might just as well pack up their [sic] bags and leave town." *Corpus Christi Caller-Times*, June 11, 1962.

John Dunn became the culprit because he had stripped
the garments of simulated decency from the popular idol
—the reflected image and ambition of the gross and corrupt who admired him, as well as the immoral nature o
the government policies which had made him.

John Dunn, the man who had dared to seek and speak
the truth, was destroyed. He was threatened, hounded and
condemned. His business holdings were sacrificed. The
City Council barred him from practice in the municipal
hospital on vicious, trumped-up charges of malpractice.
He fought the issue against a stacked tribunal in public
hearing where, in diabolical perversion of the finest and
highest virtue of the medical practice—the warm sympathy of the real physician for his patient—he was pic-
tured in the public mind as guilty of lust for a negro
woman whose life he had saved. By corrupt and ruthless
power in his home town, he was destroyed, professionally
and financially and in virtual penury was forced to move
away to seek another start in anonymity.

Dr. John Dunn was guilty of but one thing and that
was mistaken judgment. He had dared to believe that
truth and virtue would prevail where public apathy con-
dones illicit power, and he had paid the price exacted by
faith while denied in reason. This is the second profound
historic principle—and tragic truth, that his marvelous
investigation proved.

VI
AFTERMATH OF FRAUD

From here on the incidents and characters to be treated in connection with the Billie Sol Estes case may be less significant than the major features that have gone before. For example when Texas Attorney General Wilson's investigators turned up the Estes claim that he had contributed $46,000 to Yarborough's campaign fund nobody was surprised. But when Johnson's supporters contended that the Vice-President was not involved, there was widespread disbelief, with millions of Texans still unsatisfied.

They believe the fact that the principal attorney who showed up to defend Estes when his friends realized he was really in trouble, by report with a prepaid fee of $85,000, Lyndon's veteran counsel and loyal friend, John Cofer of Austin, was positive proof of Lyndon's interest.

Some three weeks before his first trial, Billie Sol, impetuous, emotional and still the born promoter, conceived the idea that he could absolve himself by going on the stand and telling the whole truth about everything and everybody. It is known that Cofer disagreed. Estes then decided to fire Cofer and hire another, the liberal lawyer, Warren Burnett, of Odessa, for a fee of $30,000. But Cofer refused to be fired. He was already paid and by report he was adamant against spreading the web of truth through confession. There was none. Billie Sol went to trial and conviction.

As the civil litigation precipitated by the collapse spread, the testimony of scores of men was searchingly sought, among these that of Douglas Lewsader, Billie Sol's loquacious pilot, who at first could not even afford a jack-leg lawyer. But when the testimony of Lewsader—the

pilot who had flown so many political notables for Este
—came to be taken his counsel was one of the most ab
and expensive in Texas—John D. Cofer.

In each case the public wonders: "Who paid Cofer?
The bankrupt Billie Sol? Then how? If not, who? And
why?

Before Cofer took over and tied a knot in Lewsader'
tongue, that knowledgeable gentleman had spilled a lot of
loose and indiscriminate information. He told of "a com
mand call" he had one night to come to Estes' home
When he got there a big, burly man with Billie introduced
himself as an agent of the Teamster's union, Hoffa's outfit that was having its trouble with Bobby Kennedy, who
had lost no love on Lyndon, but who still in his capacity as
Attorney General, the arbiter of federal justice and boss
of the FBI—might lower the boom on Billie Sol. All of
which was in the realm of political reason.

In view of the well-known fact that gangsters think
and operate in terms of blackmail and payoffs, his suggestion was logical and from the point of view of all involved, if not prudent, at least reasonable. One thing about
gangsters, they come to the point. His proposal was that
"for a million dollars we will deliver the dope on Lyndon
Johnson." It was a waste of words to elaborate upon its
possible use among men of parts and imagination. Bargained
into the hands of Bobby, it might slow the sometimes
rusty wheels of justice from grinding down on Billie Sol.
In the hands of Estes it might mean that Lyndon would
have to go all the way to keep Billie out of trouble. At least
these were the sordid implications.

His proposition made, the gentleman rose to his feet,
flipped out his card with the address of a Chicago Club
and, suggesting they check his credentials, said:

"Here's my card and here's the Club. I'll be back

a two weeks to get your answer. Whoever let's this news get out will be dead!"

According to Lewsader, on April 21, 1963, two weeks later to a day, he was back for an answer. Estes had checked the Club and confirmed his identity. Aside from the other imponderables in such dealings, however, was the uncertain question of whom he really might represent. Puzzled investigators have wondered if it might have been Lyndon, or even the Kennedys, applying the ancient materialistic test as to whether Billie Sol himself was amenable to blackmail and hence politically exceedingly dangerous.

Billie Sol, the paragon of Pecos virtue who "never took a drink, smoked, or cursed," turned the proffered professional services down. After all there is a limit to which decent men can go.

But somewhat to satiate the public's thirst for blood, somebody had to be thrown to the lions, and herein at least Washington contributed to the Roman holiday. Assistant Secretary of Agriculture James T. Ralph and his assistant William E. Morris, were among the first. Ralph, who had the earmarks of a public career man, after being high with Freeman, had slipped from favor in February—coincidental with Freeman's rather tardy answer to Lyndon over Billie Sol's cotton allotments. When the investigations disclosed that Estes had taken Ralph into the swank Neiman-Marcus establishment at Dallas and had given him a very expensive vicuna suit and some equally expensive alligator shoes,[1] this capped the climax. Ralph and his assistant Morris, both deeply involved, were forthwith fired by Secretary Freeman, while Emery E. Jacobs, deputy administrator of the Agriculture Stabilization and Conservation Service, hurriedly resigned.

Then Robert E. Manuel, counsel for the minority

Republicans on the House Sub-Committee conducting investigations, grew impatient with the closed hearings and cover-up procedure and "leaked" a 175 page Agriculture Department report on Estes' cotton allotments. It incorporated the work of the late Henry Marshall, "who was" the papers casually reported, "shot to death while investigating Estes' acquisition of extensive cotton allotments."

Manuel revealed that when Estes was in Washington in January, he had pressured Carl J. Miller, an Agriculture Department employee, by invoking the names and influence of Lyndon B. Johnson and the late Sam Rayburn. For such improper and embarrassing conduct, the Democratic-dominated House Committee at once fired Counsel Manuel.[2]

---

[1] It should be granted that the problem here was one of ethics, not illegality. There is no law in Texas against giving, nor even wearing, alligator shoes — an obvious oversight on the part of the Texas Legislature.

At one time a Texan was ready to take the stand and swear that he had seen Billie Sol buy a $395 suit and two pair of $245 alligator shoes for Orville Freeman, paying in $100 bills, possibly a case of mistaken identity. Freeman was a little too high to touch. An interesting discussion of Ralph's case is found in the *New York Time's* News Service, "Man of the News," for which see the *Corpus Christi Times*, June 12, 1962. *Ibid*, June 8, 9.

For those interested in such exotic items as vicuna and alligator and Ralph's denial of the gifts, or even the questionable prestige value of Neiman-Marcus' stuff, see the *Dallas News*, April 21, 1962; *The Daily Oklahoman*, June 9, 1962; *Fort Worth Star-Telegram*, April 19, 1962.

[2] This was not the only mention of the Johnson influence. Frank Cain, of Pacific Finance, under oath swore that when he told Estes that the FBI was investigating him, Estes retorted: "I can stop all that. I will get Lyndon Johnson on the phone," and that night Estes added, "I've got that investigation stopped." *San Angelo Standard-Times* April 21, 1962.

In proof of the fact that all this was getting too close and hot for the higher echelons of Democracy—as represented by the Kennedy administration—the President himself came out in deigned approval of the "house cleaning," but with an essentially idiotic statement, saying:

"No one speaks for American Agriculture today with more confidence or authority than Secretary Freeman." Be it so except for the evidence!

On the same day the horrifying news broke of what had happened to Miss Mary Kimbrough Jones, a gentle North Carolina lady, for eleven years an employee of the Department, of high efficiency rating, who was working in the office of N. Battle Hales. Hales, after accusing the Department of favoring Estes, had been suddenly downgraded and shifted to other work, nobody seemed to know where. When Miss Jones came in April 25, with employment records and was insistent on finding her superior, Hales, an official left the office at once ostensibly to find him. Instead a strange individual showed up and sat down at Hales' desk saying:

"I'm a doctor and I want to talk to you." Miss Jones let him know in positive Southern manner that she was not looking for a doctor; she was looking for her former boss, Mr. Hales and started to leave. "The doctor" blocked the door and with ready help dragged her down the corridor and shanghied her off to the District of Columbia General Hospital as a mental case. There she was stripped of her clothing, given only a pajama top and left hungry and alone in a room "with just a mattress on the floor and possibly a sheet ..."

Later, in defense, attendants said that "there was no *misuse* of Mary in any way [our emphasis]. But when they shut her up they said she "became hysterical," and when one Dr. Lee Buchanan, "of the department's health unit," was sent to check on her, he reported that "she screamed and yelled; [and] that he could not deal with her rationally." After such a "rational" approach? Shades of humanity! Stripped of its hypocritical pretense, here was the fine hand of "scientific" psychoanalysis.[3]

In such a case there is nothing worse for the practitioners of this evil source of power than "the news"—the naked truth. Next day the proponents of this "new treatment"; this ready agent of corruption and illicit power, rushed into print in defense: Chairman Frederick A. Thuee, of the District of Columbia Mental Health Commission, armed with a "medical certificate" from Drs. Robert H. Pine and Richard Schaengold, of the hospital's staff, testifying that Miss Jones was "a very sick girl," "in need of treatment for mental disease" and hence "dangerous to herself and others because of her mental condition."[4]

Her release was effected only after repeated public charges by Senator John Williams of Delaware, that "she was railroaded to a mental institution because she knew too much" about the Estes case; that she was "guilty of nothing other than refusing to cooperate in covering up the corruption . . ." and that Dr. Buchanan had "arbitrarily ordered" her committed to a "mental institution."

To expose the repeated lies of these psychiatrists and government agents who contended that her own doctor had concurred, Senator Williams inquired of her doctor and

---

[3] All of which did not come out until nearly three weeks later. *San Angelo Standard-Times*, May 16, 1962. *Dallas News*, May 15, 1962. Not until May 7, after long delay in getting a hearing before the District of Columbia Mental Health Commission, was she released "to the custody of her own family *with the understanding she should receive further treatment*" [our emphasis].

[4] *Ibid.*, May 17, 1962.

was told that "he had at no time ever detected anything which would even raise the slightest question as to Miss Jones' sanity."[5] Still the diabolical deed had been done, an innocent heart driven to despair and a personality possibly destroyed, simply because a gentle lady had dared to be loyal to her job and trust and bold enough to tell the truth.

Thus to the traditionally effective weapons of illegitimacy—expulsion, economic ruin, blackmail and assassination—modern science and moral perversion had added another and the worst, that of terrifying mental torture and the destruction of the most sacred sanctuary of all, the privacy and tranquillity of the human mind. The simple knowledge that it will be used, can be used, and is being used under the humanitarian pretense of "mental health" is enough in itself to drive the sane to distraction.

That it was not an isolated incident was already well-known to students of the modern world and its fiendish uses of power. If they were not directly responsible in this case, it was without doubt acceptable to Johnson and the Kennedys, as proven by their callous disregard of the matter—notwithstanding Senator Williams' sharp attack on the Attorney General—and confirmed and completely proven at Oxford later.

When the Kennedys had precipitated the tragedy in Mississippi and by brute military force overrode the sacred Constitutional rights of the State and everyone concerned, they compounded the evil deed by making an example of a distinguished American general, Edwin A. Walker. On completely fallacious, trumped-up charges, they railroaded him to the federal prison at Springfield, Missouri as "a mental case" in violation of the basic rights of all free men. In a sardonic if not a criminal way, this might be termed a sort of public service, since it made an open

[5] *San Angelo Standard-Times,* May 15, 1962.

book of the use of stark and naked power for every thoughtful American.

But the first highly dramatic use of this new and diabolically "scientific" weapon in America—this psychological terror to suppress the truth and destroy political opposition—was a facet of the sad Billie Sol Estes business. Its exposure as accepted procedure in illegitimate government could be the most profound revelation that the Estes case produced for the future. Yet its psychological roots are intertwined with the fabric of the distant past; its use implicit in Machiavelli's dictum of more than four hundred years ago, when he wrote:

> It is much safer to be feared than loved ... Men in general are ungrateful dissemblers, anxious to avoid danger and covetous of gain. As long as you benefit them, they are entirely yours, when the necessity is remote; but when it approaches, they revolt. The friendship that is gained by purchase is bought, but not secured. Men have less scruple in offending one who makes himself loved than one who makes himself feared; for love is held by a chain of obligation which, men being selfish, is broken whenever it serves their purpose; but fear is maintained by a dread of punishment which never fails. Men are so simple and so ready to obey present necessities, that one who deceives will always find those who allow themselves to be destroyed.

The evidence of the acceptance of this denial of the spiritual purpose and worth of the individual by the Kennedy-Johnson administrations is beyond peradventure of doubt. Nowhere in their past record, nor in Johnson's pledged projection of Kennedy's policies for the future, is there evidence for conclusion otherwise. This endless talk of bringing relief from general distress to all the millions of one world may sound good to the dizzy-dreamers. But the prosaic mind rebels when the sanctimonious sources of these beautiful words could not hear the screams of faithful Mary Kimbrough Jones, racked body, mind and soul on their diabolical inquisitions of power in their own city.

What was left of this poor soul, who thought that truth would prevail, fled to suffer in seclusion, while Marshall's body was being dug up by others seeking the truth in Texas.

When House Committee Counsel Manuel, "leaked" the Agriculture report with the results of Henry Marshall's investigation, he fanned the fires of suspicion smouldering in Texas. Already many were asking: "Did Marshall really commit suicide?" Outraged opinion was demanding more than a five-day deferred Justice's verdict without an inquest.

By mid-May the interest was high, Will Wilson was eagerly pushing his many-sided investigation, the public suspicion of Kennedy's and Johnson's culpability was growing and the political heat was getting uncomfortable at the top. Therefore Assistant Secretary of Labor Jerry Holleman stepped out for sacrifice by admitting a "gift" from Estes. Holleman—the former head of the AFL-CIO in Texas, who had made his political activities for Lyndon pay off with this $20,000 a year post in Washington— "volunteered" the fact of a cool thousand dollar "gift" and hastily resigned. In extenuation he pleaded actual need imposed by high but necessary living expenses at the Capitol.

By way of background, Holleman, an ultra-liberal Yarborough favorite, after long "service to the cause" in Texas, became "acceptable" to the pragmatic Johnson in

1960 as Johnson worked to heal the rifts in Democratic politics and carry his state's delegation to Los Angeles. Holleman proved handy at such things as urging Estes to pick up the tab for a fifteen hundred-dollar labor banquet given by Secretary Arthur J. Goldberg, in January, 1962, at which Vice-President Johnson was the guest of honor, but which in high moral stance Goldberg declined.

In leaving, Jerry gracefully added that he was doing so "voluntarily." In truth the high-minded President's brother, Attorney General Bobby Kennedy—who would not even glance at the sad Mary Jones case, but who would be ruthlessly railroading one of America's foremost Major Generals to a federal prison for political purposes in the same manner a few months later—Bobby, himself, with no love lost on Johnson, put on the pressure which kicked Lyndon's friend, labor leader Holleman, into political discard, but not into penury. He at once headed back for Texas for profitable but unpublicized employment with another of Lyndon's financial supporters and warm friends, another "fabulous Texan," Morris Jaffe, of San Antonio.[6]

Next in confirmation of the significance of Marshall's work, the Government assessed a penalty of $544,162.71 against Estes for fraudulent allotments. Shortly thereafter, on May 18 at Bryan, Texas, District Judge John Barron ordered a grand jury probe into "the mystery death" of Henry Marshall, "to clear the cloud connecting this with the Billie Sol Estes case . . ." and indicated that Secretary Freeman would be called to testify, particularly in view of his public statement on May 7 that much of the Estes case was cloudy because many of the facts died with Marshall."

_____

6 For the Holleman incident see the *Dallas News*, May 12, 13, 1962. He had served also as executive secretary, the President's Committee on Equal Employment Opportunities, with Johnson the well-publicized chairman.

By this time President Kennedy, in an interesting reversal, was taking administration credit for having broken the Estes exposure.[7] Attorney General Wilson, now hot on the trail of the Marshall truth, exploded this Kennedy claim. Wilson attacked also the "defensive attitude" of the Agriculture Department, which refused to tell him what Marshall was doing, or why certain Department officials believed he had been murdered. Now with a probe under way by a local grand jury, and the body exhumed for careful study, the truth would certainly come out.

For days pathologists, doctors and scientists tested, sifted and analyzed the findings. They found enough carbon monoxide in Marshall's lungs to have incapacitated him, which was strange since his body was not in his pick-up truck when found. A blow on his head was likewise serious enough to have incapacitated him. The bolt-action .22 caliber rifle, which he would have had to hold at arm's-length, the bolt operated by hand after each shot, was found at the scene. Five shots had entered his body from the front. One severed his aorta near the heart, another penetrated his liver and another had gone through his lung, any one of which could have been fatal.

For anyone who knew guns and men, the conclusion of murder was inescapable. The head investigator, Dr. Joseph Jachimcyk, the Medical Examiner of Harris County, "firmly believed it was not suicide," but for some reason was reluctant to pronounce it murder. With a Texas Ranger, seven FBI men, Attorney General Wilson, U. S. District Attorney Barefoot Sanders, and a host of other officials on hand, the investigation should have been exhaustive. The department report which Manuel had sent Wilson and had gotten Manuel fired, became an important

[7] For this pious pretense see *San Angelo Standard-Times*, May 19, 1962.

issue, being at first denied to the grand jury under the usual cover-up device of "executive privilege."

Barefoot Sanders submitted a 22-page Government censored excerpt, but Wilson joined the issue of privilege and after a conference with Robertson County Attorney Bryan Russ and Judge Barron, in the Judge's chambers, Barefoot grudgingly turned over the entire report containing Marshall's findings. Bobby Kennedy was suspected of being in daily touch with Judge Barron, and evidently decided the Government had trouble enough without making an issue of jurisdiction—of further "cover up" before a Texas grand jury. But after almost two weeks the jury, empanelled with twelve "good men and true," *were unable to agree* on whether or not Marshall was a murder or a suicide.[8]

Considering the sound common sense and character of Texans usually composing a country jury and the simple evidence—the stark reality of the gun in hand and the victim's body, than which more was superfluous—it was an absolutely incredible outcome. One wonders! Were some of these naive souls so confused by the sheer mass of scientific tests, expert testimony, legal jargon and mountains of words in argument and answer that they could do no better? Or was somebody deliberately placed upon the jury to "hang it"; to prevent a forthright honest verdict? Whatever the reason, the lack of a verdict stunned the entire state. When asked about it nearly two years later, Will Wilson shook his head and answered: "It is a complete mystery!"

It was and still is! But as such, in the light of past assassinations connected with Texas politics and deaths yet to follow in the Billie Sol Estes tragedy, it kindled to

8 See the dailies of Texas, especially *Dallas News*, May 19-31, 1962.

a higher flame the apprehensions of Texans over the nature of the political powers that seemed to hold the state in thrall.

On the night of April 4, 1962, at the western end of Texas, a ranchman came upon the body of George Krutilek in the sandhills near the town of Clint, slumped in his car with a hose from his exhaust stuck in the window. He had been dead for several days and the El Paso County pathologist, Dr. Frederick Bornstein, held that he certainly did not die from carbon monoxide poisoning.

Krutilek was a forty-nine year old certified public accountant who had undergone secret grilling by FBI agents on April 2, the day after Billie Sol Estes' arrest. The investigation concerned the Estes affair. Krutilek had worked for Estes and had been the recipient of his favors, but he was never seen or heard of again after the FBI grilling until his badly decomposed body was found. Thus the mystery mounts! What did the accountant Krutilek know about Billie Sol's business that warranted murder?[9]

The enforced inhalation of this painless killer, carbon monoxide, leaving its own traces in lungs and blood and hence almost certain immunity for the murderer, is a subtle approach that would have charmed such early imaginative practitioners of assassination as the ancient Medici. Again in a case connected with Estes, this gas was held to be the legally blameless killer of Harold Eugene Orr, the late president of the Superior Manufacturing Company of Amarillo. Orr and the Company had played a key role in Estes' finance frauds, and Orr was arrested with Estes and given a ten-year federal prison sentence.

February 28, 1964, just before he was to begin serving his term, Harold Orr went out to his garage, ostensibly to change the exhaust pipe on his car. There a few hours

9 *San Angelo Standard-Times*, April 5, 1962.

later, with tools scattered about—again by report, tools unsuited for the purpose—Orr was found dead. The Justice of the Peace pronounced it accidental death by carbon monoxide. But the stubborn disbelievers keep popping up with their questions. Was Orr, faced with prison, about to talk? And what of Howard Pratt, Chicago office manager of Commercial Solvents, Billie Sol's fertilizer supplier, found in his car, dead of carbon monoxide?[10]

While Johnson was usually far in the background at this time, he was still highly suspect of being involved with Billie Sol. Undoubtedly Estes had powerful Washington influence and backing, as proven in his preferential treatment in storage of government grain and in the handling of his warehouse bond—the guarantee exacted for delivery of the grain upon demand. His bond became one of the chief bones of contention in the investigations that followed his crash.

Toward the end of his business career the biggest single item in Billie Sol's racket was this grain storage business, where, through political influence if not outright collusion, he had, beginning in 1959, started building warehouses primarily for the storage of surplus government grain—one of the most burdensome products of the federal farm program. Washington had not yet discovered that the stuff could be given to Russia, and elevators and warehouses were bulging with the surplus. With political influence it was no problem to build storage facilities, with a guaranteed liquidation of the capital costs in about three years—that is in the Estes type of storage, if kept full. In effect this amounted to the government's gift of the facilities to the builder—free! When Estes started it did

10 This high incidence of carbon monoxide mortality is the subject of an article by Clyde Walters, *Amarillo Globe-Times*, March 26, 1964.

not take him long "to get a-going."

By the spring of 1962, with an estimated 85 million bushel capacity, he was competing for the title of "the world's largest warehouser of grain." At the time of the crash he was reported to have had 55 million bushels on hand. For the prior year the government alone, not counting his income from privately owned grain, had paid him over $5,100,000, and its monthly payments were currently near half a million dollars.

Only two things seemed requisite for fair sailing thereafter; the political influence to fill them, and keeping the warehouse bond required in guarantee of delivery. Billie Sol had both. The government issued "warehouse receipts" for all grain stored, which were negotiable paper and prime collateral. Without the bond there was no storage. The government was paying about 13½ cents a bushel annually for storage, and requiring a bond averaging about two cents a bushel. With 55 million bushels of government grain in storage, the extent of Estes' annual government income was obvious. His bond was only $700,000, which was still no shocking disparity.

But something happened and that something seemed to have been the concern among a few high Agriculture officials over the obvious favoritism and the political dangers implicit in Billie Sol's operations. These appeared after Marshall's report was suppressed, but coincident with Johnson's help in getting Estes off the hook of the illegal cotton allotments.

Significantly timed, the Department wired Estes an order, January 18, 1962, raising his bond to $1,000,000 which was close to average. For some reason his bonding company refused to go along, thus hazarding his entire government grain storage business, which, anticipated in excess of $7,000,000 for 1962 was, even in wheat far from chicken feed.

Estes flew to Washington and on January 25 showed up at the Agriculture Department where, quite possibly through Johnson's influence with Undersecretary Charles Murphy, the higher bond was waived. Thus at a critical juncture in his shaky financial affairs, he staved off the threatened loss of his warehouse receipts—and hence the loss of a vast block of collateral, and kept his monthly storage payments flowing smoothly to Commercial Solvents, the Company carrying him for immense credits for anhydrous ammonia fertilizer, whereby he was beating down the price and forcing the West Texas competitors out of business. The stakes were big and it definitely paid to have a friend like Lyndon Baines Johnson.

It was a short respite, for two months later the house of cards was crashing and Vice-President Johnson was watching closely, saying nothing, but calculating how he would play his hand. It was, as usual, played behind the scenes and as usual, with effective timing.

But in Texas Will Wilson was charging federal favoritism for Estes in grain storage, exactly what the high-placed Washington Agriculture official, N. Battle Hales, had likewise discovered and charged. C. H. Moseley, director of the Dallas Commodity office, hotly denied Wilson's assertion. The debate aroused concern as to whether or not the government grain in the Estes warehouses was still there and for awhile Moseley was sweating. But John White, State Commissioner of Agriculture, a friend of Billie's and a ready confederate of Lyndon's, popped up to reassure the public. He had just checked two of the Estes elevators and had found "the inventories exactly right"—which was not surprising to anyone who knew John White. Yet the federal officials boosted the Estes' bond from $1,000,000 to $10,000,000—which was a shallow political gesture as bankruptcy was impending.

Many of Estes' storage facilities had been built through contract with Coleman Wade, of Altus, Oklahoma, who was drawn into the sweeping investigations. Shortly after taking off in his plane from Pecos, on a return trip home early in 1963, he mysteriously crashed in the Kermit area. Government investigators swept in and instead of expeditiously cleaning up the wreckage in their routine way, kept the area roped off for days. Wade was well known to Lewsader, the Estes pilot, and this incident came near scaring him to death with its ominous overtones. Whatever the cause, another important witness was gone.

Federal Judge Ewing Thomason, of El Paso, named Harry Moore as trustee in bankruptcy and sent notices to nearly 600 creditors. When they filed their claims the vast interests and the important part Commercial Solvents Corporation of New York had played in the Estes combine became obvious. They were carrying him for $5,700,000, out of a total of some $15,000,000 of credits on their books which Billie was liquidating through assignment of his government payments. In the liquidation Commercial Solvents wanted to take over his fertilizer business more than anything else.

Prior to the crash Cosden Petroleum Company, a big producer of anhydrous ammonia, with its main operations at the West Texas town of Big Spring, had been sold to W. R. Grace and Company. By rumor Grace was close to the Kennedys and for a certainty it too wanted the Estes fertilizer outlets. Long before the crash Grace got the goods on the fraudulent nature of the Estes operations. Thus forearmed in tough business style, Grace invited Estes to New York.

According to Harold Orr's sworn testimony of Billie's account, the President of Grace began by trying to buy

Estes out. Estes declined to sell. Then the Grace boss lowered the boom, telling Estes he knew all about his fraudulent finance and if he still refused to sell, he would expose his fraud to his big backers, Commercial Solvents. Billie simply picked up the phone on the desk, handed it to the Grace official and gave him the Commercial Solvents number.

Such stories as this did nothing to settle the suspicions that somehow Lyndon B. Johnson was interested in Commercial Solvents. Undoubtedly Estes stood in high favor with the company and its President, Maynard Wheeler, who was near frantic when the grain-storage payments of about half a million monthly were shut off by the government.

With the State threatening anti-trust action, Wheeler made a public disclaimer to the effect that his connections with Estes were purely business, which had "at no time violated the anti-trust laws of the State of Texas or elsewhere." On the stand he denied the testimony of Frank Cain, a Dallas lawyer representing Pacific Finance Company—one of a number deeply involved in discounting the paper on Estes' bogus tanks—that Commercial Solvents had offered to set Estes up in Brazil, a report of unusual interest since it was once rumored that he was ready to fly there for refuge.

Despite all suspicions of Lyndon, he was never proven

---

11 E.g., on May 21, 1962, a long session behind closed doors was held with N. Battle Hales, who had charged that Estes had "profited hugely from favored treatment" in the Agriculture Department, and with Walter Berger, of Commercial Solvents. McClellan clamped "a tight lid of secrecy" on everything, with Committee members and witnesses alike forced to agree to divulge nothing. *Amarillo News*, May 22, 1962. See too, *Corpus Christi Caller*, June 13, 16, 1962; *San Angelo Standard*, June 16, 1962.

to be involved, though some tightly closed sessions of Senator McClellan's Committee, without revealing who had been heard or what had been found, indicated that the Johnson technique was being applied—and McClellan was amenable.[11]

Before the lid was clamped tight, an FBI agent on the case revealed to a friend that Commercial Solvents were suspected of gangster connections, that they had been in financial straits and it was thought that Lady Bird Johnson's money had helped pull them out.

The fact that Commercial Solvents knew what Estes was doing and evidently approved, as indicated in the story told by Billie Sol, came out in the litigation. An offical of Southwestern Fertilizer, at El Paso, later testified that in 1961 he had written to Commercial Solvents that Estes was financing his way on bogus tanks. The Company sent a man to investigate and verify the report. Yet Commercial Solvents stayed with Estes and even after he was arrested and thrown in jail, put up $400,000 in cash for him.

What the public generally awaited, however, was the revelation of the political power behind this crooked business—not just rumors that Lyndon's influence and his wife's money were involved. But it looked in vain, for Johnson's friend, Senator McClellan, to throw any light upon it. Instead the most significant hearings were tightly closed.

However the culpable elements were kept in fear lest the truth get out, perhaps through the unpredictable impulses of Billie Sol Estes. Those who knew him best believed he was, in his own mind, a religious and well-meaning person, who in conscience-ridden trouble, suffered further mental inversion while convincing himself that the way out was by honest confession—which too was in line with his denominational dogma. He repeatedly asserted to close friends that before he went to prison he would make a clean breast of the whole business.

This was his apparent intention when called before the McClellan Committee. But just before he left for Washington, those around him observed that for the first time he was all but "scared to death." He said that threats had come not only against his life but against his family. Instead of the truth for the McClellan Committee, he "took the Fifth" repeatedly.

Immediately following Kennedy's assassination, according to responsible Washington sources, a presidential order sealed the McClellan Committee findings from scrutiny, even from Congress itself. Since then various Estes friends have tried to induce him to talk, but he always answers "I can't talk unless my Austin lawyer approves." And Cofer does not.

As in the later Bobby Baker case, there were strong suspicions that the Kennedys were all set to shunt Johnson aside in 1964 because of his connections with the Estes affair. It is known that FBI agents were working on this angle immediately after Billie Sol's arrest. Dr. Dunn had numerous calls from agents inquiring specifically for leads as to Johnson's connections, the agent in charge admitting that they "had the green light" from Washington, which meant from Bobby Kennedy and his brother.

Certain minor contributing incidents were a matter of rumor if not of public knowledge; the report of Lady Bird Johnson's overnight visit at the Estes home; her brother's alleged interest in the Estes grain operations; Billie's own open allegations that he and Lyndon were going into the grain storage business under the Government Point IV program "in India"; and next it was "Johannesburg"— where Billie was to be Ambassador—as "Lyndon has it all fixed up for me"; and the persistent rumors that Mrs. Johnson's money had saved Commercial Solvents.

Whatever the investigations disclosed is known, in all probability only to the Attorney General. It may well be that they contributed to the ill-concealed enmity between him and the President and perhaps help explain his challenge to Johnson in certain state elections—such as the heavy write-in vote in the New Hampshire primaries. This made the President furious and was followed by Johnson's fast foot-work with the Wisconsin Governor, John W. Reynolds, who used the White House as a sounding board against another threatened Bobby write-in campaign, in his state.[12]

When Johnson's friend, Mayor Tom Miller of Austin died, the Vice-President flew down for the funeral in a military jet. Upon his return trip the plane skidded from the runway in landing at Dallas and Johnson continued to Washington by commercial flight. But the story got out that it had first flown to Midland, where it was parked away from the terminal and closely guarded by the secret service, while two men were escorted to it and stayed for an hour. Then the plane took off for Dallas and its mishap in landing.

In time the report of the Midland flight and the strange and secret conference leaked out. A hurried effort by a responsible person to check the Midland tower records at first went awry because of a mistake as to the date. Properly advised later, the same person returned to check the flight records, but the investigator was told that the records of that day's flights had been sealed by government order. Efforts to secure the plane's itinerary were likewise rebuffed in Washington. The two men who had

[12] For a suggestion of this thought, see Ted Lewis, "Capitol Stuff," *Washington Daily News*, March 13,1964.

by-passed the Midland terminal and spent the hour with Vice-President Johnson—they had been seen and identified as Billie Sol Estes and one of his lawyers.

Meanwhile the efforts to untangle the ramifications of the multi-million dollar financial pyramid, sometimes estimated at $100,000,000, and salvage something from the wreckage, got under way in Federal Judge Thomason's Court. With Commercial Solvents and its vast credits, with Walter E. Heller Company of Chicago and some seven million dollars involved, and a number of other big finance companies caught deep in the devious operations, it presented a problem without parallel in Texas financial history.

The Creditors' Committee was set up to represent the hundreds of others in Court, and the Trustee in Bankruptcy, Harry Moore, began the gradual liquidation of the Estes assets. Commercial Solvents wanted the Estes fertilizer business above everything else. But W. R. Grace and Company somehow managed to crowd them out.

Commercial Solvents then horned in all the more vigorously on the management of the bankruptcy, with Walter Heller and Company cooperating. Initially the management of the Estes cotton acreage was turned over to Anderson-Clayton Company, which already operated extensively in the Pecos area. But piece-meal liquidation of the giant holdings presented terrific problems.

Just at this juncture, as if providentially, Lyndon's close friend and heavy financial supporter, irreverently referred to in his native San Antonio as "Lyndon's man," was "induced" to take an interest. His approach was somewhat oblique and his methods novel, if not designing, as he moved for a foothold in the grain-storage business at Plainview.

It happened that J. C. Williamson, owner of the Williamson Oil Company of Midland, had built a fine

$1,250,000 elevator with its own rail siding and loading facilities at Plainview. But with the grain business under government control and the bulk of production going into the "government loan," an elevator was worthless without participation in government storage. But to be eligible at all the owner had to have a government certificate, which must be granted by the bureaucrats in the Commodity Credit Administration, in this case by C. H. Moseley, head of the district at Dallas. But Williamson's elevator was in the heart of Billie Sol's empire and while Williamson too was a liberal Democrat, Billie was deeper-dyed, and try as he would Williamson could not get the essential certificate.

At last he came to terms with the stark political realities, the ruthless tactics of his friends, and leased it to Estes for five years on terms assuring the payoff of his investment, but with the provision that in case of bankruptcy of the lessee, he could "repossess the leased premises . . . without prejudice to any remedy . . ." Estes made two payments and defaulted on May 1, 1962.

Alongside Williamson's Terminal elevator lay another known as the Atwood, upon which Walter Heller and Company of Chicago held a mortgage. It had no rail or loading facilities of its own and could be used only through access to Williamson's plant—which enhanced the potential value of his—that is, with the government favor of a storage certificate.

In the midst of his hassle with the government, Williamson, in mid-June 1962, got a call "out of the blue" from John White at Austin for a command meeting at Dallas. As one of liberal leaning, Williamson, hoping that things might be breaking his way, took a lawyer and flew down for a conference at The Adolphus. In came John White, a redheaded "grainman", and the pudgily-built, evasive-eyed Morris Jaffe, the financial whiz from San Antonio.

After the initial greetings they left briefly, probably for the office of Henry Strasburger, attorney of Walter Heller and Company, who held the mortgage on the Atwood elevator. Upon their return they got down to business. Jaffe asked Williamson if he wanted to sell his elevator. He did! The price—"what is against it"—a note of $800,000 held by the Midland National Bank, where the amortization payments were being made regularly.

After some parrying John White, the rabid radical who graduated at a tender age from teaching school directly to the job of running the agriculture business of the State of Texas, suggested that since it was worthless to Williamson he might as well give it to Jaffe—which so strained even J. C.'s sense of liberalism that he blew up, saying he had drilled many a million-dollar dry hole and he would just count this as another. Nursing his wrath at this New Deal double-cross by his own clan, he and his lawyer caught the Continental flight back to Midland and took his futile fight for justice to the courthouse. Meanwhile Moseley, in discussing the matter, had frankly told him that he "would never get a certificate"—and Moseley was right.

Bankruptcy proceedings were filed against Estes, April 6 and he was adjudged bankrupt, July 13, 1962, after which Williamson moved at once to recover his properties. But Trustee Harry Moore had already taken over to grab off the monthly payments on government grain and refused to surrender possession. Williamson pleaded in vain for relief, in keeping with his contract, through Judge Thomason's Court.

Significantly this approach to Williamson seemed to have been one of the first steps by Jaffe, Vice-President Johnson's warm friend, to move in on the Estes empire. A year later, in June 1963, with J. C. Williamson practically converted to the conservative cause, his splendid installation at Plainview was taken over by Jaffe's American Grain Corporation at "what was against it"—a drastically reduced note of just over $418,000 at the Midland National.[13]

Meanwhile Morris Jaffe took over—the newspapers generously said "bought"—the still vast and valuable Billie Sol Estes assets. "The news" that Jaffe, a "San Antonio businessman," had offered $7 million for them broke in the summer of 1962 and it soon developed that the fine hand of Walter Heller, through his lawyers, Henry Strasburger of Dallas and Greenberg and Schimberg of Chicago, was playing an important if not dominant role—as well it might with seven million at stake, with Commercial Solvents in the favorable position of holding a lien on the principal assets. Thus Commercial Solvents was a key party in the business. It too turned out to be prudent and progressive. Thus with the support of these two big outfits and with hidden political influence to spare, Jaffe took possession of Billie Sol's assets; some thousands of acres of the best Pecos irrigated land, ranch holdings and the multi-million dollar grain complex.

For "seven million dollars?" Goodness no! He did not propose and vigorously fought putting one red cent into the deal and only through the stubborn insistence of an attorney for other creditors that he be made to take some personal risk as surety of interest, did he finally agree to put in a token payment, possibly $100,000.

---

[13] For much of the essential detail on this "deal", see two petitions in the U.S. District Court, the Western District of Texas, Pecos Division, El Paso, viz; that of Harry Moore, November 14, 1962, and Williamson Petroleum Company, October, 1962, case 299.

The conclusion is inescapable that the Johnson-controlled political machine in Texas designedly set the stage for Jaffe's take-over, as the cleanup was without financial risk and potentially very good. As already noted, no grain storage is operated without government license through Commodity Credit. With the Estes fat in the fire, the political necessity of reassuring the public was urgent. Whereupon Moseley's outfit, Commodity Credit, made a newsworthy show of righteous concern by cancelling all the Estes storage permits and ordering the removal of the government grain. This was a palpably political move designed to assuage the public's ire. Unnoticed, however, was its tremendous impact upon the impending sale of the Estes assets.

Without government approval the facilities of "the world's largest warehouser of grain" were no longer an asset—they were a liability. In what seemed commendable, high moral dudgeon, "the government" immediately moved to "mete out justice" to Estes. But Estes was adjudged bankrupt and suffered no punishment at all therefrom. What the government was actually doing was destroying the value of his major assets, to which his hundreds of hapless creditors looked for some small percentage of recovery.

Who could say that the certificates of storage would ever be renewed? Certainly nobody among the creditors who sat around the bankrupt's bargaining table—nobody except perhaps Lyndon's warm friend, Morris Jaffe—the financial whiz from San Antonio. He alone was in position to trade and, backed by Heller and Solvents, Jaffe did.

He organized and took over through his American Grain Corporation, and expanded further with the Abbott and Williamson facilities. With Estes on trial, the Midland oil man, J. C. Williamson, after an expensive $850,000 lesson in the ruthless nature of his liberal friends, was re-appraising his political leanings along conservative lines and nearly everybody was asking:

"Who in the hell is Morris Jaffe?"

Aside from the all-important answer that Morris D. Jaffe is one of Lyndon B. Johnson's close friends, he is in his own right an interesting and unusual character whose story is pertinent in some detail. A native of San Antonio, of Mexican-Jewish parentage, he grew up in the Alamo City and became an aircraft engineering officer during the War. Upon his return from the army he and his friend, David P. Martin, organized Jaffe and Martin Builders and went into construction work.

Within a few years they got the job of building a lot of barracks at the Lackland Air Base, which on final inspection were suspected to be short of the specifications of contract. Whereupon an investigation was started which disclosed that an expensive civil engineer named McClain, who was supposedly riding herd on the job for the government, had been lavishly entertained by Jaffe. The Inspector General got interested and worked up a file, but suddenly McClain was transferred to parts unknown and the inquiry ended.

Jaffe became fast friends with a former insurance agent, Lieutenant Colonel Roger Zeller, who was Executive Officer at Lackland. Zeller, after a big synthetic buildup in the Reserve Officers Association, was shortly transferred to the Pentagon and jumped over hundreds of full Colonels to the rank of Brigadier General. Then with "influence in the Pentagon," as Jaffe put it, and high standing with Senate Majority Leader Johnson, Jaffe really hit his stride.

He "discovered" the South Texas uranium deposits, saw them appraised as fabulously rich by officials of the Atomic Energy Commission, picked up options on a vast acreage,

helped induce the government to finance a giant processing
plant, and unloaded his leases and options at a fancy profit
before the magnificent and expensive dream fizzled out like
a cheap Chinese firecracker. With Zeller's support his most
notorious operation was the Lackland Air Base skating rink,
which he managed to finance and build, at a declared cost
of $260,000, and, in order to evade the federal provision
against private ownership of property on government ground,
got it leased back to him for a ten-year pay-off period as
a concession.

But basic training for the thousands of airmen there
was under the tough-fibred American fighter, Colonel James
A. Smyrl. After a day's routine the trainees had no interest
in skating rinks. With pressure and influence to spare,
Jaffe got the Base Commander, General Herbert L. Grills,
to declare an "open post policy" once a week to give the
boys time to skate, and when skating still languished, Grills
substituted weekly skating for an hour's basic training, and
put pressure on Smyrl to force the boys to patronize the
rink. Jaffe himself threatened Smyrl if he did not "get with
the system." Smyrl, a man of integrity, was then removed
and the Commander started hauling the trainees to the rink
in buses, where, at "fifty cents" each, Jaffe's business began
to flourish. The news hit the papers, a board of inquiry was
named and Smyrl was called to show cause why he should
not be dismissed from the Air Force. Terrific pressure developed for a Senate investigation which would logically
have fallen to the Sub-Committee on Military Preparedness
—which was dominated by Lyndon B. Johnson. Even the
Secretary of the Air Force and President Eisenhower were
drawn into the controversy.

As the affair raged into the summer of 1957, Johnson
appeared to fill a speaking engagement and, when interro-
gated about the Smyrl case, answered with one of his typi-

cally lofty non sequiturs that is calculated to confound the worst critic:

"If the Air Force can be trusted with the H Bomb, it can certainly be trusted with an investigation."

Smyrl, who had flown 275 combat hours over Germany to win the Silver Star and the Distinguished Flying Cross, was brought to trial before the Board of Inquiry of three generals, September 24, 1957, on three charges; failure to carry out an order; temperamental instability; and failure to demonstrate leadership. His entire record was reviewed. The worst the Air Force could prove was that he was an impatient fighting American, dedicated to his career, lacking in humor, tireless in duty and intolerant of moral laxity and corruption.—as he had proven at the Lackland Base. In brief, his enemies proved him the very sort that the American people pray for in time of war; but find an intolerable, moralistic obstacle to soft living and corruption in time of peace. Obviously he had to go.

"The shameful farce ended...October 3, 1957." Smyrl was found guilty of being nervous and temperamentally unsuited, and of failure to "demonstrate leadership"—that is to force his men to skate and make Jaffe's concession pay. The Board recommended his removal "from the active list of the regular air force."[14]

But Jaffe's skating business rolled on—a sorry symbol

----

[14] Smyrl appealed to a review board in Washington which sustained the verdict. Through the efforts of Senator Styles Bridges, he got a fifteen-minute interview with Secretary of the Air Force Douglas—which lasted an hour. At last he won, and was sent to the Strategic Air Command abroad. Phillip A. Johnson, in charge of the Lackland Air Base Exchange, a key figure in the scandals, was fired. The bucolic General Grills was shipped to a NATO post in Italy. And Jaffe eventually sold his rink to Sam Katz, in January, 1959. David Nevin, as cited; *San Antonio Light*, Jan. 9; Feb. 12; March 11; May 1; June 24, 1958.

of the character and policy behind the basic training of the hundreds of thousands of young Americans being moulded into the vital heart of America's defense. Obviously a young man of thirty-five years who could change the basic training program of American fliers, break the proven Colonel in charge and precipitate a national scandal and furor involving everybody of note from the Lackland Base to the Commander-in-Chief, the Secretary of the Air Force and the Senate Majority Leader—with only a $260,000 racket involved, was no ordinary operator.

By the late fifties Jaffe had more to his record than some faulty barracks, a skating rink, some sour oil leases and a magnificently abortive but personally profitable boom in uranium. As the president of the Texas end of the Fed-Mart operations, he had become a merchandising tycoon.

Politics is another and most important side of Jaffe's business, and he has indicated that both are really good "since my boy became President." His political connections with and friendship for John White, Texas Commissioner of Agriculture, have had their uses. At times he flies White to Washington, probably to handle his connections with the Department of Agriculture on such matters as grain storage in the old Estes facilities, owned by his American Grain Company.

Jaffe's labor problems, if and when there are any, can be safely left to the former President of the Texas AFL-CIO, that erstwhile Assistant Secretary of Labor under Arthur Goldberg—the veteran politician Jerry Holleman. Following his frank admission of the "gift of $1,000" from Billie Sol and his sudden departure from Washington—with Bobby Kennedy's pushing, he joined Jaffe at pay estimated "somewhere between $20 and $30 thousand" a year, and has been a quiet but effective henchman ever since. He too has frequent resort to Jaffe's plane.

One of Jaffe's most notorious *compadres* is Judge Woodrow Bean of El Paso. When Fed-Mart decided to move into El Paso, Jaffe retained Bean as local counsel and at times flew him and other politicians to Austin to see House Leader Waggoner Carr on political matters. Not until Bean decided to run for Congress did the important fact—from among many others—come out that he had not paid his income tax for years, an oversight which quite often gets ordinary folks committed to federal prison. But not among Lyndon's friends! After disagreeable publicity in court, somebody paid up for Bean and the liberal Judge dropped from public sight for a while before being featured in the news as a working "cowboy on Morris Jaffe's ranch"—shades of that variegated breed!

It may be asked what became of the interests of the hundreds of other Estes creditors. A committee of Creditors was set up with the approval of the Trustee in Bankruptcy, and through agreement Jaffe took over the entire shooting match with a lien of $6,500,000, "less the amount of accrued grain storage payments"—which could have been more than two million dollars. The sale of the farm lands later should have reduced this by another two million. So it will be seen that Jaffe took over for a song, and a short one at that. If he built back his government storage to its estimated 1962 level, the facilities could have been paid off in six months. And who would doubt that he got it back—and more! For Jaffe does "have influence," not only "in the Pentagon," but in all sorts of government agencies running right into his "boy's" office at the White House. If there was ever any doubt, this became perfectly apparent to the Creditors' Committee in the Estes interests. Walter Heller, Commercial Solvents and Jaffe are running the bankruptcy, lock, stock and barrel. In early and vigorous disagreement on one issue, the Committee carried its contentions to the Trustee and to Federal Judge Ewing Thomason, an old friend of Lyndon B. Johnson, who at once slapped them down. Since then the Committee, representing many millions of dollars in claims, is simply ignored.

This in brief and far from complete compass, is something of the background of Morris D. Jaffe, the forty-year old friend of President Lyndon B. Johnson, who was unheard of in the Pecos area before he turned up to take over what was valuable and tangible after the crash of the Billie Sol Estes empire.

The high point politically of his career was his backing of Johnson for the presidential nomination in 1960 at Los Angeles. He too was there to lay his money on the line. An old-time San Antonio newspaperman came home admitting that Jaffe not only seemed to be the "money man" but "the brains and the trouble-shooter and smart beyond imagination," the most effective man behind Lyndon B. Johnson. For whatever it was worth, it was one veteran's opinion, which provoked another to add:

"When anybody's high in Johnson's organization, you can be sure he's the best. Lyndon hasn't got a bum working for him." This emphasizes a highly significant facet of Johnson's genius which makes him tremendously effective and infinitely more dangerous.

VII

COUNTERFEIT CONSERVATIVE

*" . . . a parliament [or a Congress] is not a serious
institution capable of guaranteeing to a state the securities
inherent in the democratic principle unless it possesses
and exercises the right of opposition.*

—Ferrero.

It seems incredible that anyone who has even casually
followed the news could believe that Lyndon Baines Johnson is a conservative. But the fact that many Americans
think that he is, at least "more conservative than Kennedy," whatever that could mean, is further proof of a
slanted press and the skillful deceptions of the man.

Vague generalities as to principle, evasive answers on
position, and double-talk in the political forum—such mish-
mash is his semantic dish. When he entered the Senate
he began shedding the crimson cloak of the flaming liberal,
deploring alike the "extremes of right and left" while
building the image of a man of moderation, wooing "the
radicals" from both camps with prudence and with reason and, after compromising the conservative position, almost always voting with the left.

Money and power have been his principal objectives.
With early riches assured he was able to give all his tremendous energy and talents to his eager accumulation of
power. As Senate Majority Leader he was careful to avoid
all semblance of categorical classification and label as to
basic principle and political philosophy. And he has attempted to make a public virtue of his denial of any
abiding creed.

That such a negative attitude could be successfully
paraded as a virtue in a highly complex world where orderly and civilized life, economic stability and progress

and moral and spiritual well-being are based on positive
and enduring principles, by a man who has risen to preeminent power, is a disturbing and a startling phenomenon.

Every citizen of the Republic has the right to know,
and the duty to demand to know, the basic beliefs of his
representatives in government. Lyndon B. Johnson not
only denies this, but frankly admits that he "resents" and
"bridle[s] at the very casualness" with which Americans
ask: "What is your political philosophy?"

In the same breath he mentions "our basic law—the
Constitution" and then denies its principles and purpose
when he says "it prescribes no national dogma; economic,
social or religious." The shallow if not studied insolence
of this remark is obvious. "Basic law" implies the limitations and force of fixed principles of morality codified
to govern human behavior, whereas their designation as
"dogma" can be the result only of ignorance of the meaning of moral and legal principle, or a calculated effort to
deny it. But Lyndon B. Johnson is far from ignorant. In
respect to the Constitution he continues:

"Nor is there any provision to require allegiance to
any dogma or doctrine."

In these statements from an article written by Johnson and originally published in *The Texas Quarterly* in
1958, he denies the spiritual essence of the Declaration
of Independence, the Constitution and the Bill of Rights.
He fails to recognize the inviolable nature of the human
soul that is the basis of freedom and he acknowledges the
authoritarian character of his conception of government.
From this denial of the essence of Americanism, he goes
on to define his philosophy.

"Were we bound by rigid dogmas [he continues, still
avoiding reference to ideals and principles] whatever their
name, there would be no more cause for assembling Con-

gress than for bringing the Soviet Presidium together. We are not so bound ..."

"This leads to a listing of the tenets of my own beliefs ...

"First, I believe every American has something to say and, under our system, a right to an audience."

"Second, I believe there is always a national answer to each national problem, and believing this, I do not believe there are necessarily two sides to every question.

"Third, I regard achievement of the full potential of our resources—physical, human and otherwise—to be the highest purpose of governmental policies next to the protection of those rights we regard as inalienable.

"Fourth, I regard waste as the continuing enemy of our society and the prevention of waste—waste of resources, waste of lives, or waste of opportunity—to be the most dynamic of the responsibilities of our government."[1]

This in his own words is the sum and substance of the principles and the political philosophy of Lyndon Baines Johnson—summarized for all to read and ponder. There is not a word in support of the Christian concepts that are the core of individual freedom, or of the principles embodied in the great liberal charters of the Christian time.

His first belief indicates a recognition of the right of free speech and petition, which is all to the good since, despite his sweeping denial, these are a part of our "basic doctrine"—not dogma.

His second, in belief of "a national answer to each national problem," could imply faith in our deliberative process, though not necessarily so since national answers are possible under other forms of government.

[1] See Booth Mooney's *The Lyndon Johnson Story*, Farrar, Straus and Co., 5th ed., pp. x-xii.

The third, regarding "achievement of the full potential of our resources" is completely outside our basic law, but sounds good, especially when qualified by "the protection of those rights we regard as inalienable." But these "inalienable rights," which are actually *unalienable,* are set forth for Americans in the Preamble to the Declaration of Independence, the Constitution and the Bill of Rights —which Johnson brushes off by saying that we are bound by no "dogma or doctrine."

If Johnson really cherished individual rights, his final statement of principle would inevitably be that of the traditional and true liberal—that the principal function of government is the guarantee and protection of those rights against trespass by others and by government itself. Not so with Lyndon B. Johnson.

Instead, he believes that "the most dynamic" responsibility of government is "the prevention of waste—waste of resources, waste of lives, or waste of opportunity..." Herein he reveals his concept of government; not a government restrained by the basic law—that is by rigid limitations on its power, as laid down in the Constitution and the Bill of Rights—but a government omniscient enough to decide what is waste and powerful enough to prevent it. Implicit herein is the denial of the concept of the ownership of property and of individual freedom. Herein is the philosophy of the authoritarian state.

As an example, take again Johnson's claim that the Lower Colorado River Development with its multiple dams and its vast REA system which, as previously noted, is the biggest example of national socialism in Texas. This was his legislative pet and is his proudest achievement. He takes pride in it as an example of the abolition of the waste of resources in the chalky, cedar-covered hills of his home section. But it has been accomplished only through ruthless levy upon the property of other American communities for the particular enrichment of his own, not only in disregard of the Constitution, but in violation of a Commandment that is more than "dogma"—"Thou Shalt not Steal."

In prevention of "waste of lives" a critical sociologist might raise the question as to what he would propose for that depressing fringe of humanity native to his own heath, the cedar-cutting "hill billies," who, between reliance on government relief and a little work, seem content just to drift about, to drink, to fornicate and fight.

Who would stop this "waste of lives" and how? Obviously government, perhaps by "a billion dollar war on poverty," despite the vagaries of human nature and the Biblical reminder that we have them with us always. Or failing to lift the listless and lazy to affluence, would he have government, in extremity, fall back upon his own proposal for labor during the war—their impressment into a government work force as it drafted others into the army?[2]

It should be borne in mind that the final outcome of professional humanitarianism is "homicidal mania," wherein the humble of the earth come to be considered pawns in the hands of men in power. Yet the truth of Lord Acton's aphorism that "power corrupts; absolute power corrupts absolutely," must, it seems, be re-learned by bitter experience in every age.

As proven over and over again, Johnson knows and relishes power, as is characteristic of the "modern" authoritarian liberal. Yet there is nothing "modern" about it, for The Marquis de Custine observed one hundred and

[2] Johnson seriously proposed this terrible measure for unemployed men and women in his first senatorial campaign. See the *Fort Worth Star-Telegram*, May 24, 1941.

twenty-five years ago that "despotism is never a greater menace than when it claims to do good . . . it excuses its most revolting acts by its intentions; and evil posing as a remedy has no limits."[3]

As Roosevelt's popular appeal died down, Lyndon trimmed his sails to fit the changing winds. From an ardent liberal Congressman, as Senator he began building an image of the "prudent progressive," playing both ends against the middle and when seriously challenged by either, assuming the role of saving it from annihilation by the other.

Much has been made of his "conservative" votes for the Taft-Hartley union control act and for measures affecting oil and gas. While temporarily alienating labor leaders, his Taft-Hartley vote was considered essential to political survival in Texas; his support of the depletion allowance, with the continual threat that it was about to be lost, was essential to shaking-down his Texas oil friends for campaign cash. Prudence, based on expediency, not principle, is his guiding star.

Yet his record on practically everything else is "progressively liberal," which is in truth radical and reactionary. Careful scrutiny of his Senatorial voting record proves him worse than Kennedy; a record that gained him the warm support and the close confidence of such outstanding domestic Marxists as Martin Luther King, David Dubinsky and Walter Reuther.[4]

As Senate Majority Leader, Johnson was primarily responsible for the success of President Eisenhower's major policies—which conservative Texans believed propelled America at accelerated speed into the morasses of fiscal

---

[3] Le Marquis de Custine, *Le Russie en* 1839, iv, 436.

[4] E.g., *The A.C.A. Index* lists him with a 10% conservative voting record, Kennedy 11%.

irresponsibility, internationalism and the welfare state. He converted his party perfidy into a political asset, boasting that instead of offering opposition he was giving "responsible leadership"; that he was supporting the President better than the leaders of the Republican Party, which was true. Overlooked was the tragic fact that he was sabotaging the traditional role and purpose of the opposition party and merging political power into a monolithic instrument destructive of freedom and the republican form of government. Instead of being condemned for this subversion, he generally met with praise and the approbation of a people who had forgotten the fundamentals of a constitutional republic.

While lacking the light and ivy-league touch of President Kennedy, his record proves him just as completely dedicated to our give-away, interventionist, international policies. By report his first call upon reaching the White House after the assassination was in reassurance to Khrushchev; his next was to one of the most sinister and powerful radicals in the world, the man dominating the left-wing Labor Party of New York City, David Dubinsky. Long ago he had embraced the Party's cause, declaring:

"You say I am not a liberal. Let me tell you that I am more liberal than Eleanor Roosevelt and I will prove it to you. Franklin D. Roosevelt was my hero." Herein at least Johnson was as good as his word. Were there any remaining doubt, he has dispelled it since becoming President.

In foreign affairs, he went every step with Hopkins, Acheson and Roosevelt. He consistently voted for our tremendous outlays in foreign aid. He voted for subsidies to Russia's satellites and communist countries like Poland and Yugoslavia. He voted for aid to those expropriating American property. He led in abdication of the Senate's treaty responsibilities, in violation of the Constitution. He was firmly for the reciprocal trade agreements whereby American capital and labor have been sold out on everything from beef to ball bearings, simply as a concession to internationalism. All this is proven by his voting record.

Overlooked generally is his early advocacy of the progressive disarmament of America in the face of a dangerous and hostile world. Since this first became official policy under Kennedy, critics have been inclined to place the onus upon him and his hay-wire Harvard advisors. This however is a grave disservice to Johnson and his just historic due. Four years before Kennedy outlined his plan for disarmament, which the great American historian Dr. Charles Callan Tansill aptly termed "the pattern of betrayal," as set forth in State Department Publication 7277 called "Freedom From War," Senator Johnson had sketched the plan in bold and nationally suicidal strokes.

In New York City, June 8, 1957, before the United Jewish Appeal banquet, he called for "a new world policy" in defense. In an astonishing revelation he began by repudiating the basic spiritual heritage and hope of America by invoking, not the blessings of Divine Guidance, but humanistically, the "rule of reason," saying:

"Mankind's only hope lies with men themselves. Let us insist that the case be submitted to the people of the world." After having thus disposed of Omnipotent God in favor of the collective passions of Katanga, the Congo, Russia and many others, he suggested our future national policy—an "open curtain" program of disarmament through "the controlled reduction of military forces", the suspension of nuclear testing, the reduction of our stock piles of weapons, an "open skies" inspection system, and "a world-wide agreement, backed by absolute safeguards," which he as a prudent man left to speculation.

He failed to say that in 1927 Russia had advanced the same program, calling for "dissolution of all land, sea and air forces," the destruction of all military supplies, the abolition of compulsory military training, the destruction of air and military bases, and the discontinuance of military funds and the manufacture of war supplies. Thus Johnson's "new world policy" paralleled that of the Communists, set forth for us to follow just twenty-two years before.[5]

But by December 4, 1957, his crusade for universal disarmament in New York turned to a warning for preparedness in a growingly militant Texas, after his realization that this "nation has been completely outstripped in the field where we thought we were supreme," namely, sputnik and space. Notwithstanding his leadership of the Democrats in their censure of Joe McCarthy for his patriotic warnings of sabotage and our missile lag, Lyndon now became our foremost advocate of "mastery of space."

From urging disarmament in June, he took off in oratorical orbit at Council Bluffs, December 8, to tell the world that "out in space there lies the power to control the weather of the earth . . . Out in space is certainly the potential of tomorrow's navigation . . If outer space goes by default to tyranny, the world will become only the tail to the tyrant's kite."[6] If gaseous effusion could have got him there, Lyndon would have been the first man on the moon.

---

[5] For Johnson's speech, see *Dallas News*, June 9, 1957. For the Russian proposals, see Eugene A. Korovine, Professor of International Law, Institute of Soviet Law, Moscow, "The U.S.S.R. and Disarmament," in the *International Conciliation Pamphlet*, No. 292, Sept. 1933. For Kennedy's policy, see *Freedom from War*, State Dept. Pub. 7277, 1961.

[6] *Fort Worth Star-Telegram*, Dec. 9, 12, 1957.

Yet as Vice-President he presided over the Senate, pushing his and Russia's disarmament proposals in bills which empowered President Kennedy, at his own discretion, to disarm America or give away our defenses, from navy to air force. Johnson then rammed Kennedy's treaty on nuclear testing through the Senate, which flew in the face of all the lessons of survival in history, as well as the intuitive wisdom of every healthy American.

This betrayal of America was by careful plan, but with a frankness that was amazing. As Johnson was bulldozing the legislation and the treaty on disarmament through Congress, his influential confederate with a highly questionable security rating, Walt W. Rostow, was plainly setting forth the essential feature of our "new world policy" in his book, *The United States in the World Arena.* Therein he said:

"... it is a legitimate national objective to see removed from all nations—including the United States—the right to use military force to pursue their own interests," and urged "an end" to American "nationhood as it has been historically defined."[7] Could the proposal to abolish the United States of America be more frankly stated?

As President, Johnson has continued the craven appeasement of the criminal Castro, continues to sell-out American fighting men in Vietnam, apologizes for the American students who ran up the flag over our territory in Panama, and negotiates with the gangsters there who refused to abide by their nation's solemn treaty of the past.

From consideration of Johnson's foreign policy, Americans can turn with but little less confidence to his devious budget proposals. His political legerdemain in this regard seemed to fool only those big businessmen more anxious

7 Rostow, as cited, 549.

to suck the teat of government subsidy than to rustle for themselves on the ranges of free enterprise. Nobody short of Johnson's monumental ego would have dared the fraud of proposing a hundred billion dollar budget as an "economy" measure—even when "cut to $98 billion," which, with back-door spending and Johnson's pragmatism means absolutely nothing. In his State of the Union message he pledged "utmost thrift and frugality," adding that "the government will set an example of prudence and economy." The sheer hypocrisy of this vulgar pretense, even to his shallow showmanship in shutting off the White House lights, was quickly proven by the disclosure that his initial spending exceeded that of any other President in history.

In 1959, Johnson referred to the $77 billion Eisenhower budget as a determination by "black magic," contending that "the test of a budget is whether it serves the needs of the American people." A year earlier, when sputnik had thrown him into a dither, he had observed that "we must learn to live as though there will never be a tomorrow," and as for financial stability, that too was in orbit, since, he said: "The ground beneath us ... has been largely swept away ... control of outer space ... renders irrelevant the bookkeeping concerns of fiscal officers."

Yet even Senator Harry Byrd would have been proud of him when, speaking at the University of Houston, June 3, 1958, he made an eloquent attack on foreign aid and our "reliance upon dollars alone to buy what cannot be bought." In a conservative vein he charged that:

> The result of trying to buy respect with money instead of gaining it by unswerving adherence to our traditional principles is that men and nations everywhere that we had counted on as on the side of freedom, are challenging openly and

angrily our own assumption that we are secure
as leaders of all free men.

But three days later, when foreign aid of almost four
billion dollars was voted, with funds for "friends" and
Communist countries too, he not only voted for it but
paid "high tribute to the distinguished Senator Theodore
Green", Chairman of the Foreign Relations Committee,
who had been "floor manager for the bill."[9]

Johnson obviously subscribes completely to Josef
Stalin's observation, as set forth in his volume, *Marxism
and the National Colonial Question,* that "it is essential
that the advanced countries should render aid—real and
prolonged aid, to the backward nationalities in their cul-
tural and economic development." For before the Houston,
Texas, Bonds for Israel dinner, November 16, 1959, he
followed Stalin by saying that: "Either we give ourselves
to the tasks of raising the world's standards to ours—or
else we shall be forced to lower our standards to those set
by communist designs." Before the American Medical Association in Dallas he repeated this staggering idea adding:
"I don't think there is any option."[10]

In 1960 the Texas chairman of the National Committee of Business and Professional Men for Kennedy and
Johnson frankly contended that their election "will insure
a more equal distribution of wealth than at present among
all segments of our economy." From disavowing socialism
before a convention of Texas bankers in March 1962,
President Johnson, on January 15, 1964, confirmed his
socialism before "senior citizens" in the White House by
assuring them that "We are going to take all of the money

9 *Southern Conservative,* Forth Worth, June, 1958; *Congressional Records,* p. 9387.

10 *Houston Chronicle,* Nov. 16, 1959; *Texas Councilor,* Dec.
5, 1959.

that we think is unnecessarily being spent, and take it from the 'haves', and give it to the 'have nots' that need it so much." Yet five days later in his first economic report to Congress, he was promising an "early warning system" against inflation, while calling for a billion dollar program "to enable every individual to build his earning power to full capacity," and "to assure all citizens of decent living standards regardless of economic reversals or vicissitudes of human life and health"—something never before conceived in the finite mind of man. He charged that "minor injury is a major tragedy ... honesty can become a luxury and ambition a myth ... Worst of all, the poverty of the fathers is vested upon the children." It was the first time an American leader had relegated to limbo the infinite diversity of human nature, the American economic system and Christian ethics in two short sentences.[11]

His intolerance of opposition is well-known in Washington. After allowing advocates several days of testimony before the Senate Sub-Committee on State Department appropriations, he shut the patriotic Bryton Barron, former high officer in the Department, off in *"eleven minutes"* when he appeared to testify and suggest economies on the basis of his own experience—especially through the firing of pro-communists in the Department.[12]

Johnson's voting has consistently been anti-business and pro-socialist. He has favored cooperatives, especially the REA and giant federal power projects, as in his vote for the Hell's Canyon dam in preference to seeing three smaller ones built by private industry. He is a strong supporter of slum clearance and federal housing, of giant sub-

[11] For these disclosures see *Southern Conservative*, Sept., 1960; *Fort Worth Press*, Jan. 20, 1964; *Human Events*, Feb. 1, 1964.

[12] *The Tablet*, Brooklyn, June 7, 1958.

sidies for agriculture and of continuing foreign aid. While
an ardent champion of the restrictive agricultural policies
that have steadily depopulated the country side, as a presidential aspirant, in the Kansas farm belt on December 8,
1959, he unblushingly charged the Republicans as being
dedicated to "clearing the farmer off the land." While the
government, under his own favorite measures, was paying
a billion dollars a year for storage of surplus grain—he
denied any surplus, saying there was only waste by those
"who have allowed to pass from their concerns the concerns of man ... We must find the way in America to take
our food out of the warehouses ... and put it into the
hands of the earth's hungry millions."[13] Four years later,
as President, he had! By forcing through legislation to
give it to the "tyrants" of Russia!

On December 11, 1959, in Phoenix, as the man most
responsible for the appropriation of the funds, he is said
to have "captured a capacity audience" by his scathing
attack on Secretary of Agriculture Ezra Taft Benson, the
"granddaddy of all spenders"—who Johnson charged,
"had allowed farm income to drop 17 per cent while spending 35 billion dollars on the farm program" [14] for which
expenditure there had been no stronger advocate than
Majority Leader Johnson.

But one of his first moves as President was to force
through farm legislation still based on government subsidies and controls, despite the overwhelming repudiation
of such policy by the farmers in a national referendum
the year before. At the same time he was firmly in favor
of the new meat treaties, with only a temporary token
cut on imports and escalation clauses for annual increases
to "guarantee" Australia and New Zealand "their fair

13 *Fort Worth Star-Telegram*, Dec. 8, 1959.
14 *Arizona Republic*, Dec. 11, 1959.

share in the growth of the American market"—at a time when many cowmen and feeders were facing bankruptcy. As a sorry sop to the industry, however, he did have such ready confederates as A. W. Moursund of Johnson City and Jay Taylor of Amarillo prowling the cattle ranges assuring hard-pressed producers that the President, unlike the Republicans, was still concerned "with the concerns of men"—even cowmen, "but there is nothing he can do about it."[15]

Johnson has steadily moved to the left in alliance with the extreme factions of American labor, voting to deny the union men a secret ballot on strikes, voting against prevention of the use of union dues for political purposes, against limiting federal contributions to the radical International Labor Organization when Communists delegates voted at their meetings, against prevention of secondary boycotts and against the right of unions to determine their membership, as in forcing racial integration upon them. But he is for David Dubinsky, Walter Reuther and George Meany and they are all out for him. Yet it has not always been so. Labor leaders in Texas, along with the radical-liberals nationally, distrusted him for years and threw their support behind Texas Senator Ralph Yarborough in the long-drawn feud between the two. Yet while Johnson is an avowed friend of union leaders, strangely his TV-radio interests have never been unionized, and former employees are currently suing his company for an accounting

15 Judge Moursund, Johnson's trustee, tried to cultivate a favorable reception for the treaties. Jay Taylor, past president of every Texas and national cattlemen's group of prominence and a political figure behind the scenes for years, is an inveterate idolator of Lyndon B. Johnson. For more about the beef treaties, see J. Evetts Haley, "Up the Potomac Without a Paddle," *Texas Farm and Ranch*, Dallas, April, 1964, p. 4.

of a stock-sharing plan.

His most extreme position in denying the Rights of the States and in destroying the Constitutional rights of the individual, is his support of the 1964 Civil Rights Act—which will end the American Republic. In preparing for this revolutionary move, he had the ready cooperation of the venial portions of America's news media, which carefully cultivated the Johnson image to where the rest of the country believed he was genuinely popular, even in the South.

Yet when he was chosen as Kennedy's running mate "to hold Texas and the South" in the Democratic fold, as has been said, it was only through the combined pressure of the State and National machines, with the labor, and the controlled negro and Mexican vote—plus the widespread conviction that "Nixon is just as bad"—that he was barely able to carry his own state. In truth Johnson and Kennedy did not carry Texas and the South; the Republicans lost them as they seem determined to do so again.

There is nothing more significant in Johnson's career than the fact that he has never been known to take an unpopular position and resolutely go down the line for it. Yet this is something that no man of strong principles and convictions and long tenure in public office, especially in times of drastic change, has ever been able to avoid.

On the other hand, when the time was politically ripe, Johnson did a complete flip-flop on civil rights. He voted four times against abolition of the poll tax as a congressman, opposed an anti-lynching bill in 1940, was against desegregation in the District of Columbia in 1949 and opposed cloture to break a Senate filibuster against the FEPC in 1950. But in 1955 he came out for poll tax repeal, maneuvered the passage of his own Civil Rights Bill in 1957 and by 1960 was an opponent of all forms of segregation, favoring and practicing the use of drastic federal force against it, and as President socially integrating the White House.[16]

His perfidy was most dramatically proven in his handling of the Smith, the Bridges and Jenner-Butler bills, which were designed to limit the jurisdiction of the Supreme Court in its headlong destruction of the Rights of the States, particularly in its pro-communist school integration and subversion cases.

The month of August, 1959, may prove to have been one of the most historic for the United States Senate. After keeping the Jenner-Butler Bill bottled up for the session, Johnson finally let it out, to be tabled by an eight-vote margin. The Bridges bill to restore to the States the right to prosecute crimes of sedition—which had been taken from them by the Supreme Court's usurpation—then came up, but a motion to table it was defeated 46 to 39. Senator McClellan thereupon moved to substitute a "far-reaching measure reviving many state laws previously held unconstitutional ... " and as Willard Edwards wrote, the Senate went into an uproar as for the first time in [17] the session, Johnson was "forced to bring an explosive issue to the floor." The test on this crucial measure came August 21 on a vote to kill the bill by recommitting it to committe and thereupon, as David Lawrence said, "the betrayal of the South occurred in the Senate," [18] and Lyndon B. Johnson was its traitor.

As the vote approached it seemed certain, in view of

---

[16] Amarillo News, (quoting Congressional Quarterly,) Dec. 2, 1963; *Battle Line*, Feb. 19, 1959; Willard Edwards, "Lyndon the Great," *Human Events*, May 19, 1960.

[17] Willard Edwards, "The Senate Stirs to Life," *National Review*, Jan. 17, 1959.

[18] David Lawrence column, August 27, 1959.

the earlier test, that the conservative forces would pass the Bridges bill by a vote of 46 to 39. As the only man who knew in advance how each Senator would vote, Johnson swung into action with his famed "black magic" to reverse the anticipated action. He talked his close friend George Smathers, of Florida, who favored the bill, into pairing with the absent Mike Monroney, who was for recommittal, which cut the favorable margin from 45 to 39.

He put pressure on Senator Milton Young, of North Dakota, a supporter of the bill, "to take a walk"; he induced Senator Allen Frear, of Delaware, who was likewise with the Southerners, to hide out at the time of the vote; and he induced Senator Frank Lausche, who had pledged the Southerners his support, to change his position, which cut the margin from 42 to 40.

While the vote was being taken, he sent his friend and protege, Bobby Baker, to the cloakroom—where Senator Kerr was "waiting for his name to be called so he could vote with the South"—to tell Kerr that it was going to be a tie vote if the Oklahoma Senator voted with the Southerners, and that Vice-President Nixon would then vote the tie off in favor of recommitting the bill, which would give him credit for a liberal victory and enhance his stature in the North as a presidential candidate.

While Kerr was being held in the cloakroom by Bobby Baker with these dismal forebodings, thus reducing the margin 41-40, Johnson hurriedly sent Dirksen to the Senate cloakroom where Republican Wallace Bennett, of Utah, was waiting to vote with the South, to warn him that this would tie the vote, thus putting Republican Vice-President Nixon "on the spot" by forcing Nixon to vote the tie off and thus, no matter which way he voted, hurting his presidential candidacy in one or another section of the country. Bennett finally gave in and emerged from the cloakroom to vote with the liberals, to defeat, 41 to 40, the last great Congressional effort to restrain the left-wing usurpations of the Court, to restore the Constitution and to re-establish the Republic.

Except with the prostituted press, the condemnation of Johnson was widespread and bitter throughout the South, with newspapers from Richmond to Shreveport branding him as the "Counterfeit Confederate," "The Texas Yankee," "a political charlatan," "the Southern Benedict Arnold," a "political polygamist" and "a traitor to the South." [19] But these reactions are entirely too sectional to point up the real significance of the tragedy. They simply indicted the unusual concern of the South, which, by virtue of being closer to the immediate problem, was more aware of the imminent danger. It was not a Southern but a national issue, and with Machiavellian skill and purpose, Johnson had not simply sold out Texas and the South. He had betrayed America.

From that time on he moved with firm resolution to court the radical forces in his campaign for the presidency. Yet his sophistry was so smooth and artful as to charm such correspondents as Holmes Alexander into finding him "totally devoid of demagoguery ... Who else would have thought of a right-to-vote bill?" Alexander wrote. "Or a federal agency on space? Or of a civil rights bill with a conciliation service in it?"[20] Devoid of demagoguery?" This is its finer essence!

He has built this reverse twist, this inverted English, into a deceptive art. Upon his return from taking the

19 Karr Shannon in the *Arkansas Democrat*, June 14, 1960; James Jackson Kilpatrick in *Human Events*, Aug. 25, 1960; *The Columbia Record*, Aug. 23, 1958; David Lawrence, Aug. 27, 1958.
20 *Fort Worth Star-Telegram*, Feb. 4, 1959.

Democratic precinct control from the Governor Allan
Shivers forces in Texas in 1956, at the B'nai B'rith
Convention Dinner in Washington on May 8, he had
hailed his victory as the rejection of "the vicious attempt
to inject racial hatred" into Texas politics. But as in the
case of the "religious issue" in the campaign of 1960, only
he and the liberals had injected it.[21]

By this time Johnson had perfected his parliamentary
technique, which was to round up the wildest proposals
the radicals trotted into the legislative arena, chouse them
around with a simulated show of concern, crowd them
through his own Senatorial chute, spray them with his
plausible double-talk, burn the LBJ brand deep into their
Congressional hides and turn them out to trample and
gore the American public. The liberals caught on to the
fact at once that the legislative outlaws stampeding over
the rights of the States were still their own, while the
"Main Street conservatives" rubbed the goose-grease of
moderation on the saddle-sores of the real Constitutionalists, congratulating them for having "been saved from
the extremists" by that great Texas genius, Lyndon Baines
Johnson.

This sophistry has been successful many times, but
never more completely than when the liberal Republicans
had their civil rights bill stolen from them in 1957 by
the man "devoid of demagoguery"—in the obtuse Holmes
Alexander phrase. Yet in 1949, in opposition to a feature
of an F.E.P.C. proposal to grant the Attorney General
injunctive powers to speed integration, as Senator Mc-
Clellan recently pointed out, Johnson had said: "If the
Federal government can by law tell me whom I shall
employ, it can likewise tell my prospective employees for

<hr>

21 *Dan Smoot Report*, Dec. 23, 1963; *Sweetwater*, (Texas)
Reporter, May 9, 1956.

whom they must work. If the law can compel me to employ a negro, it can compel that negro to work for me. It might even tell him how long and how hard he would have to work ... such a law would do nothing more than enslave a minority."

Yet on August 28, 1957, the moderate-wing *Washington Star* praised the Majority Leader as he came "riding a high, rolling wave of victory" to a party at the Mayflower "celebrating his forty-ninth birthday." "Straight from Capitol Hill," the *Star* continued, "where he helped engineer the vote of 12 members of the Texas House delegation for the civil rights bill (and where he helped make history by breaking Texas away from the solid South), Senator Johnson was in fine form."

Sam Rayburn helped do the honors and Johnson reciprocated by congratulating him on "the greatest thing that you and twelve other Texans" have "ever done"— which was to vote out the bill, in violation of the rights of all the States, to the particular detriment of Texas and the South; fulsome praise for being traitors to a peaceful way of life.

Thus did Johnson steal the radical Republicans' civil rights thunder in 1957 with the first "force bill" since Reconstruction. Not only that, but he converted it into a political asset, as with incredible irony, he made himself the Party's choice for second place in 1960 "to hold the Solid South in line." It was a phenomenal performance that bespeaks no less "the political genius" of the man, than the sodden apathy and political stupidity of the leaders of Southern people.

It might have been excusable had the voters not known better, but his duplicity was a matter of clear and abundant record. Early in the same session he was writing constituents in Texas wondering where they "could have

got the idea that I am supporting the 'so-called bill for
civil rights legislation now before Congress.' ... *The bill
that has been introduced*" (our emphasis) he continued,
"*is one to which I am very much opposed,* as I do not
believe it would advance any legitimate cause." Again he
wrote, "I have always been opposed to forced integration,
and I have not changed my mind on this issue. It has
been my hope that these problems could be worked out by
wise leaders at the local levels." [23] And yet just four months
later he was congratulating Rayburn for "the greatest
thing" he had "ever done" — namely, for passing Lyndon's
civil rights bill and, incidentally, proving again that Lyndon was a traitor to the South. From then on there was
no let-up in his appeal to racial bigotry to promote his
candidacy. Still the ultra-liberals, who were delighted when
he double-crossed his "conservative friends," feared he
would be guilty of dirty politics by doing the same thing
with them.[24]

The legend that Johnson was more conservative than
Kennedy resulted in part from his early vigorous antipathy
for Kennedy, and in part from the obeisance paid him by
many wealthy oil men and other business socialists from
Main to Wall Street. The *ACA Index* of voting records
listed Kennedy as 11% conservative, Johnson as 10%; and
the AFL-CIO index lists his 1960 voting record as better
than two to one over Kennedy in labor's favor; while the
ADA found his record far less commendable than Kennedy's. In ACA's breakdown into seven categories, Ken-

[23] *Congressional Record,* Feb. 5, 1964, pp. 1899-1900; Lyndon B. Johnson to A. H. Hall, Corpus Christi, Texas, July
11, 1959; *Richmond News Leader,* Feb. 11, 1964.
[24] In Texas they accused him of having "surrendered" to
President Eisenhower, rating him below Kennedy, Symington and Humphrey. *Texas Observer,* Nov. 13, 1959.

nedy was given a more conservative record than Johnson on money and inflation, on economy versus waste, on private competition as against government interference, and for individual liberty as against government coercion.

Johnson has voted 80% of the time for the "welfare state" programs and in the *ACA Index* ranks one point more liberal than Senator Sparkman, five more than that screaming liberal, Paul Douglas of Illinois, is on an exact par with Proxmire of Wisconsin and Engle of California, and has a voting record just half as conservative as Fulbright of Great Britain, One World, and Arkansas. As Senator he voted 133 times with Hubert Humphrey for "inflationary spending bills, aid to education, foreign aid, defense and agriculture." And as the *Dan Smoot Report* shows, on important issues between 1955 and 1959, he is credited with only seven conservative votes.

The reason that he is more dangerous than Kennedy is that he is so much more skillful and plausible and so much more effective with Congress. Counting upon his control of Southern politicians to hold the South in line, he calculatingly set out to woo the radical elements everywhere in his ambition to be President. For with him politics is simply "the art of the possible."[25]

By midsummer 1959, that darling of the internationalists, Senator Wm. J. Fulbright, came out for him for President. Fulbright, with the professional liberal's belief in compulsion, wanted him because the United States needed "a tough President to *make Democracy work*"; because Johnson had shown his *"ability to manage Congress"*; because the President *"must overpower local prejudices and interests"*; and because Johnson had "demon-

---

[25] *Dan Smoot Report*, May 30, 1960: Willard Edwards, mss., as cited; James J. Kilpatrick, "Lyndon Johnson: Counterfeit Confederate," *Human Events*, Aug. 25, 1960.

strated the capacity *to make this almost unmanageable system operate*" (our emphasis).[26]

This statement by one of America's foremost egg-headed internationalists is a frank and revealing declaration—not only for its proof of Fulbright's positive belief in the substitution of force for Constitutional freedom, but for his sound appraisal of the real nature of Johnson as another authoritarian. All of which should have been clear to the people of Arkansas, Fulbright's home state, since Johnson did not even raise a murmur of disapproval when Eisenhower raped the Constitution and shocked the sensibilities of free men everywhere by sending the army into Little Rock—even as he was a silent if not ready confederate of the Kennedys in their bloody business at Oxford.

Fulbright was right in observing that Johnson had shown his "ability to manage Congress." But with a people who understand the tenets of freedom and are dedicated to its perpetuity, this above all should condemn him as completely unfit for the presidency.

For the Congress of the United States of America was not conceived by the founders as a perfunctory gesture to the republican principle. It was instead created as an equal and coordinate branch of the federal government, representing the individual states and the hundreds of Congressional districts, with the right of having all their diverse views, interests, ambitions and prejudices heard in free and unlimited debate. To "manage" and "over-power" these "local prejudices and interests" and "make democracy work" is to destroy the Constitution and the fundamentals of human freedom. For the Congress, in spite of Senator Fulbright's antipathies for Constitutional liberty, is not supposed to be a Soviet Presidium, nor was

26 *Austin American,* June 8, 1959.

the presidency designed as a seat for a Khrushchev or a Hitler.

The veteran Capitol Hill correspondent of the *Chicago Tribune,* Willard Edwards, seemed to have been the first observer to see and reveal the significance of Johnson's high-handed management of the Congress—especially the 85th, which Johnson dominated completely, in close collaboration with President Eisenhower. As the Edwards commentaries revealed, Johnson not only effectively used his rare talents of gagging, of compromise, personal cajolery and ruthless pressure to effect his power, but surrounded himself with the symbols and trappings suggestive of an oriental potentate.

In defiance of the Majority Leader's usual practice of dropping committee chairmanships, Lyndon held on to six, the Democratic Policy Committee, Steering, Conference, Appropriations sub-committee, Armed Services Preparedness, and Aeronautical and Space. He had more than twenty suites of offices scattered throughout the Capitol for himself and these committees, principal of which was an affair near the Senate Chamber that capitol correspondents called his "throne room." There, as Edwards wrote, he was wont to "give visitors his most stirring performances. He whispers, he shouts, he gesticulates, rises up and down, strides, sometimes leaning over his listener and bruising their ribs with a ramrod finger." Here he gave political notables from over the country "the treatment" in preparation for his race for the presidency, as with Governor David L. Lawrence of Pennsylvania, whom he "left breathless but unconvinced."[27]

Johnson's ideal was to hold the Senate to a minimum of debate, passing bills "unanimously." He had no use

27 Willard Edwards, unpublished mss., and *Chicago Tribune,* Dec. 21, 1958.

for James Madison's dictum that the Senate was a conservative, deliberative forum where "legislation was to be considered with more coolness, with more system and with more wisdom than the popular branch," the House. On the contrary Johnson's system was what Edwards aptly called "assembly-line legislation," where many bills were passed without being read, simply on the assurance of "the leadership" that they were desirable. As Edwards pointed out:

> In a summary of the 85th Congress achievements ... Johnson hailed "nonpartisan" unanimous votes on three major measures ... The Senate, he exulted, had eliminated "strife" where once it had created it. No dissent was voiced in a Chamber established by the framers of the Constitution as a check upon "the turbulence and follies of democracy." No member arose to suggest that strife over legislation was not necessarily evil; that it has in the past even killed bad legislation, as when Taft of Ohio in 1946 stopped a stampede to authorize conscription of strikers ...
>
> The record of the last session shows what it means to reach "agreement without discord." It means brief and perfunctory debate; a lack of intelligent questioning; sparse attendance; the absence of quorum calls to summon absentees; the omission of record roll calls without which the public can never know which senators were present and how they voted; and the approval of legislation in obvious ignorance of it meaning.[28]

The Omnibus Housing bill of three billion dollars

---

[28] Willard Edwards, "The Senate Stirs to Life," *National Review*, Jan. 17, 1959; and "Lyndon the Great," *Human Events*, May 19, 1960.

was negotiated to passage without even being read or explained, and the billions thus appropriated without a quorum call to bring in seventy-five absent Senators, made into law without even a vote, recorded or vocal, was acclaimed by Johnson as a "tribute to the 'patriotism and dedication to the national interest' of those present." When Senator William E. Jenner, of Indiana, absent at the time, returned and demanded reconsideration, Johnson gave him just ten minutes to argue his motion.

In similar manner the Export-Import Bank bill to increase the Bank's lending authority to two billion dollars, was declared passed after "three minutes" debate, with only a few Senators on the floor and no vote taken. Legislation authorizing the "civilian space agency" and posing again the old and vital issue between military and civilian control—which would ordinarily have involved days of debate, took just "two hours," with Johnson holding the floor in reassurance of lack of conflict and with only thirteen senators on hand when the voice vote was taken.

When the dangerous issue of transfer of atomic materials and information to "our allies" came up, proposing relaxation of "secrecy provisions which had guarded nuclear weapons since 1946," the debate of this "radical departure from post-war policy" took less than three hours before a handful of Senators, without record vote or a quorum call.

These were the three measures posing vital policy and issues that Johnson hailed for their "nonpartisan," unanimous Senate votes.

Proof of further abdication of the Senate from its Constitutional duty is found in foreign policy. When Eisenhower arrogated authority to send troops into Lebanon, possibly to plunge America into war without the Constitutional Congressional approval, Majority Leader

Johnson pled for unity behind the President.[29]

David Lawrence condemned the record of the 85th as "the worst in half a century"; especially for its failure to pass any law "to punish those who openly preach the overthrow of our government by force", to stop the drift into bankruptcy and inflation, to restrain the Supreme Court in its obvious usurpations, to curb union coercion and monopolies and "to face up to the Communist menace to American institutions." With Johnson's masterful backstage strategy, it had, however, kept the American people more completely in the dark as to what was going on than at any time in the history of the Republic. [30] Yet politically, it was considered Lyndon B. Johnson's greatest triumph, though few Americans seemed to know or care what it meant.

What it really meant was that Johnson had destroyed the purpose and function for which the Congress was created. By destroying its deliberative nature, he had destroyed Congress itself. This is the stark significance of such legislative "unanimity of thought" on vital issues.

Thus through his power and ability to "manage Congress," Johnson had done more than any other man to precipitate the United States of America into a period of parliamentary decline, from vigorous vigilance and deliberation, to unanimity and legislative impotence. It should be recalled that in the great Republics of the past, this has been the preliminary and traditional role of all illegitimate rulers. For the Dubinskys, the Reuthers and the Fulbrights, this was Lyndon at his best; but by the verdicts of history, this was Caesar at his worst.

---

29 Edwards, mss., as cited.

30 David Lawrence, column of Aug. 27, 1958.

VIII
TOWARD THE WHITE HOUSE

After a long and skillful effort to divorce himself of all suspicion of "provincialism" and to emerge with the image of a national figure, the first ironical and inescapable political necessity facing Johnson and his old mentor, Rayburn, was to re-establish himself at home as a Texan. For unless the LBJ brand was that of a favorite son for President, he would cut a poor figure elsewhere.

Three considerable difficulties lay in the way; first, a steady drift in Texas away from the nostrums and panaceas of Lyndon's pseudo-liberalism; second, the conservative political control of Texas under the leadership of Governor Allan Shivers, who had little love for Lyndon; and third, the ultra-liberal faction in the Democratic Party led by Ralph Yarborough who loved him even less.

Upon the sudden death of Governor Beauford Jester, July 11, 1949, Lieutenant-Governor Shivers moved into the office under unusually favorable circumstances. He was young, handsome, ambitious, financially independent, politically experienced and a tough-fibered fighter. He came into office without obligation to any individual, special interest, or faction and consequently was in a strong position to make Texas an outstanding governor.

Many Texans were weary of the New Deal by 1948, when the States-Rights campaign was launched behind Fielding Wright and Strom Thurmond. The State Democratic Convention refused to endorse President Harry Truman and the conservative leadership had hopes of carrying Texas out of the Party with the Southern defectors until Governor Jester, under Washington pressure, pulled out of the movement after having led the rebels to believe he would join them.

Six years later the Texas conservatives hoped that Governor Shivers, with two full terms behind him, would challenge Johnson for his Senatorial seat. In 1952 Shivers, in control of the Democratic machinery in Texas and at the height of his popularity had, with a sense of strategy and of timing, capitalized upon the growing resentment by leading Texas out of the Democratic fold to support General Eisenhower. Not only was Shivers riding high in Texas, but he was being looked upon by the South as the spearhead of sectional opposition to domination from Washington.

But in 1956 Shivers was in high favor with Eisenhower, who was anything but a conservative, and he was toying with the idea of taking second place on a coalition ticket, being secretly planned with the President in a move that was carefully designed by modern Republicans and other internationalists to sink the rising conservative cause. This move was calculated to sabotage the flaming Southern revolt, destroy the old-line Republican leadership in Congress —even to their ranking tenure on important committees and put Shivers in position as Eisenhower's logical successor.

These plans were well along until exposed on March 29, 1956, by the veteran political correspondent, John O'Donnell, in the *New York Daily News*. In revealing the plan and its dangerous significance for the conservative cause generally, O'Donnell said: "This would be consolidation and fusion with a vengeance. It would be a regrouping of political forces, but not the new realignment that has been trying to be born since 1940—the conservatives of the nation on one side, the socialistic groups on the other. It would be a political consolidation . . . with Eisenhower on the top."[1]

With the exposure the plan fizzled out. The able but coldly-calculating Shivers had, unwisely for his political

[1] John O'Donnell, "Capitol Stuff," *New York Daily News*, March 29, 1956.

future, passed up the challenge to take on Lyndon in 1954 and instead had won a third elective term as Governor of Texas, to garner the growing animosities of long tenure, and the adverse political effects of the far-reaching land and insurance scandals that broke in his last administration.

Lyndon, with little effort, went back as Senator, to begin at once, with Rayburn's effective help, the promotion of his candidacy for President. Aside from building his synthetic national image the first serious step was to re-capture the party from the Texas conservatives so as to make him the favorite son.

Senator Ralph Yarborough, with consistency of purpose, and unusual energy and persistency in the face of repeated defeats, had built himself into the deserving idol of the ultra-liberal cause. On the State level, he, not Lyndon John-son, was the favorite of the left-wing labor leaders, the rising racial minorities and the Socialist-Democrats generally of Texas. He knew as well as anyone the designing and tricky nature of Lyndon, while Lyndon knew he could have no open truck with Ralph except on pain of losing his Texas pseudo-conservatives, without whom he could not hope to capture the Texas Democratic machinery.

Another prominent figure in this complicated political picture was Price Daniel, the bland but ambitious Texas Attorney General and a mild moderate conservative in the public eye. With Shivers entrenched in the Governor's office and Yarborough perpetually challenging him from the liberal front, Daniel had, in 1952, decided to forego his ambition to run for Governor, challenged the ailing Tom Connally and was elected to the United States Senate. With the Shivers cause in a near shambles in 1956, and Yarborough again taking the hustings for Governor of Texas, an element of big businessmen, with their usual lack of political sense and strategy came up with the panic-stricken idea that "nobody but Price can beat Ralph Yarborough." Thereupon they launched a campaign to get Price to return and run for Governor, despite the certain tragic and obvious consequences for the conservative cause.

In the first place, Ralph would be no pushover. In the second, Daniel himself was far from a confirmed conservative. In the third, even if elected, his resignation would leave the Senate seat to be filled in a special election by a simple plurality vote, in which case Yarborough, if defeated for Governor, would run again, and with his dedicated following be the certain winner. All this was pointed out to the "conservative oil men" backing Price's return but to no avail. Senator Daniel was flown into Austin at night in a Hughes Tool Company plane, surreptitiously called on Shivers by the back entrance of the Mansion and got the Governor's blessings—which was not openly wanted on account of the raging scandals. But Shivers had an organization and knew how to get money—which Daniel needed.

With the campaign in full swing, the Democratic Convention in May, at Fort Worth, resolved itself into a bitter battle between the Daniel and Yarborough forces. At its height it became obvious that Yarborough, if he but launched a vigorous offensive, would almost certainly take over the Convention. For the hard core of the Yarborough camp had no confidence in and no use for Lyndon B. Johnson, who, with "Mr. Sam"—that is, House Speaker Rayburn—were directing the play from the wings, and the cue those two called was one of peace and harmony behind Price Daniel—whom Shivers too was supporting. And peace they had to have to take over the state machine. Ralph hesitated and in hesitation he lost. But he was hard pressed for campaign funds, the election had far to go and "hoping to keep from making Mr. Sam mad"—well-knowing what he and Lyndon could do to him between then and the run off—

Yarborough decided not to push his popular advantage and hence lost the convention.

With the support of Lyndon and Rayburn, and covert help from Shivers, Daniel squeaked through the runoff to win by less than four thousand votes out of more than one and a third million cast. But by double-crossing the liberal wing of the Democratic Party in Texas and forming a coalition of moderates, pseudo-conservatives and portions of the Shivers forces with their federal machine, "Mr. Sam" and Lyndon managed to take over the Party organization in Texas. Even so, Lyndon was forced to compromise with the ultra-radical bloc by naming its flaming financial angel, Mrs. R. D. Randolph of Houston, as National Committeewoman from Texas.

Yarborough took on the big field in the election to fill Daniel's unexpired term. Ex-Congressman Martin Dies became the conservative contender. The Texas Republicans split the vote by taking a big bloc for their modern Republican candidate, Thad Hutcheson and, as anticipated, Yarborough rolled handily into the United States Senate on the wave of his dedicated following, with no obligation to and still no love lost on Lyndon.

But with the Democratic machinery in his hands, Lyndon still found the political waters far from serene in Texas. The old liberal-loyalist faction maintained its separate state organization, the DOTs—The Democratic Clubs of Texas, who nourished their wrath for Lyndon by recalling that he had hidden out during the 1956 campaign, barely giving token support to their idol, Adlai Stevenson, and fanned their feelings to high heat with every fresh rebuff to their state hero, Senator Yarborough. They wanted no part of Lyndon as a favorite son.

Likewise bitterly against him were the Texas conservatives. When in 1958 the large Fort Worth delegation met

in pre-convention caucus, it voted three to one condemning
Johnson for his sabotage of the Smith Bill, that was designed to curb the Court, in a resolution to be submitted for
approval to the San Antonio State Convention.

By Convention time, Governor Daniel, New Deal National Committeeman Byron Skelton and other Johnson
professional politicians, had raided the ultra-liberal camp
by their successful wooing of labor, negro and Latin votes
at the precinct level, and enticed away some of its leaders.
Daniel indicated their success when, shortly in advance of
the Convention, he predicted that "statewide labor forces
would switch support from the DOT to the new coalition"
—that is from Yarborough to Johnson and many did.[2]

With Governor Daniel and other pseudo-conservatives
helping hold the line and with Johnson's henchmen in
charge, the Convention was well under control. The resolution of condemnation somehow got lost and instead one
endorsing Johnson was gavelled to doubtful passage amid
widespread boos and hisses. Again both the Texas liberals
and conservatives had been double-crossed by the Johnson
conspiracy in Texas.[3]

Between then and the next State election, bitter criticism continued to come from the disappointed liberals, who
irreverently referred to the House Speaker as "Czar Rayburn", grumbled over Johnson's alliance with the Shivers
forces in the convention, complained of his collusion with
Daniel and the moderates, wherein he had "engaged in the
old 'harmony' sellout, and kicked his friends while reward-
ing his enemies," castigated him as "Pussyfoot Johnson,"

[2] Garth Jones' AP report, Aug. 16, 1958.
[3] For the background of the political play, see Sam Wood,
Amarillo Globe-News, May 30, 1958; *The Southern Conservative*, Oct., 1958; *Texas Observer*, Jan. 17, 1958 and May
2, 1959; Oct. 7, 1960.

"the Great Manipulator", who "has chosen the padded foot rather than the firm tread of intelligent opposition", and demanded to know, "Can anyone . . . fancy Lyndon playing with a political deck that was not stacked in advance."[4] They too had come to know his duplicity and they liked it no better than the conservatives.

But his plans were effectively under way. In the spring of 1960 the Texas Legislature was pushing through his dual candidacy, special privilege bill, sponsored by a leading conservative, State Senator Dorsey Hardeman. Hardeman, who had strongly supported a Texas Resolution urging passage of the Smith Act, which Lyndon scuttled, was now the champion of a bill to allow Lyndon to run for Senator and President or vice-president at the same time.

To make it especially convenient, the Legislature proposed to move the primary dates up, so that Lyndon's renomination as Senator would be out of the way before the National Conventions. Even in the bizarre history of Texas politics, it was an astonishing, but from the standpoint of Johnson's flexible ethics, a prudent and progressive proposal. The fight in the Legislature resulted in the reversal of the usual liberal and conservative positions.

Senator Yarborough spent a busy week on the telephone with his Texas Legislative friends, urging them to defeat the proposal—which was obviously the conservative thing to do. Johnson pressured his friends to vote the bill to passage—for which unusually liberal purpose the leading conservative legislators were prime protagonists. With Governor Daniel's support the bill rolled to passage—as further proof of Johnson's pragmatic efficiency and the shambles he generally makes of political parties and ideals.[5]

4 *Texas Observer*, Jan. 17, 1958; May 2, 1959; Jan. 29, 1960.
5 *Fort Worth Press*, April 13, 1959; *Texas Observer*, May 2, 1959.

A young conservative Democrat, Michael E. Schwille, of Dallas, challenged the Constitutionality of the statute, but was slapped down in the Courts.[5a] Senator Barry Goldwater humorously observed that with such a precedent, he foresaw the day when a candidate might be permitted to run for every office on the ballot, whereby, under the law of averages, he should be expected to win some of them.

While things were going well in Texas, in Washington Lyndon's liberal colleagues were restive under his iron-handed control of policy and procedure. Senator Proxmire led an incipient rebellion, while Joseph Rauh, Walter Reuther's lawyer and former National Chairman of the Americans for Democratic Action, charged both Rayburn and Johnson with "having scrapped party unity and principles in favor of 'personal cloakroom-and-dagger' tactics." Rauh described Rayburn as a "venerated hierarch presiding over one House"; Johnson as "an admired and feared autocrat" ruling the other and charged that both were without principles or fixed policies. And for once Rauh was right.

In April, 1959, the left-wing Committee for an Effective Congress attacked Johnson, charging that he, "a master of the immediate," was "doomed to failure" unless he could "yoke his labors to a new national spirit—" by which they meant a liberal and integrationist one. Robert W. McCormick, in his NBC program "Emphasis USA," on January 4, 1960, let loose a devastating blast, holding that no Texan would ever get the nomination and touched upon the rawer aspects of Johnson's nature; his "incredibly bad temper," his habit of snapping and snarling at his overworked staff, and the fact that after twenty-one years as an all out FDR New Dealer his fiery liberalism had given

5a Schwille vs. Steakley et al. Civil No. 1157. James P. Donovan and Wm. F. Billings for plaintiff; John D. Cofer, Abe Fortas, and Leon Jaworski for Johnson.

way to the tactics of a "sneak conciliator."[6] At a Democratic fund raising dinner in Washington thereafter, Texas National Committeewoman, Mrs. R. D. Randolph, informed the Party leaders that she was not for Johnson for President, adding icily: "I didn't know he was running."[7]

Johnson, however, was working feverishly to gain favor with the liberals—especially with the radical labor and racial groups. He had voted against Senator McClellan's "bill of rights" amendment in protection of the union men, he switched to a compulsory F.E.C.P. stand and, despite the flouting of the law by Congressman Adam Clayton Powell, had voted against investigation of Powell's affairs in blatant approval of corruption and in a bid for the negro vote.[8]

With his renomination as Senator in the rearranged Texas primaries out of the way, Johnson went into the Texas Democratic Convention of June, 1960, with the Party machinery under control—but still far from running smoothly. His raids on the liberal camp through outright deals with labor, Latin and negro leaders so decimated Yarborough's convention support that when the issue was joined, the annihilation was all but complete. Mrs. Randolph tried to regroup the liberals for a demonstration at Los Angeles, and the conservative faction booed and shouted at every mention of Johnson's name. Senator Yarborough, having read the sign, "was the most conspicuous man at the convention by his absence."[9]

---

6 *Dallas News*, March 20, 1959; *Fort Worth Press*, April 4, 1959; and notes on McCormick broadcast of date.

7 *Texas Observer*, Jan. 15, Feb. 5, 1960.

8 *Congressional Record*, vol. 106, pp. 8729; *Texas Observer*, June 17, 1960.

9 For a revealing commentary see the account in the *Texas Observer*, June 17, 1960. For an extended comment on the campaign, see Prof. Douglas Weeks, *Texas in the 1960 Election*, 80 pp., Austin.

It was a mere formality to bull-doze through an endorsement of "the illustrious Senate Majority Leader" for President. But it had taken some real "doing." It won him high praise among his purblind business idolators and the accolade of the notoriously corrupt Judge Woodrow Bean, of El Paso, as "the greatest living American." Thus again the Texas liberals and conservatives had been sold out through the master maneuvering, pressure, trading and deception of Lyndon Baines Johnson, through an alliance of leading labor, Mexican and negro politicians with the political eunuchs — the pious advocates of moderation, and those big business interests always ready to "go along to get along."

It left deep and ineradicable scars. It gained Johnson the bitter-end opposition of Senator Yarborough and the most ardent of his liberal followers—who went down the line against him in favor of Adlai Stevenson at Los Angeles. Thus were the ultra-liberals in Texas finally confirmed in their views that Johnson was a traitor to their cause; a ruthless enemy who would double-cross and destroy anybody who opposed his march to power. Even the conservatives, so rarely in agreement, appreciated their point of view.

In this pragmatic age politics is no longer the means to high national policy predicated on spiritual purpose, but simply "the art of the possible." And therein Texas had the best. Johnson had been named as the Lone Star's favorite son for President and, for the intoxicating moment, that was all the news media mentioned, and what else could really matter?

Johnson is reported to have raised a million dollars preparatory to his campaign, principally from the "conservative oil men of Texas," and was ready to go to Los Angeles armed with all his obtrusive vanity and determination to gain the presidency. Betimes however, he kept venting his vitriolic spleen upon his urbane, sophisticated and front-running competitor, until it would seem that conciliation, compromise and concord were impossible.

For what could Jack Kennedy, the scion of arrogant and inherited wealth, polished in the best ivy league tradition, ideologically drifting upon the high and liberal seas, doubly impelled by Irish resentment over ancestral rebuffs and his own ambition for power, well-armed with and aware of the prestige of money and somehow boyishly charming withal —what could he find in common with this hard, practical, corn-ball extrovert from the poor and uncultured hills of Texas? Those who thought there was no common ground reckoned not with the "lust for power over the souls of men," especially among those who had once drunk its strong and heady brew.

Johnson excoriated Kennedy unmercifully as the convention approached. He had John Connally circulating among the correspondents of Washington suggesting that they print a story that Kennedy had bought the West Virginia primary, after which he would present the proof. Naturally those wily observers suggested the proof in hand and then they would break the story. Johnson's delayed announcement had not helped. For the anti-Southerners, he was still a Southerner in spite of all he had done to deny it; with the Southerners he was a copperhead and a traitor. The ultra-liberals of Texas denied him; and his name was still anathema to such radicals as the ADA and the labor leaders in the North and East.

His strange combination of Texans ranged from high party faithful to such veteran oil figures as H. L. Hunt and the parvenu tycoon, Morris Jaffe, who gathered to beat the drums, carry the money bags and mingle with such case-hardened New Deal Johnson friends as Oscar Chapman, Dean Acheson, Tommy Corcoran and Benny Cohen at Los Angeles.

By Convention time the Johnson temper toward and hatred for Jack Kennedy had grown in proportion to Kennedy's startling campaign progress. Kennedy's dislike for him was returned in kind. In reference to his own late announcement, Johnson, in cutting sarcasm toward Kennedy's extended Senatorial absences, had explained that he had "a post of duty and responsibility" in Washington "as the Majority Leader," and unctuously added, "because of that duty, a duty to all the people, I cannot be absent when there is public business at stake . . . Someone has to tend the store." From then on the fighting got dirty.

In Independence Missouri, Harry S. Truman tried to slow the Kennedy stampede by charging that the Convention was already rigged. When the health issue intruded at the convention, John Connally called a press conference to report that Kennedy was a secret victim of the incurable but controllable Addison's disease—which little brother, Robert F. Kennedy, branded as "malicious and false." In leaving Washington, Johnson and Rayburn had, in a typical power play, simply recessed Congress to put their colleagues on notice that after the Convention they would still have to contend with them to get their pet bills and appropriations through. But it did not help. In Los Angeles, brother Bobby was already boasting that Senator Kennedy had the nomination in the bag. With Adam Clayton Powell's support already bargained and bought, Johnson, on arrival at Los Angeles, was goaded by Bobby's charge that Hoffa was in his camp too. Lyndon as usual deplored "guilt by association" and bitingly recalled that the Kennedys had been "running against" Hoffa for years.

Johnson made little actual headway until he baited Jack to appear at the Biltmore ballroom in a meeting billed as a historic debate between the leading contenders. In bitter and biting sarcasm, he attacked the sweating, trembling Kennedy to his face for his extended absenteeism from Congress, reversed the religious issue against him, charged him with weakness on civil rights and scorned his immaturity and inexperience generally—to the delight of the room packed with Johnson's friends. It was a brutal assault as revelatory of Johnson's nature as it was of Kennedy's weakness.

But it was a useless effort. Johnson fought on, hitting Kennedy with everything in the book, bemeaning his inherited wealth while bragging that he had made his own, accusing him of McCarthyism while he, Lyndon, was helping suppress it, and scathingly charging that old Joe Kennedy's opposition to America's involvement in war was because of his sympathy for Hitler and his Nazis. Bitter assault or not, there was no stopping the Kennedy juggernaut, built with magnificent organization, money, discipline and brains. Harry Truman had been right; the convention *was rigged*. America had grown so corrupt throughout the years of Democratic and modern Republican rule that the nomination was up for sale and the Kennedy clan had all it took to buy it. What Johnson lacked was not purpose and design but money.

When, on the night of July 3, 1960, Kennedy rolled to victory on the first roll call and the Convention erupted into turmoil, "the Texas delegation sat stunned, still and grim." Upon the motion to make his nomination unanimous, only one Texas hand was seen to go up while the entire delegation held their seats. As the ovation ran on, Rayburn and Connally finally rose, Connally turning and nodding to the delegates behind him, who grudgingly got up, except for Governor Price Daniel, who angrily kept his place.

In speaking to his forlorn followers after the die was cast, some felt that for once Johnson almost rose to greatness. But the nature of the power-mad politician reasserted itself and there are varying versions of what followed. John S. Knight reported, decidedly in line with Johnson's character, that when Bobby Kennedy called, he and Rayburn demanded that Johnson be given second place. Bobby could not believe it. They assured him they were in deadly earnest and that if it were not peacefully granted, they would take the floor and fight for it. Bobby reported to Jack, who called first hand to get the "ultimatum." Kennedy demurred, wishing to put it up to leaders of several state delegations.

"Tell 'em," Lyndon added, "that I deserve the vice presidency and intend to get it." Jack carried the news to Mayors Daley of Chicago and DeSapio of New York and Governor Mike DiSalle, of Ohio, who were equally astonished—as Stuart Symington was their choice. After hours of sober debate they capitulated and sent word that after all LBJ was their man.[10]

The news was hardly a bigger bombshell in the Kennedy than in the Johnson camp. The utter cynicism of the deal left the honest partisans on both sides absolutely dumbfounded, while everybody groped for a reason. Nobody accepted Chester Bowles' superficial explanation that the bitter attack could be explained away "in the heat of politics." Neither did the soothing suggestion that Johnson took the place to save the South make sense—especially after he had let Texas and the South go their own way when Adlai Stevenson was running. The suggestion that he accepted to exercise restraining influence on Kennedy is the most asinine of all.

---

[10] Victor Lasky, in *J.F.K.: The Man and The Myth*, has traced the Convention battle in detail. For Knight's report, see *Chicago Tribune*, July 15, 1960, and the *Texas Observer*, July 15, 1960, for Texas details.

Johnson wanted power and with all his knowledge of political strategy and his proven control of Congress, he could see wider horizons of power as Vice-President than as Senate Majority Leader. In effect, by presiding over the Senate, he could now conceive himself as virtually filling both high and important positions—and he was not far from wrong. Finally, as Victor Lasky pointed out, Johnson had nursed a "lifetime dream to be President. As Majority leader he never could have made it. But as Vice-President fate could always intervene."

Along with power, Johnson loves money, and some experienced observers believe that he accepted the nomination for cold cash in hand. Of two stories widely bandied about, one from New York is to the effect that Joe Kennedy flew half a million dollars overnight to Los Angeles, to tender and be paid to Lyndon Johnson to take second place—which is entirely apart from the published report that Kennedy reimbursed him for his nomination expenditures, while others wondered what became of the million that Johnson is said to have collected in advance. Whatever the legendary character of this account, the fact remains that some responsible students of Johnson's career are convinced that he accepted second place for money.

The immediate revulsion is understandable. Veteran pros like James Farley, along with professional liberals like Schlesinger and Rauh, were appalled, while the moderates who had flocked to Los Angeles with Lyndon were stupified. Governor Price Daniel, who carried the LBJ banner high, was shocked and jarred clear back to his Baptist ancestors. He doubted that Kennedy "would carry Texas," while admitting he, Daniel, would do no more than vote for the ticket. Meany, Reuther and various negro leaders were highly critical—but of Lyndon.[11]

11 *Texas Observer*, July 15, 1960.

The disconsolate Texans headed home and began preparations for the Party's bi-annual gathering in September known as the Governor's Convention. Nobody was happy. But Lyndon's forces were still in control of the machinery and nothing too untoward was feared. On September 20, 1960, the loyal-faithful along with the betrayed gathered in the convention coliseum at Dallas to hear the conciliatory Governor Daniel open the session with the declaration that there would be "harmony", even if he had "to fight for it." Sardonic fate decreed differently. Instead of the "dignified, orderly convention" for which he hoped, be it said to the everlasting credit of Texas that it came nearer to being a riot from start to finish.

With the Johnson partisans and the moderates in control of the credentials committee, the giant Harris County (Houston) delegation of conservatives was barred, but milled around impatiently, champing the bits at the barriers until they were let in, about an hour before adjournment. High state conservatives caucused, decided to assault the convention and repudiate the national platform, and caucused again and decided otherwise.

Two electors on the ticket served notice that they would exercise their Constitutional right of voting for whom they pleased—which would be against Kennedy and Johnson. In the furor that followed one resigned and the other was kicked out. Tempers mounted as other conservative delegates were ejected. There was a first-class fist fight and a near riot when Mrs. R. Max Brooks, retiring vice-chairman of the Executive Committee, demanded that all Harris County delegates wearing miniature Confederate flags identify themselves." The giant delegation roared to its feet shouting "dictators" and "totalitarian"—drawing the retort from Mrs. Brooks that "this is a Democratic convention, not a Confederate reunion."

Yet the rebel spirit roared on. Before the credentials committee the fiery Mrs. Sam Davis of Houston admitted her editorship of the red-hot conservative sheet, *The Texas Councilor*, which was involved in the fist fight, but refused to name her associates, saying: "I take full responsibility for trying to expose Lyndon Johnson. We're supposed to tell the national party what we want—not to have it handed down to us. If we want to get this country back, it will be by the people, not by yellow-dog Democrats."

When Ed Drake, Chairman of the conservative Dallas delegation, somehow cooled toward repudiation of the national platform, his fellow townsman Giles Miller ran with the ball, saying: "We don't want to go along with Eleanor, Walter Reuther, Adam Powell and Alger Hiss. We've been betrayed and betrayed good and proper by Lyndon Johnson. How do you think you can trust these people who are running this convention?" Drake was booed for his proposal, while nobody tried to answer Miller.

In desperation the hard-pressed Governor tried to hold the line against a gathering avalanche of violent disaffection. Except for his control of the committees, it would have been a perfect riot. A roll call was avoided for fear of showing that the boiling resentment of the conservative Harris, Tarrant (Fort Worth) and Dallas County delegations might be state-wide. Johnson's name was vigorously booed whenever mentioned and the Convention resolutions did not even endorse the National ticket or call the nominees by name. They were gavelled through in growing turmoil, and in vast relief Daniel hurriedly adjourned the Governor's Convention. It is interesting to conjecture what might have happened had the party machinery not been controlled by Lyndon's friends.

The Southern Conservative noted that "hundreds of demonstrators gathered in front of the convention building even after the chairman had suddenly decided to declare the convention adjourned, to hurl vindictive threats at the departing politicos who had vainly tried to stifle and beat down the most stubborn and rugged defiance of a national Democratic ticket ever encountered in the Lone Star State."[12] In the best Texas tradition they had repudiated Governor Daniel's plea of "harmony"—than which, as a matter of policy, nothing is more enervating of freedom.

On the national level the campaign was well under way and nobody cared to ponder the meaning of the Texas turmoil. A less hardened cynic would have been embarrassed in being upon the ticket for two offices and upon two platforms antagonistic in policy and principle at the same time. For in concession to the Texas temper, the Governor's Convention had adopted a conservative platform, while the national was unadulterated, radical socialism. The Vice-Presidential candidate embarrassed? Not Lyndon Baines Johnson! Yet consider the major contradictions of the two platforms upon which he was concurrently running for Vice President and for Senator from Texas, both of which he apparently endorsed:

(1) The national party platform called for further concentration of power in federal hands, the state denounced "federal encroachment" and the "growing and menacing power in central government"; (2) the national endorsed sit-in demonstrations, the state called for the "enforcement of laws designed to protect private property from physical occupation"; (3) the national called for the closing of such "tax loopholes as depletion allowances," the state demanded the "retention of the present oil and gas depletions allowance"; (4) the national called for

12 *Southern Conservative*, Oct., 1960; *Texas Observer*, Sept. 23, 1960.

federal aid to education, the state opposed "the entry of the federal government in the general field of public education"; (5) the national called for school desegregation, the state pledged local operation and control of schools; (6) the national pledged medical care of the aged as a part of the social security system, the state deplored socialistic medical measures; (7) the national called for legislation repealing the state right-to-work laws, the state endorsed the right-to-work law as essential to a free enterprise system.[13]

It is difficult to see how the conservatives who stormed the convention could have improved upon the Texas platform had they won control. Yet, cynically, it was written by a Johnson controlled committee and approved by a Convention dominated by Lyndon's friends. It was essentially a State's Rights platform, while the national Democratic Party document was so radical that even the veteran socialist, Norman Thomas, branded it as "Utopian, if not insincere."

Yet these were the two basic statements of principle and policy upon which Lyndon Baines Johnson was running, and obviously standing, in his dual candidacy. Why bother about Socialist Norman Thomas' archaic concern with "sincerity?" "Sincerity" was not in the lexicon of the evil men who wrote the national party platform.

Lyndon belonged to the modern age and had learned his politics and his disregard of principle from such ill, designing misanthropes as Harry Hopkins, whose ethics in public policy were based on the belief that "the people are too damned dumb to understand." Maybe Harry was

[13] Victor Lasky, in *J.F.K.: The Man and the Myth*, pp. 402, 409, has an excellent comment on the national Democratic Platform. For its conflict with the Texas platform, see the *Congressional Record*, Feb. 8, 1964.

right, but there was a mob of irate Texans on hand at the Governor's Convention at Dallas in 1960 to dispute that dictum of a degenerate mind.

In the national arena Johnson repudiated completely the statement of party principles upon which he was allegedly running in Texas, while most of his pragmatic kin—the ADAs, the AFL-CIOs, the COPEs and many radical negro leaders came to tolerate, then politically embrace and finally to admire and adore him.

After all he was the seasoned and preeminent master in the use of political power. Nobody could gainsay this sordid fact, for he had abundantly proven it. And besides he was just one heart beat away from the presidency.

IX
POWER TO INCITE AND COERCE

*"Class war was meant to bring destruction and nothing
else. It was to clear away the forces of tradition, both
political and economic, to give scope to the revenge and
dominion of the forces of the underworld."*

— *Spengler.*

When, on November 22, 1963, that ready resort of
illegitimacy, the dread act of assassination, struck the
moral and healthy world dumb the vengeful wails of the
psychopathic fringe immediately rent the air in hate while
the masses were still prostrate in prayer. Capitalizing upon
the instantaneous, inflammatory potentialities of television
and radio as well as the rolling presses, the attack of the
radical left-wingers, augmented by the neurotic do-gooders,
made a mockery of tolerance and the truth.

America tends to forget that organized evil is never
stupid, never lazy, never apathetic. Its immediate design
was to blame Dallas and the conservatives; its next was to
seize upon America's grief and pervert it into a morbid
sense of shame. Shame for what? Shame for having tolerated the diseased mind of Communism that had killed
the President? Not at all!

Instead, shame for having tolerated those who had
bespoken the danger that struck the President down; for
those who had tried to expose the officials in high places
who had sympathized with the evil philosophy and ex-
pedited the international movements of the assassin; for
those who had battled to warn America that its life was
at stake. Yes, America's shame was for having people with
the courage and Christian character to stand for freedom.[1]

[1] *The Dan Smoot Report,* Dec. 9, 1963, treats of this perversion by the haters.

By perhaps the most monumental perversion of morality and justice in history, this diabolical conspiracy of underworld evil succeeded in its purpose. Corrupt information media and perverted pulpit were the ready accessories in this colossal crime.

Where the truth was not completely obscured, it was assiduously distorted in several important areas. First, President Kennedy, as the television broadcasts amply proved, was not depressed with premonitory doom, but was in high spirits throughout the morning. Second, the city of Dallas—regardless of its just antipathies for the Kennedy program, was gay and generous in its festive welcome. Third, the assassin Oswald was not just an intellectual Marxist but a calculating, trained, criminal agent of International Communism, though the media still insist on referring to him simply as a "Marxist." Fourth, the fact that if the President's brother, Attorney General Robert F. Kennedy, instead of attacking "the Right" and pursuing a campaign to play down the dangers of Communism, had lived up to his oath of office to enforce the laws of the United States, Oswald would have been registered as an alien criminal, his whereabouts known, and most likely the President's life would have been saved.

Last and most important, Oswald could never be allowed to live long enough to break and talk, or even be brought to trial. If he broke, and there were signs that he was about to, he might reveal his co-conspirators, his friends and his confederates. But even if he did not, it would have never done to allow him to be brought to trial, because this would have exposed the degenerate conspiracy that made him a criminal Communist. With Oswald on trial, Communism would have been on trial and its evil nature perforce relayed to the far corners of the world by all the news media. This could never be allowed to happen. Instead of Oswald's being tried, decent Dallas and healthy America were indicted generally as criminals —with no less a figure than the Chief Justice of the United States taking the lead in the lynching.

Surely in such a degenerate perversion of the truth, of decency and justice as this, the government of the United States would step in and see that the truth was brought out and that justice was done. Momentarily the people hoped and expected that President Johnson, a native Texan of undoubtedly tough mettle if not of courage, would move at once with every legitimate resource at his command. They expected him not only to dig out and expose the whole truth, but to calm the wave of perverted hate and shame that the Communist underworld and their psychopathic allies were so assiduously and effectively cultivating—to the criminal injustice of Dallas, of Texas and America.

On the contrary he moved at once to do the opposite. It was known in Washington that Oswald was a highly-favored Communist agent. The fact posed for Johnson a historic opportunity. But instead of laying plans to break off relations with Russia after a reasonable period for quieting of the popular passions—a move of dramatic moral resolution which would have inspired the world— his first reported action upon reaching the White House, probably at McGeorge Bundy's insistence, was to call and reassure Khrushchev of our peaceful intentions.

His next call was to perhaps the most sinister labor leader in the world, David Dubinsky of New York City.[2] In each case the intelligent, inquiring public wonders why?

2 For something of Johnson's intimacy with Dubinsky, see Victor Riesel, "Inside Labor" column, March 10, 1964. For Dubinsky's far-reaching influence, see the Hilaire du Berrier *Reports*.

Some have suggested "politics." Just a few hours after the
assassination? This thought does violence even to the
coldly pragmatic nature of Lyndon B. Johnson.

Almost certainly the reason lay in the very nature
of illegitimate power—in fear! Johnson and his fear-
stricken colleagues—suspecting "a worldwide conspiracy,"
as voiced by Johnson immediately after the killing in
Dallas, wanted reassurance. Instead of acting from courage, Johnson's calls were impelled by fear. Fear of what
Russia might think or do; fear of what might happen to
Johnson "next," unless the "worldwide conspiracy" could
be reassured. And reassured it was, if not in so many
positive words, which seems most likely, then certainly by
all important official action that followed.

For it will be recalled that when Johnson was rushed
out of Parkland Hospital at Dallas by secret service men,
friends and confederates, surrounded and crowded down
in the car where he could not be seen, and sped to Love
Field to be sworn in as President behind the curtained
windows of the presidential plane, and hurriedly flown
away to Washington, he and his associates were in obvious
terror. In rushing away from Parkland, he had expressed
concern over a possible "world-wide conspiracy"; the
thought that he might be "next"; and that those in line
of presidential succession, House Speaker McCormick and
Senator Hayden, might be marked for assassination too,
and anxiously inquired "are they prepared to get me out
of here?"[3]

This was not the reaction of brave men in the face

[3] For indications of this terror, see Johnson's comments to
Malcolm Kilduff, Newsweek Jan. 6, 1964, p. 20; Stewart
Alsop, "Johnson Takes Over," Saturday Evening Post, Feb.
15, 1964, p. 18; Fletcher Knebel, "The Ordeal of Lyndon
B. Johnson," Look, March 10, 1964, pp. 27-28.

of danger; this was the age-old response of rulers who have come to power through illegitimacy—men gripped with fear, even fear of the people they rule.

Nothing whatever was done to keep the city of Dallas and patriotic Americans everywhere from being blamed for intolerance and hate, and from being branded as accessories to the crime of killing Kennedy. The assassination of the President was unspeakably evil, but the horrible perversion of morality and of justice through the mass indictment of millions of Americans was far worse. Did President Johnson rise in righteous concern to rectify this slander of a great people stricken in anguish and in grief? On the contrary he abetted it.

On November 26, 1963, he ordered the FBI to take charge of all evidence pertaining to the assassination, with a promise that its reports would be made public immediately. On the same day, however, the official organ of Moscow in America, the Communist paper, *The Worker,* editorialized on President Kennedy's virtues, laid the blame for his death on the "ultra-right," and recommended that the President appoint a special commission, headed by Chief Justice Warren, to investigate it.

Three days later, just as the Communists suggested, Johnson appointed such a commission composed, with one exception, of ultra-liberals, with the Chief Justice—whose aid to the Communist cause is of extensive record in his Supreme Court opinions—as Chairman. Just three days later still, December 2, President Johnson rescinded his earlier promise to give America the truth, announcing that the FBI investigations and reports would not be made public, but would be turned over to the Warren Commission for "evaluation"—a shallow euphemism but an effective device for suppressing the truth.[4]

4 *The Dan Smoot Report,* as cited.

This was not only in line with the "managed news" policy of the Kennedy-Johnson administration, but in keeping with the specific suggestions of the Communists, and implicit in Warren's bias and background. For the Chief Justice, with the prejudicial nature for which he is notorious, had rendered his verdict before any of the evidence was in. In his eulogy before the Kennedy catafalque in the rotunda of the Capitol, Warren assailed "the forces of hatred and malevolence," claiming the President was assassinated "as a result of the hatred and bitterness that has been injected into the life of our Nation by bigots." Thereby the Chief Justice, positively knowing that Oswald was an avowed and known agent of International Communism, proved himself to be the leading advocate of the perversion of truth and justice in America. Obviously he had been made Chairman of the Commission to whitewash the Communist conspiracy and cover up the truth. Shortly thereafter Warren confirmed this fact by announcing that much of the evidence might not be released "in our lifetime."[5]

Thus the American people are convinced that the truth of the Oswald case, and its Jack (Rubenstein) Ruby connections, will never be known. At least not until they elect a President who believes they have a right to know the truth.

Johnson at once began his demonstrations to catch the popular eye, while consorting ever more closely with the radical elements upon whom he counted to keep him in power. He had long since decided that the left-wing leaders of labor, the liberals and the racial minorities were the key. Upon becoming President, he brought them in with a rush and a ruthlessness that would put Robert Kennedy to shame. He set himself to capture the support of the labor leaders whom he had been courting as Ma-

5 *Chicago Tribune*, Feb. 12, 1964.

jority Leader, as Vice President and as head of Kennedy's committee on fair employment. In violation of his earlier promises, he had become an ardent advocate of forced integration, bludgeoning all corporations sharing in government contracts to force the employment of negroes upon them, irrespective of costs, ability and efficiency.

On December 4, twelve days after his accession, and in blatant violation of the declared moratorium on politics, Johnson had twenty-five of the highest ranking labor leaders in the Cabinet Room of the White House at his command. Members of the Cabinet—McNamara, Freeman, Dillon, Udal, Hodges, and Wirtz were on hand. In his ingratiating manner, Johnson told the labor leaders he "wanted to know" them on a "first name basis"; he needed their "support more than" the late president, "because he had more talent than I have"; he had asked them there to find "What is on your mind?" "Tell me," he continued, "I need to know", and indicating his Cabinet, "these fellows need to know."

With Meany and Reuther sitting on either side of the President, they told him their problems. Johnson ended the conference by saying, "I want you to understand one thing, gentlemen. The doors of this house are always open to you. I want to hear from you when you have troubles and when you have ideas." Then with a gesture toward his Cabinet, he pointedly said: "And their doors are open too." And "everybody heard. Everybody understood" for this was special privilege with a vengeance and the labor leaders loved it.[6] Now nobody seems to move in and out of the White House with greater ease than the arrogant radical, Walter Reuther, the confirmed Marxist, who, with

6 Victor Reisel, "Johnson has 'Closed Door' Talk with Labor," *Human Events*, Jan. 4, 1964; *U.S. News and World Report*, Dec. 16, 1963.

his brother, had written the "Secret Memorandum" for Attorney General Kennedy suggesting the suppression of all conservative and patriotic groups, directly in line with his long-avowed "fight for a Soviet America."[7]

Notwithstanding this brazen alliance with the revolutionary leaders of labor, what is sometimes erroneously called the conservative United States Chamber of Commerce, in convention five thousand strong, April 27, 1964, greeted President Johnson with "wave after wave of applause," interrupting an hour-long speech sixty times. This can lead but to one of two possible conclusions: either Harry Hopkins was right, or they agree with Reuther's principles, though possibly, in the Hopkins phrase, they are "too damned dumb" to know it.[8] Whatever the explanation, this incredible exhibition of ignorance or depravity is positive proof of the low level to which American business leadership has fallen.

To make the vulgar display even more significant, it followed by only a few days Johnson's strong-arm tactics in "averting the rail strike." On January 3, 1964, from the LBJ Ranch, Johnson had congratulated the country upon its "low level" of strikes, boasting that the record since 1960 was "unmatched in any comparable peacetime period." Yet after one of the longest, most vicious and violent strikes on record—that against the Florida East Coast Railway, which had run without hindrance from the Federal government for over a year—in April 1964, Johnson was faced with the imminent shutdown of all the

---

7 See Walter Trohan's column *Chicago Tribune*, Oct. 18, 1963, and *Walter Reuther's Secret Memorandum*, as printed by Christian Crusade, Tulsa, Oklahoma.

8 For the account of this enthusiasm for Johnson, in spite of his record, his presently avowed intentions, and his actions, see the daily papers of April 28, 1964.

POWER TO INCITE AND COERCE

roads by strike. In "averting it" he demonstrated again his resort to pressure and power, with the resultant destruction of the rights of everybody concerned.

David Lawrence, in warning of "the true nature of the settlement ... and its implications," wrote: "This ... isn't a 'free collective-bargaining process' ... it means ... an arbitrary usurpation of governmental power without the explicit sanction of Congress." It meant that Lyndon B. Johnson, while conniving with the labor leaders, was double-crossing the laboring man and destroying collective bargaining. As a matter of policy, Lawrence continued: "The public is confronted with the realistic fact that *free bargaining has been supplanted by coercive 'mediation'* [our emphasis], and this can hardly be depended upon in the long run as a way to solve major disputes. What has happened gives an uncomfortable feeling of acquiescence in a kind of benevolent dictatorship."[9] "Benevolent"? Maybe! "Dictatorship"? Yes! The rights of millions of stockholders in the railroads and other millions of working men to protection from coercion did not count; but the counting of votes did.

The further favor with which labor leaders are regarded was blatantly obvious in another incident. Secretary of War McNamara bitterly assailed Senator Barry Goldwater, an experienced flier and a Major General in the United States forces, for questioning the adequacy of our reliance on missiles, with the implication that he was violating security restrictions. In mid-January, shortly

---

[9] David Lawrence's column, April 27, 1964. *The Dan Smoot Report*, April 13, 1964, gives an excellent summary of labor violence during the golden Kennedy-Johnson age, which the President, on January 3, proclaimed for its "industrial democracy," in which labor and management had shown their ability "to work out their destinies in a free and peaceful manner." See AP release, Jan. 3, 1964.

after the expression of Goldwater's doubts—which were
later confirmed by General Curtis LeMay—Johnson again
entertained the top labor leaders at the White House. In
open-armed reception, they were told to come to the
"social," not the "official" or business entrance, where
they were greeted by Mrs. Johnson and warmly ushered
in to a steak bordelaise lunch by their "master" host.

Again directing Meany to sit on his right and Reuther
on his left, Johnson "excited" his twenty-odd guests by
having them briefed on the Administration plans; on information and figures "which civilians are rarely privy
to." The Secretaries of Defense and State, McNamara
and Rusk, divulged "highly classified" material and Johnson gave them a preview of his state of the union message, because they represented "millions of people," he
said, and "I want you to know what we are thinking."[10]

A public policy of divulging vital information to such
an avowed Marxist as Walter Reuther, while castigating
a proven fighting American General and foremost Senator
for publicly questioning a vital factor in our defense—
may win millions of votes, but there are millions of Americans who will doubt its wisdom.

Before leaving the labor issue, it should be mentioned
that perhaps nothing better illustrates the smooth Johnson
technique and collusion with the worst in labor's camp
than the David Rabinowitz appointment to the Federal
bench in Wisconsin. This notorious Sheboygan lawyer was
known for his alliance with Walter Reuther and was legal
counsel for Local 833, UAW-CIO, throughout the long-con-
tinued criminal violence of the Kohler strike, where he
fought the maintenance of law and order by injunctive
process. President Kennedy appointed him Judge for the
Western Federal District of Wisconsin, of which he was

10 *Dallas News,* Jan. 9, 1964.

not even a resident, which raised a furor everywhere, especially in the legal profession.

His fellow attorneys, the Sheboygan County Bar Association, the Wisconsin Bar Association and the American Bar Association—as well as "a substantial segment" of the Wisconsin press and people, vigorously opposed the appointment. But Rabinowitz had long been active in Democratic machine politics, was a member of the Democratic National Committee, was Reuther's favorite and a Kennedy supporter from the first.

No matter the opposition! In the eyes of an administration that placed power politics above national interest, Rabinowitz was the man for Federal Judge, regardless of what the bar, bench and people of Wisconsin thought. A committee of the American Bar Association unanimously submitted a bill of indictments to Senator Eastland's Judiciary Committee, urging disapproval. Without action the appointment died, and the position was open when Johnson assumed presidential power and began having Reuther in by way of the "social door" at the White House.

With the new session of Congress approaching, the "master of political strategy" shifted into high gear. Johnson sent Clark Clifford, his Washington advisor-lawyer and trouble-shooter to Minneapolis, where, at breakfast with Wisconsin Democratic Governor John Reynolds and Democratic State Chairman J. Louis Hanson, with help on the side from Mrs. Mildred Jeffrey, National Democratic Committeewoman from Reuther's Michigan, who admitted her active participation in the Kohler strike, Clifford "brought up the subject" of the Rabinowitz case. With an eye on the forthcoming election Clifford returned to Washington to get the deal sealed.

Three days later, just twenty minutes before Congress was to convene, Johnson telephoned Rabinowitz that he was giving him the interim appointment, and "the Judge" scurried to take the oath before 12:00 noon—the instant Congress would convene. Since "Congress *was not* in session," Senatorial approval of the nomination was unnecessary for the interim and Judge Rabinowitz—the Sheboygan labor lawyer who had defended Reuther's lawless violence at Kohler, including brutal beatings and murder, could continue "to serve" on the Bench. The ethical lawyers of the nation were aghast, but individually silent, because most must practice for a living in Federal Courts.

The Chicago Tribune, January 8, 1964, said that this last minute action by Johnson prior to the convening of the 88th Congress, in "defiance of the Senate's Constitutional prerogative to advise and consent to appointments, was unprecedented." *The Milwaukee Sentinel* referred to it as "a raw political pay-off that demeans the bench and insults the ideal of an independent judiciary," even more objectionable than when made by Kennedy because Rabinowitz's sordid record had been aired and condemned by the nation's judiciary. Besides, it continued, this presidential "act of arrogant cynicism at worst—makes a mockery" of Johnson's statement in his first message to Congress that he "respected the independence of the legislative branch of our government." After his record as Majority Leader no further proof of his contempt for Congress should have been needed—though apparently history writes her lessons in vain.[11]

But this alliance with the ruthless leaders of labor had been cemented long before. At a private banquet for Lyndon B. Johnson while he was Vice President, arranged by the then Secretary of Labor, Arthur Goldberg, with

11 *Milwaukee Sentinel,* Jan. 4, 8, and Feb. 18, 1964; *Sheboygan Press,* Jan. 7, 15, 1964; *Chicago Tribune,* Jan. 8, Feb. 17, 1964.

that wild agglomeration of New York City radicals known as the American Labor Party, they had "drowned" the dissident past in "a series of toasts to each other." The Labor Party leaders had then and there chosen him as the "spark plug of liberalism in Washington." In their convivial drinking Johnson made it plain that "he wanted to take the place of Adlai Stevenson and Hubert Humphrey in their political hearts," and he did.

Thus in keeping with their completely pragmatic nature, they decided that a man they could not trust, especially one with great power, had incalculable value to their cause, and hence made him their own. Lack of morality and consistency offer no offense to the professional liberal; in fact it is his stock in trade. Johnson was then slated as the New York Liberal Party's principal speaker for their annual banquet, October 19, 1963—which meant he had won their stamp of approval as the 1968 successor of President Kennedy.[12]

As President, Johnson quickly held a conference with that high Olympian of loose thinking, Walter Lippman—whose pioneer services for socialism started with his undergraduate membership in the Fabians at Harvard. Right down the line came such advocates of revolutionary change as James Farmer, head of the Congress on Racial Equality; that darling of the Communists, the Right Reverend Martin Luther King, head of the Southern Christian Leadership Conference; Roy Wilkins, executive secretary of the NAACP; and Whitney Young, director of the Urban League—all of whom spent a cozy hour in conference with the President.

To clinch the bargain with the Liberals, on December 4, 1963, Lyndon came out in complete support of the civil rights bill—the one piece of legislation that would

12 *Los Angeles Times*, Sept. 16, 1963.

assuredly destroy what was left of the civil rights of all as well as the American Constitutional system. Throwing his own great influence and the weight of the presidential office behind the inflammatory and dangerous racial situation, he addressed the working men in what must have been Abe Fortas's phrase saying:

"The endless abrasions of delay, neglect and indifference have rubbed raw the national conscience." To the businessman, he added: "We've talked too long, done too little and all of it too late." The lawless, shouting, sitting, marching rioting negroes took the presidential cue and stepped up their violence—to where even the white liberals began screaming that this was "extremism."[13]

Within six weeks after Johnson became President, William S. White found that he had captured, "without firing a single shot", the liberal citadel—which "for a decade had rejected him as too 'moderate'". The utter cynicism of his union with the worst of the New York City radicals seemed of no public moment. For as White wrote, with Johnson "politics has always been a technique to power and not power itself; a means toward a purpose and not itself a purpose; a hammer in the hands of men whose proper function is to make policy and not mere argumentations."[14] White erred simply by failure to elaborate one point. Policy is meaningful with Lyndon B. Johnson only as an avenue to more personal power.

As President he hurried to court all elements of the radical left. He entered heartily into making the $50,000 tax-free award from the Atomic Energy Commission to Dr. Robert Oppenheimer. The *New York Times*, not unexpectedly, found the underlying theme one in which the "government was, in part, vindicating the honor of Oppen-

13 *New York Times*, Dec. 8, 1963.

14 *Austin Statesman*, Jan. 14, 1964.

heimer." Johnson truly played the liberal role by trying
to build back this worst of Communist sympathizers to
public acceptance, after his dismissal from government
service for security reasons following extensive investigation. No wonder the National Council of Churches joined
the Communist fellow-travelers and rushed to pledge the
President their "full loyalty and devotion," along with
Fabian Socialist Lippmann—"the trumpet that always
sounds retreat."[15]

By mid-February, 1964, there was no question that
Lyndon had the Liberals, lock, stock and barrel. Alex
Rose the International Hatter head gave his accolade and
ended with his blessing as he left the White House:

"I told President Johnson that the Liberal Party...
had been deeply inspired with his first few months in
office ... The legislative advances ... now taking place so
dramatically are in large measure due to the dynamic and
determined leadership of President Johnson." "Without
hesitation," he added that his group will "be fighting on
the side of Johnson" in the campaign. Thus at last there
could be no doubt that Johnson had won them over, as
this was right out of the horse's mouth.[16] The pattern of
radical support was now wide-spread.

As soon as he became President, the organized internationalists, socialists, do-gooders, and left-wing groups
generally had fallen all over themselves to get into line:
the eighty-group Leadership Conference on Civil Rights,
AID—the Agency for International Development, the
NEA, National Council of Senior Citizens, National
Farmers Union, Committee for a National Trade Policy,

---

[15] *Human Events*, Dec. 14, 1964; *Times-Herald*, Dallas, Jan.
19, 1964; *Milwaukee-Sentinel*, editorial "Purer Image",
Feb. 22, 1964.

[16] *Chicago Tribune*, Feb. 15, 1964.

COPE, American Public Power Association and Cooperative League of the USA, The National Council of Churches and other haywire groups too numerous to catalogue.[17] But Johnson did not stop with them.

As a part of his overall drive to capture the radical front, his appeal for colored support went hand in glove with his grasp for the labor and liberal leaders. Negro leaders flowed through the White House with the utmost deference paid during the first two weeks of Johnson's occupancy, despite his unctious "moratorium on politics," while the President served notice on both business and labor that they must accept complete integration. This campaign too had been launched with cold calculation several years before and requires review.

While Vice President, he and Mrs. Johnson began courting the negro vote on the social as well as the economic level. The May 5, 1960, issue of *The Austin Mirror,* a negro paper at the Texas capital, pridefully reported a local party of 3000 ladies honoring the Majority Leader's wife, attended by "approximately 350 negroes, many of whom had received special invitations." *The Mirror* happily reported that Mrs. Johnson had made it clear "that there was to be no racial discrimination at her party, and" with "negro ladies" helping do the honors, the paper emphasized "there was none . . . Many of her friends predict that Lady Bird Johnson will be the nation's next Eleanor Roosevelt and carry the banner for equality as did the wife of the former President. . ." *The Mirror* correctly reflected "Lady Bird's" new role.[18]

Shortly after becoming Vice President, Johnson held

---

17 The columnist Peter Edson, has commented upon this hard-core, left-wing unity behind Johnson.

18 *News and Courier,* Charleston, S.C., Nov. 6, 1961; *The Mirror,* May 5, 1960.

a "closed door" meeting with Labor Secretary Goldberg and representatives of forty-eight of the nation's biggest defense contractors. He told them in no uncertain terms that the government had the power to "cancel contracts, hold investigations in public, blacklist firms from future contracts, or seek court injunctions to force compliance with the integration order." He then blandly observed that all present had happily agreed with the administration's suggestion, adding: "I do not think that this problem will be solved by threatening people or by bullying them." Obviously there had been no "threatening"— just the implied destruction of their businesses, which was also far from "bullying."[19]

In a speech at Gainesville, Florida, October 27, 1961, Johnson made a sweeping attack on all Americans who were critical of the Supreme Court and the Executive for their police state methods against segregation, charging such people with sowing the "weeds choking out the rich strength of American life." The Communists, he said, could sit back and relax, "for good Americans, blinded by partisanship, will unwittingly do their work for them." Revolutionary demagogues always charge, and with a certain ironic logic, that the people who refuse quietly to submit to coercion and not the tyrants exacting it, are to be blamed for the social disturbances that follow. Slavery, like death, can come peacefully when there is no will to resist—which, for the cause of liberty, was answered by Patrick Henry's rousing words ringing through the ages.

Three days after the Florida speech, in the San Antonio, Texas special congressional election between the radical Democrat Henry Gonzales and the Republican John Goode, Vice-President Johnson stumped the city for Gonzales. Again he injected the racial issue, this time between

[19] *Southern Conservative*, May, 1961.

a Latin — and an Anglo-American, and melodramatically
contended that the "eyes of the world are on San Antonio"
when in truth the world did not give one particle of a
damn about what happened in the Alamo City. Still he
shouted, "They want to see whether we are bigots, whether
we are prejudiced or whether we are going to go out and
elect a good American," and it worked. One Latin-American precinct went 688 to 7 for Gonzales and the negro
boxes went 10 to 1 for the Texas-Mexican.[20] Thus Gonzales was elected by the strong, local racial bloc vote
which had been solidified further by Johnson's inflammatory appeal. This inverted use of racial prejudice, in keeping with left-wing tactics, thereafter became a favorite
Johnson device in appeal for negro votes, and it may be
well to note its further effectiveness.

     In the 1960 Texas elections, Johnson had taken both
Mexican and negro blocs away from the ultra-liberals to
support his hand-picked, moderate Democratic candidate,
John Connally, for Governor, to the utter consternation of
those liberals who still followed Yarborough as their guiding star. In the fall, the turnover of negro votes in favor
of Connally was dramatic. In Houston, ten negro precincts
that had gone more than two to one against Connally in
the primary run-off—in favor of the ultra-radical Don
Yarborough, switched almost 3 to 1 in Connally's favor
and against the Republican candidate in the general election. And Connally, by less than one percent margin—545
votes out of more than 85,000 cast—barely carried his
home county of Tarrant, and only by taking the overwhelming majority of the colored vote.[21] Thus in the show-
down, Johnson proved that he had the technique, the

20 *San Angelo Standard-Times*, Nov. 11, 1961.

21 See *Texas Observer*, Dec. 27, 1962; and transcript of Tarrant County Election Returns, 1962.

political wisdom and the power to raid the camp of his traditionally bitter enemies in his home state, and lure away the followers of a Senator who was deservedly the idol of the radical forces.

In December, 1962, he held an unreported state-wide meeting of negro leaders from over Texas as guests at his Pedernales River ranch. When the news leaked, it "stirred state-wide consternation among the insiders and liberal politicians who heard about it," while immediately a state-wide drive to pay the poll taxes of 1,187,000 Texas negroes of voting age got under way.[22] Again he raised a furor with Floridians as guest of honor at their meeting, March 11, 1963, to formulate plans for the Quadri-Centennial Celebration of the founding of Saint Augustine. After months had been spent by officials planning for a "formal cocktail party and a tremendous ... dinner at the lavish Ponce de Leon Hotel"—a traditional favorite of millionaire dowagers and ladies of means, Johnson about a week before, hit them with a bombshell. Both functions must be integrated or he would not come.

Invitations had already been sent. High state, national and foreign dignitaries were invited and Johnson had accepted long before. Yet virtually at the last minute, when nothing could be done to avert this open and studied show of contempt for good taste—in violence of Southern traditions, proprieties and way of life—he sent his "ultimatum" and threw the officials "into frantic consternation." Thereupon began the racial disturbances that have plagued Saint Augustine ever since—in reality initiated by this obscene act of Lyndon B. Johnson. No wonder the negroes there have since tried to break the barriers of protection inherent in private ownership of property and

22 *Texas Observer*, Dec. 27, 1962; *The Courier* (colored), Pittsburgh, Pa., Dec. 29, 1962.

the rights of all to be let alone—even whites. The Vice-President of the United States set the precedent by showing them how to "crash the party."[23]

Thus rolled his campaign to woo the radical minorities, which—with his Main-Street moderate and his "yellow dog" Southern Democratic vote—he expected finally to put him in the White House, still just "one heartbeat away." But do as he might he was steadily sliding in esteem. Among the Capitol press not a kind word could be heard about him, even during his Vice Presidential campaign. A poll of the Capitol press for their ten top presidential preferences, in preparation for publication at the time of Kennedy's death, showed Bobby Kennedy leading and Lyndon Johnson a poor ninth. But as President he became the perfect example of the "instant statesman."[24]

Dedicated to an enhanced image of action and pledged to carry out Kennedy's program completely, Johnson drove hard, with all his vast determination, skill, coercive pressure and energy to effect it; forcing legislation for wheat on credit to Russia, tax cuts in spite of the dangerously growing deficit, a $98 billion dollar "economy" budget, $4.4 billion public works bill, new housing program, billion dollar abolition of poverty program and, to cap the climax of federal tyranny, his civil rights bill.

In between was his play to the distaff side, insisting upon more women in government, with special emphasis on race. Among the first was Frankie M. Freeman, colored lawyer, who upon appointment boasted of her past picketing in the streets, which she would "do . . . again if the need is there." When Edward R. Murrow resigned, Johnson appointed the radical negro author Carl Rowan as

---

23 *Jacksonville Journal*, March 12, 1963: *Wall Street Journal*, Nov. 27, 1963; and personal memoranda on the incident.

24 See Lucius Beebe, *Human Events*, Jan. 25, 1964.

Director of the so-called United States Information Agency in his place, praising him as "eminently qualified to supervise this vital program of telling America's story abroad. A month later, Rowan, who became the first negro to sit in on the secret National Security Council, was in hot water with Senators Lausche and Hickenlooper for showing abroad a film depicting the American negro as living in "virtual slavery."

President Johnson met with negro Housing Administrator Robert C. Weaver, promising a building program with something for everybody, while a news story emphasized its "provisions for negroes and the opportunities to all for 'country club living'" through government guaranteed loans.[25]

Early in December, 1963, Martin Luther King enjoyed an hour's conference at the White House, advising the President that racial demonstrations would start again, and expressing his happiness "as a Southerner" that he had "a fellow Southerner ... in the White House who is concerned about Civil Rights." According to *Time* the conference resulted in "an unprecedented coalition of conscience"—whatever that means. Other Southerners, who were not exactly "fellow Southerners", were suggesting it meant "thick'ern thieves," or, in plainer idiom, "in close cahoots" in selling out America for negro votes.[26]

In an effort to "build up steam" for the civil rights bill, other wheeler-dealers in racial agitation such as Roy Wilkins of the NAACP, and Whitney M. Young of the National Urban League, paid fulsome praise. Wilkins

25 *Chicago Tribune*, Feb. 26, 1964, March 1, 1964; *San Angelo Standard-Times*, Jan. 22, 1964; *Human Events*, Feb. 1, 1964.
26 For the conference, not the idiom, see *Human Events*, Dec. 24, 1963; *Time*, Jan. 3, 1964.

pointed out that "We have very great faith in the new President's attitude on civil rights . . . " and Wilkins added, "he is emerging as a national and international figure." Young observed that "Ten years ago if we had heard a new President speaking in a deep Southern drawl, there might have been so much fear among Negro leaders that some of us might have gotten on the next boat for Ghana. But we know where LBJ stands and we realize that he is a sincere and dedicated supporter of civil rights. A magnolia accent doesn't mean bigotry."[27] Thus with the negroes on a first name basis with "Lady Bird" and "L.B.J.", at least with the press, he had them in his corner.

Significantly, President Johnson had not objected when Martin Luther King told him that the racial demonstrations, with their certain trespass upon the rights of others, would continue; he had not objected when the news broke that Rowan—whom he had praised for his "idealism and integrity"—was caught showing a film, broadly depicting the American negro as living in "virtual slavery"; he had not protested when Milton A. Glamison, the colored minister leading the boycott of the New York schools, repeatedly warned that these would continue with "possible violence"; nor did he deprecate in any way the growing avalanche of fear, disorder and mounting hatred. But upon every advantageous opportunity he did abet and incite it.

In a speech on Lincoln's day, he further incited the raging racial turmoil by implying that Americans were still being denied their rights on account of race, color and religion. He flew in to open the World's Fair by helicopter, to be sure of getting past the threatened disruption of traffic by racial demonstrators, and tried to talk while

---

[27] *U.S. News and World Report*, Dec. 16, 1963; *New York Times*, Dec. 8, 1963; *Human Events*, Dec. 24, 1963.

vast concentrations of policemen—the hall-mark of illegitimate power, swarmed about with clubs and paddy wagons in a vain attempt to keep the peace.

But his most radical step in wooing the negro vote, irrespective of all its dangerous implications, was his complete acceptance of social integration by setting the example at the White House. According to a glowing account in the March 12, 1964, issue of the *Chicago Defender*, "America's only negro daily," the President had tagged the wife of the negro Congressman, Charles C. Diggs, of Chicago, in a dance at a White House reception after which, "with some excitement" she "showed her dimples" and cooed that she had "danced with the President . . . an excellent dancer . . . twice."

At an earlier reception the colored wife of California Congressman Augustus F. Hawkins was "just as delighted . . . with the Texas charmer." While she had been dancing with a young military officer "who was apologizing for his stiffness," a voice cut in saying: "Now, let's give an expert a chance." According to the *Defender*, "Mrs. Hawkins, who has won many kudos of her own for being vivacious and charming," exclaimed: "It was the President! He was just charming, and that Southern drawl is just precious." Later "she and the First Lady were arm-in-arm as she and the Congressional wives were shown the First Family living quarters," while she found "Mrs. Johnson is so natural, you can't believe she's the President's wife."

With the predicate for complete integration by federal force thus laid, President Johnson flew into the Old South to leave no shadow of doubt that he was determined to destroy its once cherished way of life. The setting in racially conscious Georgia was carefully planned, with Senator Talmadge—a name that once symbolized militant segregation—prominently on hand. On May 8, 1964, in a

land that has long opposed federal domination with wrath-
ful recollections of the hated Sherman's march to the sea,
President Johnson plainly told all Southerners—as well as
all Americans—that their way of life and their unalienable
rights to privacy and property were gone. In reverse
demagoguery never approached in effectiveness even by
that old rabble-rouser, the original red-suspendered Governor, "Gene" Talmadge, Johnson fanned the fires of racial
feeling still raging throughout America. In heavily segre-
gated Gainesville "he thundered":

> Full participation in our society can no longer
> be denied to men because of their race, religion
> or region. The Constitution applies to every
> American of every race, of every religion, of
> every region in our country—or it applies to no
> one.

He dismissed the Southern ideals, traditions and
memories—bought with Southern fortune, suffering and
seas of blood—with obscene and ruthless cruelty. With
implications of inter-marriage and a miscegenated race,
he insisted that America is one nation and "one people,"
and in a thinly-veiled reference to Governor George C.
Wallace, and in obvious contempt for the Southern cause,
castigated "those who would come waving the tattered
and discredited banners of the past, who seek to stir old
hostilities and kindle old hatreds . . ."[28]

Did these "rabid Southerners" rise in wrath at this
gross contempt for them, their honored ideals and traditions? Did they roar in disapproval at this blatant insult
to their flags hallowed by the baths of blood of their grand-
sires and blazoned in honor by the lives and services of
such immortal patriots as Jackson and Lee to their "tattered and discredited banners of the past . . . ?"

[28] *Dallas News*, May 9, 1964.

On the contrary "hundreds of thousands" of Georgians, if the papers can be credited, poured out and "wildly acclaimed" the plain-spoken harbinger of their destruction. The more this incredible spectacle is pondered, the more shocking its sinister significance becomes. Nor can this vulgar display in approval of race and national suicide be laid alone to the unstable political nature of the people of Georgia. Something of the same frenetic disregard for the civilized future was evident far to the north the following day.

On May 10, 1964, still studiously building the image of the presidential dynamo in action, Johnson swept through the New York area emitting "a scorching blast" at "bigotry and hate" and those who "fling poisoned mud," to the thoughtless adulation of thousands of other well-wishers who cheered him on his incendiary way.[29] History is replete with its tragic parallels, but history is forgotten by people brain-washed into acceptance of their approaching doom, applauding the "popular leaders" who betray the heritage of the Western World in their insatiable lust for power.

At this stage Johnson has but one objective; continued hold on power, and everything within his orbit is geared to this selfish end. In its pursuit he has turned his back completely upon the individualistic traditions of Texas and the ways of the South, which in essence means his repudiation of the ideals and traditions of America. For despite our regional differences, the heart and soul of America—wherever they throb in dedication to freedom—are essentially the same.

This is a fateful and dangerous period for civilized people everywhere, and the fading beacon light of a free America is anxiously watched from throughout the civi-

[29] *Daily Oklahoman*, May 10, 1964.

lized world. Thus again it is requisite for Americans to recall that this struggle is not one of partisan politics, but one of basic moral and spiritual principle.

If we are to preserve this marvelous land, it is imperative that all patriots remember that the elements of taste and decency, of privacy and propriety, and of personality and property cannot be arrogated by government and bestowed upon masses of men by brute force and federal bayonets. In spiritual essence they are granted by God, to be cherished and enhanced by individual effort and worth, to grace and bless a land and its peoples.

In like manner social status in any civilized country is individually earned. It is not conferred by executive decree or imposed by government force. In her healthy, intuitive wisdom, America knows this truth; in our craven corruption we deny it. This is the hour of our decision.

If survival be our concern, it would therefore seem that the least America should expect of its President is a measure of regard for the principles, the civilized proprieties, the ideals and the ways of life that have guaranteed its growth and vigor, its power and perpetuity, its grace and spiritual worth—instead of their open denial by base political nature conniving in their destruction, simply to strengthen its hold upon illegitimate power!

A moral and spiritual people deserve as much; a healthy and courageous land would tolerate no less.

X

MAN AND CHARACTER

". . . . It is much safer to be feared than loved, if one of the two has to be wanting. Men in general are ungrateful dissemblers, anxious to avoid danger and covetous of gain. Men have less scruple in offending one who makes himself loved than one who makes himself feared . . ." [for] fear is maintained by a dread of punishment which never fails."

—Machiavelli.

Additional comment upon the nature of Lyndon Baines Johnson, the master of political pressure and illegitimate power, may appear redundant, but something of a summary of his traits and character seems in justice due.

His egomania is reflected in the proliferation of his LBJs to include his wife and daughters, ranch, radio-tv business, plane, flag and dogs—though his present little Beagle Johnsons are cutely called "Him and Her". The same trait is found in his unending showmanship, such as his sophomoric pleasure in a peripatetic press conference of seven laps around the White House grounds, ending with his remark to the panting reporters that he would probably then go for a swim as he "needed the exercise." He wished them to know that the walk, the lifting of little Beagles by the ears and dancing half the night with every lady in sight left him full of unspent vigor. The image must ever be that of the dynamo in action.

The sign that once hung in his office: "You ain't learning nothin' while you're talking," was ludicrous because, as Walter Trohan observed, visitors "do not talk to Lyndon. They listen. He is a compulsive talker." But on the political subject at hand he comes prepared, briefed in advance. His staff work has always been superb and in his ambitious grasp for power he has driven his aides relentlessly. When that power was dependent upon the Texas electorate alone, nothing of moment among his constituents seemed to be overlooked. He helped his friends and he wooed his enemies, to hold, solidify and enhance his support. No editorial bearing upon him would fail of Walter Jenkins' notice. If favorable, a letter of appreciation followed. If mildly critical, a gently remonstrative letter from Jenkins, perhaps suggesting lack of understanding of the Senator's position reached the editor. Unfavorable broadsides in important journals called for "the treatment" from the boss himself, ranging from violent invective to cajolery.

Along with his vanity, pride and acute sensitivity is a high and explosive temper and a notoriously intemperate tongue. These sometimes find vicious outlet upon the subordinates around him—which is the certain hallmark, not of nobility and breeding, but of the plebeian nature obsessed with power. He has been known to curse out a secretary who offered to call his pilots to tell them that he was on the way to his plane, so that they might be ready, and to crush another with a heartless tirade before the press for making a typographical error. He has flown into a rage with local political leaders for their failure to produce a crowd for a flying appearance; to keep his copilot, who had come to the cabin of his plane to ask a question, standing ten minutes in the aisle beside him without deigning to notice his presence; to grab a secret service man by the coat lapels and jerk him close while bawling him out for his failure to know why a White House door was locked. When he was Senate majority leader the elevator operators and other more or less subordinate capitol employees detested him for his arrogant treatment—a feeling shared by the independent members of the Washington press.

His love of the trappings of power is excessive and sometimes results in amusing incident. When, in August, 1963, he flew into the West Texas town of Graham for the funeral of a long-time aide, Glynn D. Stegall, Johnson had his secret service men call L. L. Davidson, a car dealer, for a "big black Cadillac" in which to attend the funeral. Davidson, a ruggedly conservative Texan, refused.

Two secret service men drove up at once in a Lincoln, walked in on Davidson, presented their credentials and renewed the request. Davidson told them sharply that he had already given his answer; "the Vice President cannot have a Cadillac, but", pointing to a second-hand Ford with a bold "Goldwater for President" sticker on the bumper, he said he "would be glad to lend it to the Vice President." When the agents still insisted, Davidson ushered them out, saying: "Why don't you put him in that Lincoln and pull the shades down if you are so anxious to get him to the funeral?" When Davidson's rebuff hit the news, there was such a rush of patronage that he sold completely out of Cadillacs.[1]

What other President would have had the brashness to bring his own government-paid photographer and make him a regular fixture in the White House, taking 11,000 pictures of Johnson in action during his first seven weeks in office.[2] That Lyndon loves the trappings of power was obvious from the way in which he basked in self-conscious glory beneath the spotlights of his resplendent Capitol "throne room", done in green and gold, with its chandeliers, its special plumbing, its wall-to-wall carpeting and its painted scenes suggesting the banquet hall of a Roman

[1] Author's private sources and U.P.I. release, Aug. 15, 1963.
[2] *Newsweek*, Jan. 27, 1964; *Washington Post*, Dec. 25, 1963.

Emperor, with cupids "carrying baskets of flowers and lightly clad maidens reclining in graceful attitudes[3]— "tall cotton" indeed for a politician from the cedar brakes of Texas.

He loves money, good clothes, fine liquor and luxurious living in the manorial manner. Though already owning one pretentious Washington residence, he bought the Perle Mesta mansion from "the hostess with the mostest" to live in regal style, no whit embarrassed by the fact that it carried a racial convenant preventing its sale or lease to anyone of "Negro blood or extraction, or to any person of the Semitic race, blood or origin . . ." Although a fresh and flaming convert to the New Frontier's "brotherhood of man," he did not disavow the racial restrictions. Since becoming President he has sold the $300,000 mansion.[4]

In 1961, while the mansion was being re-decorated, he "snatched a luxury apartment" of eight rooms and five baths at the Sheraton-Park Hotel from "a capital social luminary who had contracted for it, because Lady Bird . . . desired it," in keeping with their new social status as the nation's number two family. His swimming pools, with their piped in music to soothe the troubled spirit and relays of telephone connections to enable him to talk while doing the crawl, are indicative too of his love of luxury.[5]

Bobby Kennedy raised dunking in full dress to social acceptability, but it took the audacity of Lyndon to convert swimming in the nude into a social status symbol at the White House. Walter Trohan tells how it is done. Johnson leads his gentlemen guests to the locker room and then

---

[3] Willard Edwards, *Chicago Tribune*, Dec. 21, 1958.

[4] Walter Trohan, column of Oct. 11, 1961.

[5] For reflection of this trait, see Stewart Alsop, in the *Saturday Evening Post*, Dec. 14, 1963; *Fort Worth Star-Telegram*, June 9, 1961.

"astounds them" as "he invites them to strip, and they follow with some reluctance. There is apparent method in this madness, because it is impossible for the Presidential guests, everyone a great man in his own considered judgment, to be pompous in his sagging birthday suit . . . Not all guests go into the pool. One broadcasting executive sat and contemplated his navel during the swim-along with LBJ," in this new White House function called "skinny dippin' ".[6]

At times Johnson's consumption of liquor is prodigious, and Austin gossip used to point to a "sobering up" room in a local hospital, which seemed unnecessary since the nearby LBJ Ranch quarters are commodious. He has been seen to drink three double-shots of Scotch on the twenty-minute flight between Austin and his ranch, and is inclined to a mean and truculent humor when drinking. Once when John Connally and his wife had just arrived as house guests for an LBJ Ranch party covered by the press, without provocation Lyndon cursed him before other guests for being a sorry "s—o—b". The Governor and his wife retrieved their bags and left for Austin. At times Johnson seems to take a sadistic delight in being as crude, cruel and boorish as possible.

As the honor guest of the publisher of *The Amarillo News-Globe,* S. B. Whittenburg, a gentle scion of the greatest family concentration of diversified wealth in the Panhandle of Texas, Lyndon kept the dinner party at the Amarillo Club waiting for about two hours—while he continued to drink and dawdle with his staff at his hotel suite, despite the frantic efforts of a *News* editor to get him on his way. When at the dinner at last, he treated the group with boorish indifference—as befits a man drunk on power. Recently one of the most famous of his old New Deal

6 Trohan, as cited, Jan. 23, 1964.

cronies, who too had relished and fostered the growth of federal power, said in concern after seeing the President, "this man seems to think he is God!"

Jack Kennedy once observed, and with reason, that Johnson "fluctuates and is not a heavyweight thinker." Symington, who was never accused of depth either, said that the old-timers in the Senate had "never seen his kind of leadership. He operates out of his hat."[7] He does play politics intuitively, by ear, as might be expected of an apostle of expediency. A close associate observed that he doesn't really have a foreign policy," which is apparent, since he has no deep-seated government philosophy at all. The columnist Peter Edson observed his "billing as the greatest compromiser and fixer of all times"; *The New York Times* quoted his description of himself as "a compromiser and a maneuverer. I try to get something." That "something," *The Times* continued, comes "through a combination of persuasion, manipulation and discreet threat."

James Reston dwelt admiringly upon Johnson for "his boundless confidence and intuitive judgment"; Marquis Childs found him a Jacksonian looking upon government as "a legitimate source of enrichment"; Wm. S. White suggested that his "politics have always been a technique to power"; and Joseph Rauh, Reuther's ADA lawyer, from an early enemy turned into an ardent advocate, while that renowned authority on Africa, "Soapy" Williams, for whatever the lather was worth, likewise flopped over, predicting that he will make a "great president."

As usual *The New York Times,* in reference to his use of "discreet threat," tread but lightly in the realm of fact, while Walter Trohan got down to the marrow in Johnson's bones by pointing out that he "resents chal-

7 *Chicago Tribune,* Aug. 3, 1959.

lenges and will not brook any disobedience," nor will he "hesitate to whip Congress." Trohan said that "he can be persuasive but he also can be tough", as well as warm and candid, but "he can be as cold as an icy blast from the Texas Panhandle and as ruthless as a stampeding bull."

He is so sensitive to criticism as to equate political opposition with personal enmity—even with enmity to the nation. Twice in one week he hit back viciously at the press and political opposition as "alarmists and people who like to jump on their government," holding them to "be almost as much of a problem as some of our other enemies." Thus he brooks no opposition. One commentator observed that he "will fulfill himself by getting things done ... or he'll know the reason why. Let the man who bars his way recognize whom and what he is taking on." This intolerance of opposition led Dan Smoot to point out his overt threat to muzzle conservative critics when he charged that they are "irresponsibles" with "no self-limiting capacity," and hence cannot "be left to run their course."[8]

"Discreet threat?" His threats carry the brutal impact of an over-loaded blunderbuss. *The Wall Street Journal,* January 31, 1964, found him threatening business leaders who were calling upon him by saying: "I am betting the free economy and private business can do for the economic blood-stream what the Government appropriations do ... If they don't do it, I know how to spend." This became a pledge to labor when he told a union delegation: "We all still know how to ask for programs that

---

8 For this roundup of opinion, see: *Wall Street Journal,* Nov. 27, 1963; *New York Times,* Dec. 8, 1963; *Austin Statesman,* Jan. 14, 1964; *San Angelo Standard,* Jan. 25, 1964; Fulton Lewis, Jr., "Washington Report" Dec. 4, 1963; Reston, column Jan. 8, 1964; Childs, column, Feb. 3, 1964; Trohan, column, Jan. 26, 1964; *Dan Smoot Report,* Dec. 23, 1963; *Newsweek* Feb. 24, 1964.

the Government can sponsor to put people to work."

This was mild compared with his treatment of Texas oil men during the 1960 presidential campaign. Republican candidates in Texas were, as usual, short on money, because Rayburn and Johnson had bluntly warned the oil men that if they went for Nixon and the Democrats won, the Kennedy-Johnson administration would carry out the national platform pledge repealing the oil depletion tax allowance, and the oil men would be dead ducks. Thus many of the so-called "conservative oil men of Texas" capitulated and voted the socialist ticket, with its platform calling for repeal of the depletion allowance, while, incredibly, trusting in the perfidy of Lyndon for protection.[9]

Some of Lyndon's closest friends have tried to depend on him but to their sorrow. Few incidents better illustrate his ruthless nature and resort to blackmail than his tactics in keeping Congressman Joe Kilgore from becoming a candidate against Senator Yarborough. As already noted, Johnson and Yarborough had patched up their ancient feud following the assassination, and it took no seer to foresee the future. Ralph would help solidify the screaming liberals behind Lyndon, who would reciprocate by relieving Ralph of worries in the coming election.

But Lyndon's long-time friend, Governor Connally, was not in on the deal, and with support from the moderates and conservatives was privy to and sympathetic with plans to unseat the Senator. The wealthy insurance man, former Congressman Lloyd Bentsen, of Houston, decided to run. Smooth, ingratiating, experienced, and moderate enough to please the Main-Street socialists, he hired a public relations firm and rented headquarters for the race. Suddenly he backed out. Lyndon did not want him. Texas political wiseacres suggest his sudden decision was

[9] *Human Events,* Aug. 18, 1962.

due to threat of an embarrassing suit against his extensive insurance interests—charging violations of a law in a Mid-Western state in which he operated—where Lyndon's political influence was strong.

Then the conservative Joe Kilgore called on his friend Allan Shivers, who declined to run, and with the pledged support of both Shivers and Connally decided to take on Yarborough himself. Announcing that he would not be a candidate for re-election to Congress, he began lining up strong newspaper and financial support, biding the filing deadline of February 5, 1964, before announcing his candidacy.

With the conservative forces solidly on his side, Congressman Kilgore was further favored by the fragmentation of the old ultra-liberal bloc, that Yarborough had led so long, through the cynical deals and raids of Johnson— its potent leaders bought off, its racial groups lured away, its labor unity shattered. More than that, Yarborough's links with Billie Sol Estes were still fresh in the public mind, with other damaging disclosures shortly to follow. Thus Kilgore was in strong position to unseat the Senator except for one thing—the nod from his friend Lyndon B. Johnson, than which in Texas politics there is nothing more important.

With plans laid to announce at the last minute, one of Kilgore's friends and supporters called to say that Houston Harte, the most powerful figure in Texas journalism, had told a mutual friend: "I will vote for Joe but I can't support him with my papers," after Kilgore had understood that he had the complete support of Harte's powerful chain. For notwithstanding Houston Harte's ardor for Lyndon, he had never lost any love on union labor, and had even been urging Lyndon to help get a candidate out against Yarborough. Kilgore knew at once that something serious had gone wrong, and decided to call the President and get the word right out of the horse's mouth.

He did, and it was plain, forthright and brutal. Johnson told him that his entry into the race would do the President "grave and irreparable harm"; that he "must have unity in Texas"; that he "could not afford to have another Senator from Texas in Washington against him"; and that if Kilgore were elected, he would be voting with Byrd and Russell and against him on such issues as civil rights and medicare, which Kilgore admitted. Then Johnson reeled off the names of a number of Texas papers, including the Fentress and Harte chains, saying, "you think you have their support, *but you won't have!*" He named some of Kilgore's main financial supporters, adding ominously, "and *they will be having troubles.*" And after letting Kilgore know he would campaign against him, the "completely pragmatic" man of iron from Texas laid down the most important fact of political life—"you can't win."

Kilgore caucused again with Connally and Shivers and the next day, with the deadline at hand, called Walter Jenkins to inquire if there had been any change in the President's attitude. Jenkins told him to "hold a minute", and came back on the line to say there had been none. Governor Connally, who stood by Kilgore to the end, was so furious that he threatened to refuse another term, saying that he might as well retire to his ranch at Floresville "if the State of Texas is going to be run from Washington," of which, in truth, there was no doubt. Kilgore decided that if he had to run against both the President and Yarborough, he had better not run at all—though in the light of later events he would have had a splendid chance of nomination.

This is typical of Lyndon's special treatment; the

"gentle persuasion" by which he achieved "unity" among his close friends in Texas. Some writers discreetly call it Johnson's "black magic"; plain talking Texans term it blackmail.[10] Kilgore made his plans to return to private life, while Connally, musing over the double-cross, was heard sadly to observe:

"I knew Lyndon would do it to others; I did not think he would do it to me."

It would be hard to find an incident that reveals more clearly the cold and ruthless Johnson nature. He had no more compunction in forcing his life-long friend, Houston Harte, to repudiate his newspaper backing of Congressman Kilgore, than in applying the terrors of illegitimate power to shut off Kilgore's sources of financial support.

So to Lyndon's effective sabotage of the purpose of Congress he effectively adds another tool of illegitimacy, the actual dictation of the choice of candidates for public office. Yet this is why many leaders of corporate business and labor like him; simply because "Lyndon gets things done." But the favors and influence for which they gamble today will be paid for with their own fortunes and freedom tomorrow. For government at best is devoid of conscience, and illegitimacy can play no consistent favorites. Perpetuity is its sole objective. When its heartless purpose is best served, the liquidation of its friends is no more difficult than that of Kilgore's financial backers, because the power to tax, the handiest device of modern tyrants, is the certain power to corrupt, to coerce and to destroy.

Yet the same illicit technique is readily used by cor-

[10] For the background of this rough deal, see the commentaries of Jimmy Banks and Allen Duckworth, *Dallas News*, Feb. 5, 23, 1964; and Sam Kinch, *Fort Worth Star-Telegram*, Feb 3, 1964; and *Texas Observer*, Jan. 10, 1964.

242 A TEXAN LOOKS AT LYNDON

ruption to build its own glamorous image of acceptability, and as an illustration, Texas, with the pride of at last having "a native son in the White House," could be counted on to do it in a bigger if not more criminal way. But this vaunted pride was not a spontaneous surge of enthusiasm from the grass-roots; it was a sorry synthetic concoction brewed for public consumption by the practical corporate leaders of Main Street.

The profound historian of the Roman Empire, Ferrero, pointed out that "a legitimate government has no need of propaganda," and added history's testament that "no falsehood is beyond the capacity of a revolutionary" one. In Houston the nephew of the late fabulous Jesse Jones, John T. Jones, Jr., head of the multi-million dollar Jones Foundation, which owns the *Houston Chronicle* and vast hotel and banking interests, had probably never heard of Ferrero, but he really knows Lyndon and the way in by the "social" White House door. And as an eminently successful publisher he knows the value of propaganda for political purposes. From an overnight visit at the White House, he came home with the story of a forty-page, lavishly illustrated color supplement and plans for spreading it over Texas like a blanket.

This authorized biography, *Profile of a President*,[11] glorifying Lyndon B. Johnson to the verge of deification —"A Man of Mankind" whose hope for humanity, according to another subtitle, "lies in the realm of reason", was conceived and labored to life in the best traditions of political prostitution, while those called upon to pay for "the baby" were coerced into the illegitimate act without even the recompense of passing physical pleasure—so heartless is this modern brand of power.

11 Leslie Carpenter, *Profile of a President*, Feb. 9, 1964, 40 pp., *Houston Chronicle*.

The method, called "cooperation" in discreet circles, likewise illustrates the techniques of illicit power. At an exclusive and secretive luncheon on January 29, 1964, at a private dining room at the Jones-owned Rice Hotel, "Johnnie" Jones entertained some thirty to forty of Houston's civic, business and financial leaders, with good food and the best waitresses commandeered from the extensive Rice establishment. As host and master of ceremonies, Johnnie abjured his favored friends to secrecy, and told them of the Liz and Leslie Carpenter handsome insert, and that Texas had a chance to get in on it. With "a great Texan" in the presidency, its wide dissemination would, he emphasized, be a fine business thing for Texas and their area. Three great Texas dailies would carry it —his own, the *Houston Chronicle*, the *Dallas Times-Herald*, whose ownership likewise dotes on Lyndon, and the *San Antonio Express*, owned by Houston Harte, which loves Lyndon even more.

Such a massive undertaking, Jones pointed out, called for money. Invoking their pride in Lyndon and Texas and their good sound business sense, he appealed to their public spirit and their undoubted patriotism. The cost for the three papers was $28,000 each—a mere $84,000 in all. Beside the plate of each guest was an embossed, folded place card bearing the honoree's name. Inside the fold was a simple form for signature indicating his support, with a space for the amount he might like to pledge for the project. All the guests had to do was sign or not, as they wished, and in keeping with the Texas proprieties nobody would ever know the difference—that is nobody except John T. Jones and Lyndon B. Johnson, though this obvious truth was never even breathed.

Mr. Jones emphasized his view that Goldwater did not have a chance, which was particularly interesting since

among his guests were wealthy men who had contributed
to the Goldwater campaign. Hence here was a real opportunity to get in early on the winning side. As may be sure,
his guests were formidable figures, such as A. G. McNeese,
president of the Bank of the Southwest, John McLean,
president of the New Texas Bank of Commerce, Marcus
Greer, president of the City National, General Maurice
Hirsch, lawyer and patron of the fine arts, William G.
Farrington, member of the Council of Foreign Relations,
with international financial connections, Milton Under-
wood, securities investment banker and others with vast
oil and moneyed interests.

They were all men of affairs and means, "progressive
and prudent" enough too, to quote a famous Texan, to
realize the life and death power of government over them
and their interests, and hence susceptible to coercion and
fervent philanthropic feelings. Thus in support of such a
worthy civic and patriotic purpose they signed up right
willingly. In this way a near million copies of this life of
Lyndon—the man who, to quote this handsome history,
"loves the land" and "is quick to help others"—reached
the Texas public.

This should be proof enough even for a Georgia Democrat that Lyndon is "a man of action who knows how
to get things done." And in this frightful age, if the polls
be honest, this is the sort of leader the brain-washed people
want. Revert again to this Houston incident and consider
what appalling power! These Texans were not underlings
but men of wealth, influence and prestige of their own,
though hardly "independent." Thus does illicit power
coerce the men of corporate capital and burnish the image of the "popular" leader who is destroying them. But
somewhere in the distant future, as their enslaved grandchildren grope for liberty, the truth as to how their grand-

sires bargained freedom away may help a little in their tragic struggle.

Since this *Profile of a President* assures Texans that Lyndon "loves the land", it should do no violence to justice to illustrate how completely. Millions of Americans, in intuitive harmony with the strong elemental traits of the human race, love the out-of-doors and its creatures. With most of these hunting is more than a sport and a diversion; it is a physical challenge and a re-creation of the spirit. Lyndon too, with his business partner, Judge A. W. Moursund, loves to hunt, and his skilled markmanship is a matter of newspaper record. Not so well known are the methods and devices by which his remarkable prowess has been won. The average sportsman, reading the news, may envisage this vigorous man with quick and unerring aim bringing down the fleeting Texas buck with a quick shot. But truth seems at variance with the legend.

In the timbered Texas hills north of Johnson City, on the Johnson-Moursund hunting preserves, these two cronies sometime ago built a high and sumptuous hunting tower. Access from the ground is by elevator, and capping the tower is a glass-enclosed room, where hosts and guests may loll and drink and gamble in ease while waiting in the cool of evening for the hapless game to be tolled into open range by the luscious growth of winter-oats in a field below. It was here that Lyndon, in keeping with his "regal propensities," had the noted newspaper men, Roy and Jack Howard, along with Walker Stone, chief editorial writer for Scripps-Howard, as his hunting guests. Their experience, as one of these awed guests described it, "equalled hunting with the Maharajah of Mysore, who invites his guests to shoot tigers from a royally equipped and danger proof structure in the jungles of India."

Here in Lyndon's glassed-in and heated tower forty

feet high, his guests found themselves comfortably situated with toilet facilities, and lavish food and drink, while ranch hands waited below to "service" the party. When dark enticed the unsuspecting bucks from the surrounding timber to graze in the lush field, Lyndon, the doughty huntsman and host, got up and switched on a searchlight, played it upon his prey, laid his rifle across the rampart, focused his telescopic sights upon the buck and as a true "Dead-Eyed Dick" of the New Frontier, unerringly brought him down and ordered his hands to retrieve and haul him away. His guests were dumbfounded at this modern and effective wrinkle in what was the ancient royal sport.[12]

Lyndon and Moursund are likewise fond of hunting doves—the lovely bird that flies south through their section in fall migration by the thousands, offering beautiful shooting as the flights come into the "watering places" late of afternoon and early evening. While Lyndon was recuperating from his heart attack, he, Moursund and the local banker, Ernest Stubbs, with a negro to pick the birds, hied themselves away one evening for shooting at a private tank on the Moursund ranch properties. As it happened Captain E. M. Sprott, head of the law enforcement division of the Texas Game and Fish Commission, along with two of his wardens, were hunting on an adjoining preserve. By Texas law shooting stops at sundown, but while Sprott and his boys lingered to pick their birds, bombardment continued on Moursund's range nearby. As the game officials drove out to the public road leading into Johnson City at dusk, the Captain stopped and sent Warden Grover Simpson in by car, as provided by Texas law, to check

12 For reference to this marvelous sporting device and its effectiveness see Williard Edward's column, *Chicago Tribune*, Dec. 21, 1958. For elaboration, ask the natives of Lyndon's home range.

on the game bags to see that the neighboring hunters were within their limits.

Shortly Simpson returned to report that he was having trouble; that Judge Moursund and his party, claiming the sanctuary of hunting on his own land, would not let him check their bags. Sprott drove back to mediate the controversy, explaining to the Judge, the only hunter so far identified, that the law required them to do so. Moursund still hotly objected and the warden, Grover Simpson, a thoroughly independent Texas officer who strangely believed that when he took an oath to uphold the law he should do so—no matter who was involved, got "hottern' a pistol barrel" as the discussion continued. On the front seat of Moursund's car in the near dark loomed an unidentified figure with hat pulled down over his face and both hands cupped over his ears—though far "from covering them." Finally the fiery warden, disgusted with the delay, turned to Judge Moursund demanding: "Who is that big-eared s—o—b in the front seat?" That gentleman was Senate Democratic Majority Leader, Lyndon Baines Johnson.

Captain Sprott explained to the Judge that as officers of the law they had no choice, in view of his refusal to let them check their game, but to go into Johnson City and file on them for violation of the hunting laws of Texas. This Sprott and his wardens did. In such cases both defendants and the State are notified of the date set by the Court for hearing. But inexplicably for those who do not know politics, the next Sprott and the State of Texas heard was that Blanco County Judge Moursund's case had been called and in the absence of the State, Justice W. E. Stevenson had dismissed the case. The "dumbfounded" Captain Sprott, indicating that "five days notice" was usually given, said the Game Department had absolutely no notice, but added, "I guess they know what they are doing." Obviously "they" did.

It might be thought that Judge Moursund and his sporting companions would be anxious to let this incident lie. Not the vindictive Lyndon B. Johnson. Herbert Frensley, president of Brown and Root, who had been appointed to the Game Commission, was needled by Lyndon to fire the Director of the Department, Howard Dodgen, Captain Sprott and Warden Grover Simpson. Frensley demurred. The years passed, but Lyndon does not forget. When he had put his friend Connally into the Governor's office, the time for retribution had arrived. Howard Dodgen had to go and the easiest way to do it seemed to be by reorganization of the Department.

Governor Connally decided to appoint Blanco County Judge A. W. Moursund—whom a neighboring Texas judge charged was "the worst game outlaw" in the area—to the Texas Game Commission—the department's governing board. Plans were then announced to reorganize it into the Texas Parks and Wildlife Commission, and career man, Howard Dodgen, after eighteen years in the service, but still short of full retirement benefits, was, despite the Governor's earlier reassurance fired by Lyndon's henchmen.[13] Thus some seven years after the hunting incident did Texas salvage its public honor and assuage the feelings of its leading citizen, who, in Leslie Carpenter's apt phrase, not only "loves the land" but is "quick to help others."

One further tragic incident may be taken in illustration of Lyndon B. Johnson's many-sided character. In keeping with his frenetic spirit and tremendous energy, he has long been an avid user of planes. When he began flying a half million-dollar Convair, incurably skeptical

[13] *Houston Chronicle*, April 4, 1964; *Texas Observer*, May 1, 1964, p. 1, and numerous interviews by the author.

Texans at times wondered how he got it. Widely bandied rumors variously credited contractor H. B. Zachry, of San Antonio, Brown and Root and Billie Sol Estes—all favored friends of Lyndon. Still little notice was taken until the Convair crashed.

Friday night, February 17, 1961, was extremely foggy and wholly unfit for flying in the Austin, Texas area. Vice President Johnson was at his Pedernales River Ranch, sixty-odd miles west in the Blanco County Hills. "His plane," the plush white Convair 240, N94256, was safely parked on the ramp at the Austin Airport; its first-rate pilot, thirty-nine year-old Harold Teague and his co-pilot, Charles Williams, thirty-seven, were as usual standing by for instant and imperious call. Johnson ordered the plane flown to the ranch—where the paved strip was lighted, but where no ground control instruments had been installed, with only a two-way radio at the ranch for communication with the plane. When the strip lights could not be seen and flying was blind, all that the pilots had for calculating their position was the crossing points of the radio beams from the Austin and San Antonio stations, which, with a fraction of error at more than sixty miles would throw them off the field.

Harold Teague consulted "the tower" at Austin and was advised against the flight. He then talked, it is said by radio, with Lyndon at the ranch, telling him they should not try to make it. Johnson is said to have exploded, venting his profanity upon the pilot, demanding to know "what do you think I'm paying you for?", and again ordering him to "get that plane" to the ranch.[14] Teague called his wife to tell her that they had been ordered to

---

[14] At the time newspapers reported that this conversation was taped in the usual fashion by the Austin tower— though it has not yet been produced in proof.

leave, and at 7:16 p.m., February 17, 1961—when motorists were having to dim their lights to see the road directly before them — Vice President Johnson's Convair roared into the murky night, above the hilly terrain, with the strong hands of two eager but anxious young Texans fingering the controls.

Strangely not until three days later, Monday, February 20, did the news get out that the plane "was overdue" at Johnson's ranch, sixty-odd miles away, though the papers did print the reassuring news that the Vice President "was safe." The charred ruins were found where the pilots, hopelessly groping down for lights they could not see, had at last flown into a cedar-covered hill. For the tragic moment the mourning widows left behind in Austin were highly resentful, while others who knew the demanding nature of the man who had ordered them out, and his reckless disregard of the laws and safety regulations imposed by federal decree when in the air himself, mourned with mixed emotions at the funeral.

Texas was seized with an eager interest in the origin and the ownership of the plane. Rumors were rife that it belonged to Billie Sol Estes, and then to Zachry, whose paid pilots had at times flown Lyndon; while a report crept into a San Antonio paper that it was owned by Brown and Root. But the registration and ownership of planes are a matter of record with the Federal Aviation offices at Oklahoma City. Somehow for days there was much confusion, and the suggestion is boldly made among fliers, service men and others in Texas aviation, that there was a fast juggling of ownership papers right up to the top, at Oklahoma City—so that there could be no question but that the plane belonged to Lyndon Baines Johnson. Nor does the evidence refute them.

By report the title to the crashed Convair passed

from the Alamo Aviation Service, Inc., of which H. B.
Zachry, was president, on February 20, 1961—*three days
after the crash*—to the "Brazos 10th Street Corp." of
Austin, "wholly owned" by Donald and Jane Thomas.
This corporation did not even have a telephone. But it
did have the same street address as the LBJ Company,
and Donald Thomas has for years been the Company's
lawyer, while another Johnson friend, Edgar Perry III,
of Austin, was shown to have been one of the Brazos
incorporators.

When questioned about the matter, Warren Wood-
ward, vice-president of the LBJ Company, said that the
plane had been leased by the Brazos 10th St. Corp. from
Alamo Aviation during the 1960 campaign with an option
to buy; that the option had been exercised "this month"
—the month of the crash, and the records of the F.A.A.
at Oklahoma City seem to bear him out.

Insurance of "between $200,000 and $300,000" on the
plane was carried by The Insurance Company of North
America, while the pilots were, in the gross phrase, "covered" by policies of $100,000 each.[15] Behind these shifts of
recorded corporate ownership of Lyndon's Convair CV
240, including that through his dummy device, the Brazos
10th St. Corp., is an interesting story to the effect that
the plane originally belonged to John W. Mecom, a prominent Houston oil man. It is said that Mecom agreed to
lend it to Lyndon for his 1960 presidential campaign with
the understanding that they would cover up the adverse
political truth of his being flown around the country by a
big Texas oil man by signing a bogus lease with an option

[15] The author's investigations into this tragic incident cover
private and for obvious reasons confidential sources. For
equally obvious reasons, the newspaper accounts were
sketchy. See e.g., *Austin American*, Feb. 20, 21, 1961.

to buy—which accounted for the ridiculously low price of $200,000 for a $500,000 plane.

The story further holds that when the campaign was over and Mecom demanded the return of his plane, Lyndon replied that he wanted to buy it. Mecom protested vigorously, reminding Lyndon that there was really no agreement to sell, but just a campaign trick for Lyndon's protection. Lyndon is said to have retorted that they had signed a contract, that he was standing on his option, and that he was going to buy the plane. And he did.

His 6000-foot paved runway, somehow superimposed on the four-hundred-odd acre LBJ Ranch and designed for jets is still another story, of which a minor feature must suffice. In Congress on April 11, 1962, Congressman Heistand charged that the Vice President had been the recipient of "political payola" in the sum of $29,265 for "navigational lights and radio instrumentation" on his private field in Texas. When Heistand called the F.A.A. to inquire about the installations, he said the Agency "had not even heard of Johnson City." But when he called back again, he reported that they had done "a cover-up job" by designating the strip as the Johnson City Airport—though the village of some six hundred-odd people was fifteen miles away.[16]

In view of this public subsidy willingly accepted by Vice President Lyndon B. Johnson for his private field, it is interesting to note that, as a presidential candidate in 1964, he refuses to let his ranches participate in subsidy programs. Mrs. Johnson, when confronted with the embarrassing news of "the deplorable" status of the negro renters in the shacks on her Alabama land, had her "manager" suggest that this is in part due to the small return on her timber lands because of "her attitude toward ac-

---
16 *Congressional Record*, April 11, 1962, p. 5915.

cepting . . . government aid."[17] Thus it is good to know that at last the Johnsons have set the high example of spurning government subsidy—at least during a political campaign.

In conclusion it should be admitted that ordinarily it is presumptuous to inquire into the religious attitude, affiliations and beliefs of any individual—for there man trods on private ground. Yet the fact that America was founded as a Christian nation—with freedom flowing only from Christianity's fundamental concept of the inviolability of the individual and his accountability to God, plus the further fact that the present epochal struggle for survival is essentially spiritual, place a moral imperative upon every citizen to assay America's leadership primarily in terms of spiritual worth. For in the end what else can really matter?

Lyndon Baines Johnson has repeatedly said that man's best "hope lies in the realm of reason." With no desire whatever to argue his point of view, the author—as a weary chronicler of history and a battered cowboy of the sunlit ranges of Texas, feeling no personal obligation for logical defense of his own spiritual faith—simply wishes to say that he could not be more confirmed in disagreement.

Johnson's humanistic leanings, indicating his faith and hope "in the realm of reason" instead of Almighty God is something for Johnson himself to explain if he wishes. Along with many Americans the author felt a grating harshness and a sense of shock in the way the President, in his first public statement, called for "your help and" as if in afterthought, "God's." In a time of tragedy and trial the appeal of most moral men is first and foremost to Almighty God.

---

[17] AP report from Billingsley, Ala., May 20, 1964.

Certainly Johnson's idolatrous proposal of "a fitting memorial to God," to be built with private funds solicited "from all faiths"—believers and unbelievers alike—was not meant as open sacrilege. But it was so shocking that it moved even the *Washington Star* to comment that:

> It was a 19th century philosopher, Friedrich
> Nietzsche, who decided that God was dead. But
> it took a 20th century American President, Lyn-
> don B. Johnson, to propose a memorial.

Memorials are built for the dead and not the living. Whatever purpose Johnson may have had, this proposal bespeaks at best a strange spiritual nature and an essentially superficial mind.

In the beginning the author made the gravely serious charge that nothing in Johnson's public record and statements emphasized any abiding spiritual and moral creed, nor dedication to any firm political and philosophical principle. The author ends this study, a far from prideful record for a native Texan and proud American to set down, with a reaffirmation of that judgment, fully aware of the terrible recriminations of illegitimate power that may, with certainty, be expected to follow.

The true historian as a moral man is under a dual compulsion; that not only of seeing but of recording the truth. The modern pragmatic age cannot comprehend the compulsions of history, honor and tradition. But the ancestral blood and spirit of my forebears—from their participation in the capitulation of Cornwallis, through San Jacinto's battle for Texas freedom down to the present, with the responsibilities to grandchildren romping now in zestful expectation on my ranches, demand no less.

In age I cannot live with betrayal and dishonor, and I have no desire or intention of doing so.

ORDER FORM

Palo Duro Press
P. O. Box 390,
Canyon, Texas

Send me .... copies of **A TEXAN LOOKS AT LYNDON:**
A Study In Illegitimate Power

Payment of $............ is enclosed (send check or money order.)

Name ....

Street ....

City and State ....

(Please Print)

THIS CRUCIAL YEAR OF 1964 . . .

. . . may be the most important in American history, as well as in determining the fate of the Christian World and hence of human freedom. Thus the moral and spiritual character of our leadership has never been of more vital importance.

Please read and circulate this book on the career and character of Lyndon Baines Johnson, *A STUDY IN ILLE-GITIMATE POWER* by J. Evetts Haley.